ROBERT ALTMAN

INTERVIEWS

CONVERSATIONS WITH FILMMAKERS SERIES
PETER BRUNETTE, GENERAL EDITOR

Photofest

ROBERT ALTMAN

INTERVIEWS

EDITED BY DAVID STERRITT

UNIVERSITY PRESS OF MISSISSIPPI / JACKSON

http://www.upress.state.ms.us

08   07   06   05   04   03   02   01   00   4   3   2   1

∞

Library of Congress Cataloging-in-Publication Data

Altman, Robert, 1925–
        Robert Altman : interviews / edited by David Sterritt.
                p.   cm. — (Conversations with filmmakers series)
        Includes index.
        ISBN 1-57806-186-5 (alk. paper). — ISBN 1-57806-187-3 (pbk. :
        alk. paper)
        1. Altman, Robert, 1925–   Interviews.   2. Motion picture
        producers and directors—United States Interviews.   I. Sterritt,
        David.   II. Title.   III. Series.
        PN1998.3.A48A5   2000
        791.43'0233'092—dc21
                                                                99-26928
                                                                CIP

British Library Cataloging-in-Publication data available

CONTENTS

INTRODUCTION

OF THE MANY THEMES running through Robert Altman's interviews over the years, one that stands out prominently is his affection for his own career. "You name somebody that's had a better shake than I have," he challenged two *Film Comment* editors in 1992. "I can't think of anybody," he continued. "I have done almost 40 films . . . theater, opera. . . . I've had great commercial successes, great critical successes; there are schools that teach my films; almost all the films that I've made are still being shown somewhere in retrospectives." If a skeptic were to point out that he isn't exactly a household name among Saturday-night moviegoers—or Academy Award aficionados, or box-office profiteers—he has an answer for that, too: "The best work I've done, the most creative work, has been between those peaks that the general public sees."

This is a fascinating comment, given the fact that most feature filmmakers view responses of the "general public" as a crucially important factor—perhaps *the* crucially important factor—in their ability to maintain reasonably stable careers in an industry famous for its fickleness and volatility. While he welcomes healthy ticket sales as much as the next director, Altman seems to regard them as more an afterthought than a *raison d'être*.

Equally surprising are his good feelings about the overall trajectory of his professional life, which started hesitantly, developed gradually, and has taken more than its share of potentially disastrous downturns. Pondering its problematic aspects, one could imagine Altman becoming disillusioned, cynical, embittered. In fact, something very different appears to have happened. Of course he has seized on his moments of conventional success to shore up his status as a bankable, audience-friendly director—when *M*A*S*H* became an international hit, for instance, or when such ambitious pictures as *Nashville* and *Short Cuts* earned him best-director nominations in the Oscar sweepstakes. When faced with less prosperous periods, however, he has drawn from them a different sort of capital, seeing hostile criticism as proof of his uncompromising creativity and commercial distress as a sign that his artistic energies have simply outpaced popular taste for the moment. What fails at today's box office, after all, may be the toast of tomorrow's retrospective.

Above all, if Altman had a good time making a picture, he counts it a personal triumph whatever the rest of the world may think. And those good times evidently happen with striking regularity. "I've not made a film yet that I do not consider a success," he told Michael Wilmington in 1991, implying that "success" is a loose enough label to include the chilly *Quintet* and the clunky *O.C. and Stiggs,* among other commercial calamities. His measuring stick is "the collaboration of the people" who work on a movie, and the "treasure" and "pleasure" of his work is found in the "process" rather than the product that the "general public" eventually sees.

Such an attitude could only be held by a notably extroverted person, and Altman fits that category well, notwithstanding the accusations of sourness and misanthropy leveled at his movies by some detractors. He talks openly with journalists and scholars who seek him out for interviews. He speaks frequently and fondly of his favorite performers, telling *Film Criticism* in 1983 that when the camera rolls "the artist that's creating . . . is the actor and not me." Film critics, treated with opportunism or condescension by some directors, receive his respect as conscientious professionals who make it a point to stay "in touch with . . . the several millions of people in the country, or the world, who are film oriented," as he told *Playboy* in 1976.

His attitude toward the public is more complicated, and he has opened himself to charges of elitism and arrogance with remarks like his *Film Heritage* comment that the "artist and the multitude are natural enemies," doomed to mutual misunderstanding because of the artist's determination "to carry people into areas they don't want to go into." Yet a few moments later he told the same interviewer that "art appreciation" is facilitated by "taking away the fear that the multitudes have," stressing his desire to "simplify" art and make it "accessible to the most . . . people." This goal doesn't always sit easily with his passion for the "mystery" of life, or with his insistence on viewing the human condition through his own idiosyncratic lens regardless of how many others can make sense of the perspectives it provides. At the heart of his artistic philosophy, though, one senses a persistent need to communicate his vision to friends and strangers alike, and an abiding regard for the ability of moviegoers to become active partners in the creative process when given a chance by the few directors who dare to challenge Hollywood formulas. "I feel that once an audience has to work to help make the story by the way they perceive it," he said to Wilmington, "and they're picking . . . their own clues out on the way . . . it becomes more enjoyable for them. They become a participant." His implicit respect for the viewer becomes explicit when he admits to Pat Aufderheide that "all I need to sustain me in my vision is one person. One person who says, I got it, I was really moved."

All of which points to what may be the central paradox in Altman's career. The director who expresses such confidence in the audience's creative power, and takes such sustenance from a single spectator who understands what he's attempting to say, has been charged repeatedly—perhaps more than any other filmmaker of his generation—with holding far too many of his characters in a chronic state of contempt. Asked about this by his more aggressive questioners, he stresses his role as an "observer" rather than a "propagandist," contending that his films are descriptive rather than judgmental, simply presenting the facts of contemporary life as any fair-minded person might see them. He has never succeeded in quieting this issue down, however. Certain provocative moments in his work—the mortification of Hot Lips Hoolihan in *M*A*S*H* is a particularly pointed example—have been resurrected by any number of interviewers, providing one of the most provocative threads woven through the conversations in this book and revealing not only the complexity of Altman's views but also the diversity of opinions held by critics vis-à-vis his work. "There seems a pattern in your films of women being humiliated," said *Sight and Sound* interviewer Peter Keogh to Altman in 1992, only a year after *Film Comment* interviewer Beverly Walker noted the director's "propensity to portray women sympathetically" and as "real contenders, neither passive victims of some type of male violence nor supportive sidekicks to a man who engineered the action." Such divergent views foreground the pervasive ambiguity—stimulating, infuriating, or both—that has made

Altman's films impossible to ignore even by those who hold them in varying degrees of suspicion.

An overall grasp of Altman's unorthodox career is necessary for an appreciation of his wide-ranging interviews. Born in 1925 in Kansas City, Missouri, he had an unexceptional Midwestern upbringing that included education in parochial schools and a military academy. A stint in the Air Force brought him into the thick of World War II, where he participated in more than 20 bombing missions. His first filmmaking experiences came under the distinctly unglamorous aegis of a Kansas City production company that cranked out industrial documentaries. The glamour quotient increased a little but not much during the next 20 years, as he worked on a handful of extremely minor theatrical and television films and became a dependable, if unpredictable, contract director for various network TV series. By the middle 1960s he appeared to have found his niche as a hardworking craftsperson whose occasional bursts of originality would be more a hindrance than a help to any future progress.

This outlook changed a bit in 1968, when his science-fiction adventure *Countdown* made it to theaters on a double bill with John Wayne's war movie *The Green Berets*. It changed more in 1969, when *That Cold Day in the Park* earned the first serious reviews of his two-decade-old career with its intense (if uneven) depiction of a sexually obsessed woman. And it changed drastically the following year with the release of *M*A*S*H,* which delighted adventurous critics, amused widespread audiences, won the highest prize at the Cannes filmfest, and garnered several Academy Award nominations including best picture and best director.

The obvious move for Altman at this point would have been to cement his growing fame with another freewheeling crowd-pleaser. Then as now, however, he had little patience with the obvious. His follow-up movie came quickly, confidently, and disastrously. *Brewster McCloud* pleased the limited corps of critics who had valued *That Cold Day in the Park* and *M*A*S*H* for their avant-garde tendencies rather than such garden-variety elements as the mannered acting of the former and the football-game foolery of the latter. But the new picture displeased everyone else, encouraging a growing sense within the industry that Altman was too creative, original, and audacious for his own professional good.

Subsequent releases did little to alter this perception, even though some of them — most notably *Thieves Like Us* and the brilliant *Nashville* in the middle 1970s—earned ecstatic reviews along with their mediocre box-office returns. His independent spirit received support from the sympathetic Hollywood producer Alan Ladd Jr. and from an entrepreneurial maneuver of his own—setting up the Lion's Gate production company in 1976—but movies that appeared to be commercial (*Buffalo Bill and the Indians, A Wedding*) earned almost as little as movies that didn't appear to be commercial (*3 Women, Quintet*) over the next several years. An argument with Paramount Pictures over the budget and revenues for *Popeye* gave a bitter ending to what might have been an ideal project, joining Altman's flamboyant style to a suitably delirious subject, and spurred him to put Lion's Gate up for sale. He turned his sights to television (especially the new arenas of cable TV and home video) and to live theater, embarking on a decade dominated by stage productions and stage-to-screen adaptations.

Again the future seemed clear—with Altman permanently ensconced as a Hollywood has-been, plying his trade on the margins of the business—and again the auguries proved false. The theatrical film *Vincent & Theo* won widespread notice in 1990, and two years later *The Player* marked a full-fledged comeback at the box office, in the critical columns, and in the Academy Award race. Altman has been a player ever since, even though financial returns fell short of the good reviews earned by *Short Cuts* and the similarly sweeping *Ready-to-Wear* was wanly received. More recent projects, from *Kansas City* with its jazzy riffs to *The Gingerbread Man* with its neo-*noir* edginess, have reconfirmed the flexibility that has marked Altman's career as a whole, and proved that a 70-something director with a reputation for high living and eccentric habits can still keep movie-watchers around the world in a state of continual guesswork as to what direction he'll turn in next.

The interviews in this book were conducted by critics, journalists, and scholars who share a serious interest in Altman's work. As indicated, they do not always have a sympathetic attitude toward particular aspects of that work—many are wary of the cynicism or misogyny sometimes imputed to it, for instance—and the diversity of implicit or explicit commentary embedded within the articles is one criterion that I have used in selecting which ones to include. I have also sought to cover all the phases of Altman's feature-film activity from the period of his first major contributions—discussed in a groundbreaking *New York Times Magazine* article of 1971—to the recent jazz-movie experiment *Kansas City,* explored in my own 1996 interview. I have given a particularly large amount of attention to the key years of 1976, when Altman and others were endeavoring to sum up his initial burst of career-changing creativity, and 1992, when *The Player* had revivified his reputation and *Short Cuts* was a highly promising gleam in the auteur's eye. Any collection of interviews with a single artist will result in some degree of repetition and reiteration, but it is a tribute to the continually self-inventing nature of Altman's aesthetic that all of these pieces, even those originally published during a single year, reveal new and enlightening facets of his *oeuvre*.

Aljean Harmetz was one of the earliest film-industry reporters to recognize Altman's importance, and even the title of her article — "The 15th Man Who Was Asked To Direct *M*A*S*H* (And Did) Makes a Peculiar Western" — captures the flavor of his work at a moment when nobody could predict whether it would soar like *M*A*S*H*, plummet like *Brewster McCloud,* or blaze a new path with the genre-bending *McCabe and Mrs. Miller,* then in production. Connie Byrne and William O. Lopez use the intricacies of *Nashville* as the springboard for a discussion of his still-escalating experimentalism and the growing political implications of his work. The important *Playboy* interview by Bruce Williamson touches on many issues raised by Altman's career up to and including the failure of *Buffalo Bill and the Indians* to rekindle the excitement of *Nashville,* and finds the director in particularly crisp rapport with a like-minded journalist who nonetheless raises a number of keenly challenging questions.

F. Anthony Macklin's article from *Film Heritage* examines Altman as movie mogul, looking into the economics of the newly formed Lion's Gate Films and his function as producer of pictures by Alan Rudolph and Robert Benton as well as his own *3 Women,* a daring project by any standard. Charles Michener elicits Altman's side of the story vis-à-vis the underrated *A Wedding* and the very different moods of *Quintet* and *A Perfect Couple,* which were still in the production pipeline. Andrew Sarris focuses attention on video just when it became a major concern for Altman — and the motion-picture world in general — at the beginning of the 1980s. Richard Combs and Tom Milne run the gamut from *Popeye* to *Quintet* to *Health,* weaving Altman's remarks into a revealing monologue that offers further insights into his sociopolitical ideas. Matters of technique and American attitudes toward art and life are among the subjects explored by Harry Kloman and Lloyd Michaels during Altman's theatrically oriented period,

and Patricia Aufderheide brings her characteristic flair for ideological analysis to questions about *Secret Honor,* one of his most openly political works.

Also using a single film as the primary focus for a wide variety of
inquiries, Michael Wilmington interrogates Altman on *The Long Goodbye*
and its portrait of a "Rip Van Marlowe" inspired by Raymond Chandler's
private-eye hero of the 1940s but transplanted to the 1970s where circumstances rarely match his sensibility. Beverly Walker seizes on a phrase used
by Altman in her discussion with him — "People who watch don't die" —
to crystallize not only a message of *Brewster McCloud* but a theme of conflict
between artist and audience that has underlain much of his work. Geoff
Andrew does something similar with a *Popeye* motto, "I yam what I yam,"
seeing this as an antic slogan for Altman's own emphatic individuality.
Peter Keogh and Janice Richolson use *The Player* to launch differing inves-
tigations of the filmmaker's views on commercialism, materialism, and
other Hollywoodian traits. Gavin Smith and Richard T. Jameson cover just
about everything in their joint *Film Comment* interview conducted in 1992,
as does Graham Fuller in his remarkably far-sighted conversation. My interview from Cannes in 1996 solicits Altman's views on a single late-career
production and some of the issues that have preoccupied him for decades.

Looking once more at the themes that surface and resurface through
these conversations, one can't help being struck by Altman's ability to com-
bine an open, generous approach to the interview process with a lurking
suspicion of the pernicious results it may have. "What I'm doing right now
is a very dangerous thing for an artist to do," he told Williamson during
their 1976 session, adding that "when you start trying to explain what you
do . . . well, once you find out, you probably won't be able to do it again."
And five years later to Combs and Milne, "The danger of these kinds of
conversations and interviews to me is that . . . I don't really want to know
why. The minute I articulate it . . . I begin to believe what I say. I narrow
everybody's view of what that film can be." One sympathizes with the artist's
need to preserve the intuitiveness, the nonverbal acuity, the reliance on
notions and hunches (also revealed in some interviews) that distinguish
his films, the best and the worst of them, from those of anyone else in cinema today. At the same time, however, people who engage with Altman's
art often feel a strong desire to know *why* — why he works the way he does,
why he makes the decisions that render his movies so singular in their
effects, why he has refused to carve out the conventionally successful

career that could clearly have been his if he hadn't turned his talents in such offbeat directions. Through his compulsive cooperation with gifted interviewers, he has provided his admirers — and detractors — with an enormous number of tantalizing clues. Like audience members wrestling with one of his densely layered sound tracks, it's up to us to put them together and read their messages.

To paraphrase Altman, cooperation from others has constituted the pleasure and treasure of this project, so I wish to offer hearty thanks to the many writers, editors, and publishers who enabled its completion. Special thanks go to Graham Fuller for facilitating my use of his excellent article, and above all to Shirley Sealy for helping me pin down the invaluable *Playboy* interview by Bruce Williamson in the difficult weeks after Bruce's death; during the many years when we worked and socialized together he proved himself again and again to be one of the most talented, knowledgeable, and companionable critics I've had the pleasure to know, and while his contribution would have been a highlight of this book under any circumstances, I hope its presence will serve as a remembrance of his irreplaceable personality as well as a testament to his journalistic and cinematic expertise.

My sharp-eyed and quick-witted research assistant, Leilah Broukhim, has been of inestimable help with her untiring labors in various libraries and repositories. Seetha Srinivasan and her associates at the University Press of Mississippi have distinguished themselves by their patience as well as their skillfulness and support. My critical and academic colleague Peter Brunette was kind enough to invite my participation in the Conversations with Filmmakers series. And a very deep bow is due to Robert Altman, whom I first interviewed at Cannes in 1974 — where he was very upset that Pauline Kael had dubbed *Thieves Like Us* a "masterpiece," thus making it sound like "a big hard book you have to read in school" — and have had the enormous pleasure of meeting and conversing with on sundry occasions since.

My deepest gratitude goes to my wife Ginnie, who helped me prepare the final manuscript; our sons Craig and Jeremy, who have watched and discussed Altman movies with me more times than I can count; and Tanya Van Sant, who's about to join the family. This book is dedicated to them.

— David Sterritt, New York City, March 1999

CHRONOLOGY

1925   Born in Kansas City, Missouri.

1931   Becomes a student at St. Peter's, a well-regarded Roman Catholic school in Kansas City.

1938   Graduates from St. Peter's, enrolls in Rockhurst High School, another Catholic school; leaves after a few months to attend Southwest, a public school.

1941   Switches from Southwest to the Wentworth Military Academy in Lexington, Missouri, during his junior year.

1945   Joins the Air Force; trains at a base near Los Angeles for combat service in World War II, where he serves as copilot for more than 20 bombing missions.

1946   Marries first wife, LaVonne Elmer.

1947   Takes a job with the Calvin Company, a Kansas City production company specializing in industrial films, for which he eventually makes approximately 60 films. Cowrites the original story (uncredited) of the United Artists production *Christmas Eve*. Appears as an extra in *The Secret Life of Walter Mitty,* a popular Danny Kaye comedy. Christine, his first child, is born.

1948   Cowrites the original story of *Bodyguard,* an RKO production in the currently popular *film noir* style.

1951   Cowrites the screenplay of a musical-comedy spoof, *Corn's-a-Poppin'*.

1953–54   Directs and coproduces the television police series *Pulse of the City* for a Kansas City network.

1955   Writes, produces, and directs *The Delinquents*, a low-budget drama.

1957   Produces, directs, and edits *The James Dean Story*, a documentary. United Artists releases *The Delinquents*.

1957–66   Directs a wide variety of episodes and pilots for Hollywood television series, including *Alfred Hitchcock Presents, U.S. Marshall* (*Sheriff of Cochise*), *The Whirlybirds, Oh! Susannah* (*The Gale Storm Show*), *The Millionaire, Hawaiian Eye, The Troubleshooters, Sugarfoot/Bronco Hour, The Detectives, Lawman, Maverick, Bonanza, Surfside Six, The Roaring Twenties, Peter Gunn, Route 66, Bus Stop, M Squad, The Gallant Men, Combat, Kraft Mystery Theatre, Kraft Suspense Theatre, The Long Hot Summer,* and *Chicago, Chicago* (*Night Watch*).

1964   Produces and directs the melodrama *Once Upon a Savage Night,* about the hunt for a serial killer, for Universal's television division; Universal gives it a limited theatrical release as *Nightmare in Chicago.*

1967   Shoots the science-fiction drama *Countdown,* about a trip to the moon.

1968   *Countdown* is released on a double bill with John Wayne's version of the Vietnam War, *The Green Berets.*

1969   Directs his first film with personal thematic and stylistic touches, *That Cold Day in the Park,* a drama of sexual obsession starring Sandy Dennis as a mentally troubled woman who holds an apparently mute teenager captive in her home.

1970   Makes a commercial and critical breakthrough with the antiwar comedy *M*A*S*H,* using the Korean War as the backdrop for sardonic adventures of U.S. Army surgeons who oppose the horrors of war with an attitude of cynical humor; the film's episodic structure, roving camera work, and multilayered sound attract much notice as aspects of a distinctive personal style; it goes on to win the Palme d'Or at the Cannes International Film Festival and Academy Award nominations for best picture, director, supporting actress, and editing, taking the Oscar for best screenplay. Altman follows up quickly with *Brewster McCloud,* a surrealistic comedy about a young man building a flying machine in the depths of the Houston Astrodome; it receives a half-hearted release from MGM and does poorly with critics and audiences, although Altman's personal touches are again noticed, boosting his reputation as a director with a distinctive style. Altman begins shooting *McCabe and Mrs. Miller* in October in Vancouver, British Columbia.

1971   *McCabe and Mrs. Miller* is released, its sound and visual quality suffering from poorly processed prints; it receives mixed reviews and lackluster box-office returns, although its reputation starts to rise almost immediately when properly finished prints become available and critics begin discussing its unusual qualities.

1972   Shoots the psychodrama *Images,* a highly subjective account of a mentally troubled woman progressively losing touch with reality, in Ireland with British funding; it does poorly at the box office after yet another unenthusiastic release by its distributors, although Susannah York wins the best-actress award at the Cannes filmfest. Altman returns to Los Angeles to begin work on *The Long Goodbye,* applying experimental touches to the popular Raymond Chandler novel.

1973   *The Long Goodbye* marks another commercial disappointment coupled with mixed reviews, but United Artists agrees to back another project, *Thieves Like Us,* based on Edward Anderson's novel of love and crime in the 1930s; this begins Altman's collaboration with writer Joan Tewkesbury, designer Scott Bushnell, and cinematographer Jean Boffety.

1974   Influential critic Pauline Kael proclaims *Thieves Like Us* a "masterpiece" but box-office response is lukewarm, again exacerbated by studio uncertainty as to marketing and promotion. Altman starts work on the gambling comedy-drama *California Split,* an MGM project originally intended for Steven Spielberg; it earns a modest profit upon release.

1975   Directs the epic *Nashville* from Joan Tewkesbury's screenplay, fully indulging his penchant for multilayered sound, restless visuals, and improvisatory performances; it earns many rave reviews, fairly good box-office returns, and five Academy Award nominations despite a limited release by Paramount, which is concerned about its unconventional aspects.

1976   Directs the offbeat western *Buffalo Bill and the Indians, or, Sitting Bull's History Lesson,* based very loosely on Arthur Kopit's play *Indians;* postproduction is completed on an accelerated schedule; reviews are unenthusiastic and distribution is very limited. Altman establishes Lion's Gate Films, his own production company.

1977   Directs the highly surrealistic *3 Women,* based on a dream, with backing from Alan Ladd, Jr. at Twentieth Century-Fox, earning many respectful reviews and a best-actress prize for Shelley Duvall at the Cannes filmfest. Produces the offbeat private-eye drama *The Late Show* for director Robert Benton and the Altmanesque comedy-drama *Welcome to L.A.* for director Alan Rudolph.

1978   Directs the ambitious comedy-drama *A Wedding,* doubling the character count of *Nashville* from 24 to 48; reviews and financial returns are weak, although it is selected for Lincoln Center's respected New York Film Festival as the prestigious opening-night attraction. Begins work on *Quintet,* continuing his association with Twentieth Century-Fox. Produces *Remember My Name* for Alan Rudolph.

1979   Completes the dark fantasy *Quintet,* partially filmed above the Arctic Circle, with an international cast in a dreamlike story about diverse characters playing a deadly game in a perpetually frozen world; reviews and box-office results are disastrous. Still at Twentieth Century-Fox despite Alan Ladd, Jr.'s exit from the studio, Altman moves quickly into the romantic comedy-drama *A Perfect Couple,* which receives a minimal release. Serves as executive producer of *Rich Kids* for director Robert M. Young.

1980   Returns to his large-canvas style for *Health,* a comedy about personal and political intrigue at a health-foods convention, hoping to premiere it during the year's Presidential campaigns; Twentieth Century-Fox refuses to release it. His unconventional approach becomes an asset when he sets off to direct the big-budget musical *Popeye* in Malta, but weather problems and challenges raised by the production's comic-strip style result in widespread reports that the picture is in trouble; it turns a profit when released but reviews are mixed and Altman is again branded too risky for mainstream projects.

1981   Puts his Lion's Gate production company on the market, prompted by financial disputes with Paramount over the *Popeye* budget and the collapse of *Lone Star,* a tentative MGM/UA project; sells the company during the summer to producer Jonathan Taplin for $2.3 million. Expresses interest in nonstudio projects for cable television and home video, and begins a period of directing live theater productions, including the Broadway production of Ed Graczyk's drama *Come Back to the 5 and Dime, Jimmy Dean Jimmy Dean,* which receives weak reviews, and *Two by South,* a pair of one-act plays by Frank South ("Rattlesnake in a Cooler" and "Precious Blood") that is well-reviewed Off-Broadway and in Los Angeles.

1982   Directs a film version of *Come Back to the 5 and Dime, Jimmy Dean Jimmy Dean* in super-16mm for cable television; it also has a limited theatrical release, earning better reviews than the stage production had received; this begins a collaboration with cinematographer Pierre Mignot that continues for several years. Directs and produces a television version of *Two by South.* Directs a visually stunning large-scale production of Igor Stravinsky's opera *The Rake's Progress* at the University of Michigan in Ann Arbor, where he is a visiting lecturer. *Health* receives a bare-bones release from Twentieth Century-Fox two years after completion.

1983   Directs a long-delayed film version of David Rabe's drama *Streamers,* about soldiers in the Vietnam War, winning awards for its ensemble cast at the Venice Film Festival. Films the teenage comedy *O. C. and Stiggs* for MGM/UA, which refuses to release it.

1984   Directs a film version of *Secret Honor,* a one-character play about President Richard Nixon that Altman had produced on the stage; it earns solid reviews but limited financial returns.

1985   Completes a film version of Sam Shepard's drama *Fool for Love* for Cannon Films, considerably expanding the play's size and scope; reviews and returns are disappointing. Stays in Paris, where postproduction for that film was completed, to direct a television version of Marsha Norman's play *The Laundromat* with Carol Burnett and Amy Madigan.

1987   Directs television versions of *The Dumb Waiter* and *The Room,* two plays by Harold Pinter, for ABC in Montreal; directs a film version of Christopher Durang's comedy *Beyond Therapy* that fails critically and commercially. *O. C. and Stiggs* has a very limited release four years after completion.

1988   Contributes to *Aria,* producer Don Boyd's compilation film based on operatic music, by directing the short "Les Boréades," depicting a rowdy audience listening to three excerpts from Jean-Philippe Rameau's eponymous opera. Directs a television version of Herman Wouk's play *The Caine Mutiny Court-Martial.* Films the experimental miniseries *Tanner '88* for Home Box Office, in collaboration with "Doonesbury" cartoonist Gary Trudeau; this comedy about a presidential campaign, produced and broadcast during the actual 1988 election campaign, wins considerable acclaim and earns Altman an Emmy award for best director.

1989   Agrees to direct *Vincent & Theo,* about Vincent van Gogh and his brother.

1990   *Vincent & Theo* is released to very favorable response.

1991   Begins an effort to finance *L.A. Shortcuts,* based on short stories and a poem by Raymond Carver.

1992   Completes *The Player* from Michael Tolkin's screenplay about a movie producer who murders a screenwriter; the self-reflexive Hollywood satire is greeted with enthusiastic reviews and solid box-office earnings, and Altman is nominated for the best-director

Academy Award. Arranges to direct *Short Cuts*, which goes before the camera in late summer.

1993   Completes *Short Cuts*, a sprawling collection of stories set in Los Angeles; it wins best-picture and best-acting awards at the Venice filmfest and opens the New York filmfest, although its box-office returns do not equal its strong critical reception. Goes to work immediately on *Prêt-à-porter*, a large-canvas comedy about the Paris fashion world.

1994   Shooting of *Prêt-à-porter* begins in spring; its December opening, under the title *Ready-to-Wear*, brings a disappointing critical and commercial response.

1996   Releases the jazz-oriented drama *Kansas City*, which opens to mixed reviews and unimpressive box-office receipts.

1998   Completes *The Gingerbread Man*, a crime drama based on an original story by suspense novelist John Grisham; response is respectful, confirming Altman's current status as a bankable director. Starts work on *Cookie's Fortune*.

1999   *Cookie's Fortune* has its American premiere in January at Robert Redford's influential Sundance Film Festival in Park City, Utah, a closely watched showcase for independent productions; it opens commercially three months later.

FILMOGRAPHY

D—director; P—producer; S—screenplay; Ph—cinematography;
E—editor; M—music; C—principle cast.

1957. *The Delinquents*. D, P, S—**Robert Altman**; Ph—Charles Paddock;
E—Helene Turner; M—Bill Nolan; C—Tom Laughlin, Peter Miller, Rose-
mary Howard, Richard Bakalyan, James Lantz, Lotus Corelli, Leonard
Belove, Helene Hawley, George Kuhn, Pat Stedman, James Leria, Norman
Zands, Kermit Echols, Jet Pinkston, James Leria, Joe Adelman, Christine
Altman. United Artists. 75 min.

1957. *The James Dean Story*. D, P, E—**Robert Altman**, George W. George;
S—Stewart Stern; M—Leith Stevens; C—Martin Gabel. Warner Bros. 82 min.

1964. *Nightmare in Chicago (Once Upon a Savage Night)*. D, P—**Robert
Altman**; S—Donald Moessinger, from the William P. McGivern novel *Death
on the Turnpike*; Ph—Bud Thackery; E—Danford B. Greene, Larry D. Lester;
M—Johnny Williams; C—Charles McGraw, Robert Ridgeley, Ted Knight,
Barbara Turner, Philip Abbott, Douglas A. Alleman, Charlene Lee, Arlene
Kieta, Robert C. Harris, John Alonzo. Roncom/Universal. 81 min.

1968. *Countdown*. D—**Robert Altman**; P—James Lydon; S—Loring Mandel,
based on Hank Searls's novel *The Pilgrim Project*; Ph—William W. Spencer;
E—Gene Milford; M—Leonard Rosenman; C—James Caan, Robert Duvall,
Barbara Baxley, Joanna Moore, Charles Aidman, Michael Murphy, Ted

Knight, Steve Ihnat, Stephen Coit, Charles Irving, John Rayner, Bobby Riha Jr. Warner Bros. 101 min.

1969. *That Cold Day in the Park*. D—**Robert Altman**; P—Donald Factor, Leon Mirelli; S—Gillian Freeman, from the Richard Miles novel; Ph—Laszlo Kovacs; E—Danford B. Greene; M—Johnny Mandel; C—Sandy Dennis, Michael Burns, Suzanne Benton, Luana Anders, John Garfield, Jr., Michael Murphy, Doris Buckingham, Alicia Ammon, Edward Greenhalgh, Frank Wade, Rae Brown, Linda Sorensen, Lloyd Berry. Commonwealth. 110 min.

1970. *M*A*S*H*. D—**Robert Altman**; P—Ingo Preminger; S—Ring Lardner, Jr., from the novel by Richard Hooker (H. Richard Hornberger and William Heinz); Ph—Harold E. Stine; E—Danford B. Greene; M—Johnny Mandel; C—Donald Sutherland, Elliott Gould, Sally Kellerman, Tom Skerritt, Jo Ann Pflug, Robert Duvall, René Auberjonois, Bud Cort, Roger Bowen, Fred Williamson, Gary Burghoff, Fred Williamson, G. Wood, John Schuck, David Arkin, Michael Murphy, Kim Atwood, Tim Brown, Indus Arthur, Ken Prymus, Dawne Damon, Carl Gottlieb, Tamara Horrocks, Bobby Troup, Danny Goldman, Corey Fischer, J. B. Douglas, Yoko Young, Fran Tarkenton, Ben Davidson, Howard Williams, Jack Concannon, John Myers, Tom Woodeschick, Tommy Brown, Nolan Smith, Buck Buchanan. Twentieth Century-Fox. 116 min.

1970. *Brewster McCloud*. D—**Robert Altman**; P—Lou Adler; S—Doran William Cannon; P—Lamar Boren, Jordan Cronenweth; E—Louis Lombardo; M—Gene Page; C—Bud Cort, Sally Kellerman, Michael Murphy, William Windom, René Auberjonois, Shelley Duvall, John Schuck, Margaret Hamilton, Jennifer Salt, Stacy Keach, Corey Fischer, G. Wood, Bert Remsen, William Baldwin, Amelia Parker, Pearl Coffey Chason, Gary Wayne Chason, William Henry Bennet, Ellis Gilbert, Verdie Henshaw, Robert Warner, Keith V. Erickson, Thomas Danko, W. E. Terry, Jr., Dixie M. Taylor. Metro-Goldwyn-Mayer/Adler-Phillips-Lion's Gate Films. 104 min.

1971. *McCabe and Mrs. Miller*. D—**Robert Altman**; P—David Foster, Mitchell Grower; S—**Robert Altman**, Brian McKay, from Edmund Naughton's novel; Ph—Vilmos Zsigmond; E—Louis Lombardo; M—Leonard Cohen; C—Warren Beatty, Julie Christie, William Devane, Keith Carradine, John Schuck, René Auberjonois, Shelley Duvall, Michael

Murphy, Bert Remsen, Jack Riley, Hugh Millais, Corey Rischer, Anthony Holland, Jace Vander, Elizabeth Knight, Manfred Schulz, Robert Fortier, Jackie Crossland, Elizabeth Murphy, Linda Sorenson, Maysie Hoy, Linda Kupecek, Carey Lee McKenzie, Janet Wright, Tom Hill, Jeremy Newsom, Jack Riley, Wayne Robson, Wayne Grace, Wesley Taylor, Anne Cameron, Graeme Campbell, J. S. Johnson, Harry Trader, Edwin Collier, Joe Clarke, Terence Kelly, Brantley F. Kearns, Don Francks, Lili Francks, Rodney Gage, Derek Deurvorst, Alexander Diakun, Harvey Lowe, Joan McGuire, Claudine Melgrave, Gordon Robertson, Eric Schneider, Milos Zalovic. Warner Bros. 121 min.

1972. *Images.* D, S—**Robert Altman**; P—Tommy Thompson; Ph—Vilmos Zsigmond; E—Graeme Clifford; M—John Williams, Stomu Yamash'ta; C—Susanna York, René Auberjonois, Marcel Bozzuffi, Cathryn Harrison, Hugh Millais, John Morley. Lion's Gate Films/Hemdale/Columbia. 101 min.

1973. *The Long Goodbye.* D—**Robert Altman**; P—Jerry Bick; S—Leigh Brackett, based on Raymond Chandler's novel; Ph—Vilmos Zsigmond; E—Lou Lombardo; M—John Williams; C—Elliott Gould, Nina Van Pallandt, Sterling Hayden, Mark Rydell, Henry Gibson, Jim Bouton, Jo Ann Brody, David Arkin, Warren Berlinger, Ken Sansom, Jack Riley, David Carradine, Arnold Strong (Arnold Schwarzenegger), Jack Knight, Pepe Callahan, Vince Palmieri, Rutanya Alda, Kate Murtagh, Tammy Shaw, Danny Goldman, Sybil Scotford, Steve Coit, Tracy Harris, Jerry Jones, Rodney Moss. Elliott Kastner/Lion's Gate Films/United Artists. 113 min.

1974. *Thieves Like Us.* D—**Robert Altman**; P—Jerry Bick; S—Joan Tewkes-bury, Calder Willingham, **Robert Altman**, based on Edward Anderson's novel; Ph—Jean Boffety; E—Lou Lombardo; C—Keith Carradine, Shelley Duvall, Bert Remsen, Louise Fletcher, Tom Skerritt, John Schuck, Ann Latham, Joan Tewkesbury, Al Scott, John Roper, Rodney Lee, Jr., Mary Waits, William Watters, Lloyd Jones, Dr. Edward Fisher, Joesphine Bennett, Pam Warner, Howard Warner, Eleanor Mathews, Walter Cooper. United Artists. 123 min.

1974. *California Split.* D—**Robert Altman**; P—**Robert Altman**, Joseph Walsh; S—Joseph Walsh; Ph—Paul Lohmann; E—Lou Lombardo; M—Phyllis Shotwell; C—George Segal, Elliott Gould, Ann Prentiss, Gwen

Welles, Joseph Walsh, Edward Walsh, Jeff Goldblum, Bert Remsen, Barbara Ruick, John Considine, Joanne Strauss, Jack Riley, Barbara London, Jay Fletcher, Barbara Colby, Vince Palmieri, Alyce Passman, Sierra Bandit, Eugene Troobnick, Richard Kennedy, John Winston, Mike Greene, Bill Duffy, Tom Signorelli, Sharon Compton, Harry Drackett, A. J. Hood, Winston Lee, Thomas Hal Phillips, "Amarillo Slim" Preston, Ted Say, Marc Cavell, Mickey Fox, Arnold Herzstein, Carol Lohmann, Alvin Weissman. Columbia. 109 min.

1975. *Nashville.* D, P—**Robert Altman**; S—Joan Tewkesbury; Ph—Paul Lohmann; E—Sidney Levin, Dennis Hill; M—Richard Baskin; C—Lily Tomlin, Ned Beatty, Keith Carradine, Henry Gibson, Ronee Blakley, Geraldine Chaplin, Ned Beatty, Keenan Wynn, Michael Murphy, David Arkin, Shelley Duvall, Lauren Hutton, Barbara Harris, Allen Garfield, Karen Black, Barbara Baxley, Christina Raines, Scott Glenn, Jeff Goldblum, Gwen Welles, Robert Doqui, Bert Remsen, Richard Baskin, Timothy Brown, David Hayward, Allan Nicholls, Sheila Bailey, Dave Peel, Julie Christie, Elliott Gould, James Dan Calvert, Donna Denton, Vassar Clements, Sue Barton, Patti Bryant, Merle Kilgore, Carol McGinnis, Jonnie Barnett. ABC/Paramount. 159 min.

1976. *Buffalo Bill and the Indians, or, Sitting Bull's History Lesson.* D, P—**Robert Altman**; S—**Robert Altman**, Alan Rudolph, based on an Arthur Kopit play; Ph—Paul Lohmann; E—Peter Appleton, Dennis Hill; M—Richard Baskin; C—Paul Newman, Geraldine Chaplin, Will Sampson, Joel Grey, Burt Lancaster, Harvey Keitel, Shelley Duvall, Kevin McCarthy, John Considine, Bert Remsen, Frank Kaquitts, Robert Doqui, Pat McCormick, Denver Pyle, Allan Nicholls, Mike Kaplan, Bonnie Leaders, Evelyn Lear, E. L. Doctorow, Noelle Rogers, Ken Krossa, Fred N. Larsen, Jerry Duce, Joy Duce, Alex Green, Gary MacKenzie, Humphrey Gratz, Pluto Calcedona. Lion's Gate Films/Dino De Laurentiis/United Artists. 123 min.

1977. *3 Women.* D, P, S—**Robert Altman**; Ph—Charles Rosher; E—Dennis Hill; M—Gerald Busby; C—Shelley Duvall, Sissy Spacek, Janice Rule, Robert Fortier, John Cromwell, Craig Richard Nelson, Ruth Nelson, Belita Moreno, Beverly Ross, John Davey, Sierra Pecheur, Leslie Ann Hudson, Patricia Ann Hudson, Maysie Hoy. Lion's Gate Films/Twentieth Century-Fox. 123 min.

1978. *A Wedding.* D, P—Story—**Robert Altman**; S—John Considine, Patricia Resnick, Allan Nicholls, **Robert Altman**; Ph—Charles Rosher; E—Tony Lombardo; M—Tom Walls, John Hotchkis; C—Lillian Gish, Vittorio Gassman, Desi Arnaz, Jr., Ruth Nelson, Howard Duff, Nina Van Pallandt, Dina Merrill, Pat McCormick, Carol Burnett, Paul Dooley, Mia Farrow, Pam Dawber, Amy Stryker, Geraldine Chaplin, Lauren Hutton, Belita Moreno, Allan Nicholls, John Considine, Allan Nicholls, Ann Ryerson, Lauren Hutton, Dennis Christopher, Cedric Scott, Robert Fortier, Patricia Resnick, Bert Remsen, John Cromwell, Gavan O'Herlihy, Marta Heflin, Dennis Franz, Viveca Lindfors, Craig Richard Nelson, Beverly Ross, Virginia Vestoff, Luigi Proietti, Mary Seibel, Margaret Ladd, Gerald Busby, Peggy Ann Garner, Mark R. Deming, Jay D. Jones, Jeffrey Jones, Amy Brand, Chris Brand, David Brand, Jenny Brand, Courtney MacArthur, Paul D. Keller III, Maureen Steindler, Mona Abboud, Maysie Hoy, Margery Bond, Harold C. Johnson, Alexander Sopenar, Jeffrey S. Perry, Lesley Rogers, Timothy Thomerson, David Fitzgerald, Susan Kendall Newman, Ellie Albers, Tony Llorens, Chris La Kome. Lion's Gate Films/Twentieth Century-Fox. 125 min.

1979. *Quintet.* D, P—**Robert Altman**; S—**Robert Altman**, Frank Barhydt, Patricia Resnick; Ph—Jean Boffety; E—Dennis M. Hill; M—Tom Pierson; C—Paul Newman, Vittorio Gassman, Fernando Rey, Bibi Andersson, Brigitte Fossey, Nina Van Pallandt, Monique Mercure, Tom Hill, David Langton, Craig Richard Nelson, Max Fleck, Maruska Stankova, Anne Gerety, Michael Maillot, François Berd. Lion's Gate Films/Twentieth Century-Fox. 110 min.

1979. *A Perfect Couple.* D, P—**Robert Altman**; S—Allan Nicholls, **Robert Altman**; Ph—Edmond L. Koons; E—Tony Lombardo; M—Tony Berg, Allan Nicholls, Tom Pierson; C—Paul Dooley, Marta Heflin, Titos Vandis, Henry Gibson, Belita Moreno, Dimitra Arliss, Ann Ryerson, Allan Nicholls, Ted Neeley, Dennis Franz, Poppy Lagos, Margery Bond, Mona Golabek, Terry Wills, Susan Blakeman, Melanie Bishop, Fred Bier, Jette Seear, Heather MacRae, Tomi-Lee Bradley, Steven Sharp, Tony Berg, Craig Doerge, Butch Sandford, Jeff Eyrich, David Luell, Art Wood, Ren Woods, Tom Pierson. Lion's Gate Films/Twentieth Century-Fox. 111 min.

1980. *Health (HEALTH).* D, P—**Robert Altman**; S—Frank Barhydt, Paul Dooley, **Robert Altman**; Ph—Edmond L. Koons; E—Tony Lombardo,

Dennis Hill, Tom Benko; M—Joseph Byrd; C—Lauren Bacall, James Garner, Glenda Jackson, Carol Burnett, Paul Dooley, Alfre Woodard, Henry Gibson, Donald Moffat, Diane Stilwell, Ann Ryerson, MacIntyre Dixon, Robert Fortier, Allan Nicholls, Dick Cavett, Georgann Johnson, Mina Kolb, Margery Bond, Nancy Foster, Julie Janney, Diane Shaffer, Patty Katz, Nathalie Blossom. Lion's Gate/Twentieth Century-Fox. 96 min.

1980. *Popeye*. D—**Robert Altman**; P—Robert Evans; S—Jules Feiffer, based on comic-strip characters created by E. C. Segar; Ph—Giuseppe Rotunno; E—Tony Lombardo, John W. Holmes, David Simmons; M—Harry Nilsson, with additional score by Tom Pierson; C—Robin Williams, Shelley Duvall, Paul Dooley, Ray Walston, Richard Libertini, Wesley Ivan Hurt, Paul L. Smith, Roberta Maxwell, MacIntyre Dixon, Donovan Scott, Donald Moffat, Dennis Franz, David Arkin, Linda Hunt, Peter Bray, Allan Nicholls, Bill Irwin, Klaus Voorman, Van Dyke Parks, Robert Fortier, David McCharen, Susan Kingsley, Michael Christensen, Sharon Kinney, Geoff Hoyle, Wayne Robson, Larry Pisoni, Carlo Pellegrini, Ray Cooper, Noel Parenti, Karen McCormick, John Bristol, Julie Janney, Patty Katz, Diane Shaffer, Nathelie Blossom, Carlos Brown, Ned Dowd, Hovey Burgess, Judy Burgess, Roberto Messina, Pietro Torrisi, Margery Bond, Saundra MacDonald, Eve Knoller, Peggy Pisoni, Barbara Zegler, Paul Zegler, Pamela Burrell, Roberto Dell'Aqua, Valerie Velardi, Doug Dillard, Stan Wilson. Paramount/Walt Disney. 114 min.

1982. *Come Back to the 5 and Dime, Jimmy Dean Jimmy Dean*. D—**Robert Altman**; P—Scott Bushnell; S—Ed Graczyk, based on his play; Ph—Pierre Mignot; E—Jason Rosenfield; C—Sandy Dennis, Cher, Karen Black, Sudie Bond, Kathy Bates, Marta Heflin, Mark Patton. Sandcastle 5/Mark Goodson/ Viacom. 102 min.

1983. *Streamers*. D—**Robert Altman**; P—**Robert Altman**, Nick J. Mileti; S—David Rabe, based on his play; Ph—Pierre Mignot; E—Norman C. Smith; C—Matthew Modine, Mitchell Lichtenstein, David Alan Grier, Michael Wright, Guy Boyd, George Dzundza, Albert Macklin. Mileti Productions/United Artists Classics. 118 min.

1984. *Secret Honor*. D, P—**Robert Altman**; S—Donald Freed, Arnold M. Stone, based on their play; Ph—Pierre Mignot; E—Juliet Weber; M—George

Burt; C—Philip Baker Hall. Sandcastle 5/in cooperation with University of Michigan, Los Angeles Actors' Theatre. 85 min.

1985. *Fool for Love.* D—**Robert Altman**; P—Menahem Golan, Yoram Globus; S—Sam Shepard, based on his play; P—Pierre Mignot; E—Luce Grunenwaldt, Steve Dunn; M—George Burt; C—Sam Shepard, Kim Basinger, Randy Quaid, Harry Dean Stanton, Martha Crawford, Sura Cox, Louise Egolf, Jonathan Skinner, April Russell, Deborah McNaughton, Lon Hill. Cannon Group. 107 min.

1987. *Beyond Therapy.* D—**Robert Altman**; P—Steven M. Haft; S—**Robert Altman**, Christopher Durang, based on Durang's play; Ph—Pierre Mignot; E—Steve Dunn; M—Gabriel Yared; C—Julie Hagerty, Jeff Goldblum, Glenda Jackson, Tom Conti, Genevieve Page, Christopher Guest, Cris Campion, Sandrine Dumas, Bertrand Bonvoisin, Nicole Evans, Louis-Marie Taillefer, Laure Killing, Gilbert Blin, Matthew Lesniak, Sylvie Lenoir, Vincent Longuemare, Françoise Armel, Annie Monnier, Jeanne Cellard, Hélène Constantine, Yvette Prayer, Joan Tyrell. Sandcastle 5/New World Pictures/ Roger Berlind. 93 min.

1987. *O. C. and Stiggs.* (filmed 1983). D—**Robert Altman**; P—**Robert Altman**, Peter Newman; S—Donald Cantrell, Ted Mann; Ph—Pierre Mignot; E—Elizabeth Kling; M—King Sunny Ade and his African Beats; C—Daniel H. Jenkins, Neill Barry, Paul Dooley, Jane Curtin, Dennis Hopper, Melvin Van Peebles, Ray Walston, Louis Nye, Tina Louise, Martin Mull, Cynthia Nixon, Laura Urstein, Jon Cryer, Donald May, Clara Borelli, James Gilsenan, Victor Ho, Bob Uecker. Metro-Goldwyn-Mayer/United Artists. 109 min.

1988. "Les Boréades," in anthology film *Aria.* D, S—**Robert Altman**; P—Don Boyd; M—Jean-Philippe Rameau; C—Jennifer Smith, Anne Marie Radde, Phillip Langridge. Lightyear Entertainment/Virgin Vision/Miramax Films. 90 min (entire film).

1990. *Vincent & Theo.* D—**Robert Altman**; P—Ludi Boeken; S—Julian Mitchell; Ph—Jean Lepine; E—Françoise Coispeau; M—Gabriel Yared; C—Tim Roth, Paul Rhys, Jean-Pierre Cassel, Johanna Ter Steege, Wladimir Yordanoff, Bernadette Giraud, Adrian Brine, Jean-François Perrier, Hans

Kesting, Anne Canovas, Jip Wijngaarden. Belbo Films/Central Films/La
Sept/Telepool/RAI Uno/Vara/Sofica-Valor/Arena Films. 138 min.

1992. *The Player.* D—**Robert Altman**; S—Michael Tolkin; M—Thomas
Newman; C—Tim Robbins, Greta Scacchi, Peter Gallagher, Whoopi
Goldberg, Fred Ward, Cynthia Stevenson, Vincent D'Onofrio, Brion James,
Richard E. Grant, Dean Stockwell, Dina Merrill, Sydney Pollack, Gina
Gershon, Lyle Lovett, Randall Batinkoff, Elliott Gould, Sally Kellerman,
Nick Nolte, Cher, Jill St. John, Burt Reynolds, Julia Roberts, Jack Lemmon,
Lily Tomlin, Jeremy Piven, Michael Tolkin, Stephen Tolkin, Frank Barhydt,
Marlee Matlin, Bruce Willis, Buck Henry, Anjelica Huston, Steve Allen,
Richard Anderson, Joel Grey, Harry Belafonte, Shari Belafonte, Rod Steiger,
Mimi Rogers, Sally Kirkland, Michael Tolkin, Joan Tewkesbury, Scott
Glenn, Karen Black, Robert Carradine, Kathy Ireland, James Coburn, Gary
Busey, Ray Walston, Cathy Lee Crosby, Brad Davis, Martin Mull, Teri Garr,
John Cusack, Marvin Young, Leeza Gibbons, Andie MacDowell, Peter Falk,
Jeff Goldblum, Adam Simon, Robert Wagner, Brian Tochi, Susan Sarandon,
Alan Rudolph, Annie Ross, Jack Riley, Patricia Resnick, Bert Remsen, Guy
Remsen, Alexandra Powers, Jennifer Nash, Jayne Meadows, Malcolm
McDowell, Sally Kellerman, Maxine John-James, Steve James, David Alan
Grier, Dennis Franz, Louise Fletcher, Kasia Figura, Felicia Farr, Thereza Ellis,
Paul Dooley, Michael Bowen, René Auberjonois, Charles Champlin. Avenue
Entertainment/Spelling Films International. 123 min.

1993. *Short Cuts.* D—**Robert Altman**; P—Carey Brocaw; S—Frank Barhydt,
Robert Altman, based on Raymond Carver stories; Ph—Walt Lloyd; E—
Geraldine Peroni, Suzy Elmiger; M—Mark Isham; C—Jennifer Jason
Leigh, Annie Ross, Lori Singer, Tim Robbins, Lyle Lovett, Lili Taylor, Lily
Tomlin, Tom Waits, Bruce Davison, Madeleine Stowe, Matthew Modine,
Anne Archer, Peter Gallagher, Fred Ward, Frances McDormand, Robert
Downey, Jr., Andie MacDowell, Jack Lemmon, Buck Henry, Huey Lewis,
Julianne Moore, Chris Penn, Jarrett Lennon, Robert Doqui, Walt Lloyd,
Zane Cassidy, Margery Bond. Fine Line Features/Avenue Pictures/Spelling
Films International. 189 min.

1994. *Prêt-à-porter (Ready-To-Wear).* D, P—**Robert Altman**; S—**Robert
Altman**, Barbara Shulgasser; Ph—Jean Lépine, Pierre Mignot; E—Suzy

Elmiger, Geraldine Peroni; M—Michel Legrand; C—Marcello Mastroianni, Sophia Loren, Jean-Pierre Cassel, Kim Basinger, Chiara Mastroianni, Lili Taylor, Stephen Rae, Anouk Aimée, Rupert Everett, Rossy de Palma, Tara Leon, Georgianna Robertson, Ute Lemper, Forest Whitaker, Michel Blanc, Tom Novembre, Richard E. Grant, Anne Canovas, Tim Robbins, Julia Roberts, Lauren Bacall, Danny Aiello, Lyle Lovett, Tracey Ullman, Sally Kellerman, Linda Hunt, Teri Garr, Jean Rochefort, François Cluzet, Harry Belafonte, Katarzyna Figura, Sam Robards, Tapa Sudana, Laura Benson, Laurent Lederer, Constant Anee, Yann Collette, Christy Turlington, Alexandra Vandernoot, Jocelyne Saint Denis, André Penvern, Maurice Lamy, Pascal Mourier, Adrien Stahly, Denis Lepeut, Paola Bulgari, Serge Molitor, Claude Montana, Anello Capuano, Thierry Mugler, Cher, Tatjana Patitz, Helena Christensen, Sonia Rykiel, Gamiliana, Eve Salvail, Elsa Klensch, Nicola Trussardi, Jean-Paul Gaultier, Christian Lacroix, Issey Miyake, Gianfranco Ferre, Susie Bick, Björk, Naomi Campbell, David Copperfield, Claudia Schiffer. Miramax Films. 133 min.

1996. *Kansas City.* D, P—**Robert Altman**; S—**Robert Altman**, Frank Barhydt; Ph—Oliver Stapleton; E—Geraldine Peroni; M—John Cale; C—Jennifer Jason Leigh, Miranda Richardson, Harry Belafonte, Michael Murphy, Dermot Mulroney, Steve Buscemi. Electric/Sandcastle 5/CiBy 2000. 115 min.

1998. *The Gingerbread Man.* D—**Robert Altman**; P—Jeremy Tannenbaum; S—**Robert Altman** (as Al Hayes) from John Grisham's original story; Ph—Changwei Gu; E—Geraldine Peroni; M—Mark Isham; C—Kenneth Branagh, Embeth Davidtz, Robert Downey, Jr., Daryl Hannah, Robert Duvall, Famke Janssen, Tom Berenger, Mae Whitman, Troy Beyer, Julia Ryder Perce, Danny Darst, Sonny Seiler, Vernon E. Jordan, Jr., Walter Hartridge, Lori Beth Sikes, Michelle Benjamin Cooper, Rosemary Newcott, Wilbur Fitzgerald, David Hersberg, Paul Carden, Christine Seabrook, Bob Minor, Myrna White, Jim Grimshaw, Stuart Greer, Gregg Jarrett, Nita Hardy, Ferguson Reid, Benjamin T. Gay, Mark Bednarz, Chip Tootle, Grace Tootle, Sonny Shroyer, Mike Pniewski, Jay S. Pearson, L. H. Smith, Wren Arthur, Jesse James, Angela Costrini, Vanessa Young, Lydia Marlene, Bill Crabb, Jin Hi Soucy, Richie Dye, Chad Darnell, Nathalie Hendrix, Doug Weathers, Jeremy Cooper, Beth Eckard, Brad Huffines, Bill Cunningham,

Patrick Prokop, Mike Manhattan, David Jordan, Gregory Alpert, George Lyndel Brannen, Gregory F. Pallone, Alice Stewart, Angela Beasley, Alyson Beasley, Scott Troughton, Shane James, Herb Kelsey, William Thorpe. Enchanter Entertainment/Island Pictures. 114 min.

1999. *Cookie's Fortune.* D—**Robert Altman**; P—**Robert Altman**, Etchie Stroh; S—Anne Rapp; Ph—Toyomichi Kurita; M—David A. Stewart; C—Patricia Neal, Charles S. Dutton, Glenn Close, Julianne Moore, Liv Tyler, Lyle Lovett, Chris O'Donnell, Ned Beatty, Courtney B. Vance, Donald Moffat. October Films. 118 min.

Industrial and commercial films

Approximately 60 films for the Calvin Company of Kansas City, Missouri, including *Better Football, King Basketball, The Builders, The Dirty Look, Honeymoon for Harriet, The Last Mile, The Magic Bond, Modern Baseball, Modern Football, The Perfect Crime,* and *The Sound of Bells.* Other early films made outside the Calvin Company including *Fashion Faire, Grand Stand Rookie,* and *The Model's Handbook.*

Miscellaneous shorts

ColorSonics productions including *The Party.* Personal films including *Pot au Feu* (1966) and *The Life of Kathryn Reed* (M—John Williams; C—Ted Knight).

Television specials

1982. *Two by South.* D, P—**Robert Altman**; S—Frank South; C—Leo Burmester, Guy Boyd, Alfre Woodard. Alpha Repertory Television Service.

1985. *The Laundromat.* D—**Robert Altman**; P—Dann Byck, David Lancaster; S—Marsha Norman; Ph—Pierre Mignot; E—Luce Grunenwaldt; M—Alberta Hunter, Danny Darst; C—Carol Burnett, Amy Madigan, Michael Wright. Byck-Lancaster/Sandcastle 5.

1987. *The Dumb Waiter.* D, P—**Robert Altman**; S—Harold Pinter; Ph—Pierre Mignot; M—Judith Gruber-Stitzer; C—John Travolta, Tom Conti. Secret Castle Productions/ABC.

1987. *The Room.* D, P—**Robert Altman**; S—Harold Pinter; Ph—Pierre Mignot; E—Jennifer Auge; M—Judith Gruber-Stitzer; C—Linda Hunt, Annie Lennox, Julian Sands, Donald Pleasance, David Hemblen, Abbott Anderson. Secret Castle Productions/ABC.

1988. *The Caine Mutiny Court-Martial.* D—**Robert Altman**; P—**Robert Altman**, John Flaxman; S—Herman Wouk; Ph—Jacek Laskus; E—Dorian Harris; C—Eric Gogosian, Brad Davis, Jeff Daniels, Michael Murphy, Peter Gallagher, Kevin J. O'Connor, Daniel Jenkins, Danny Darst, Ken Michels, David Miller, Matt Molloy, David Barnett, Ken Jones, Brian Haley, Matt Smith, L. W. Wyman. The Maltese Companies/Wouk/Ware Productions/ Sandcastle 5 Productions/Columbia Pictures Television.

1988. *Tanner '88.* D—**Robert Altman**; P—Scott Bushnell; S—Garry B. Trudeau; Ph—Jean Lepine; E—Alison Ellwood, Judith Sobol, Ruth Foster, Dorian Harris, Sean-Michael Connor; C—Michael Murphy, Pamela Reed, Cynthia Nixon, Kevin J. O'Connor, Matt Molloy, Jim Fyfe, Daniel Jenkins, Ilana Levine, Veronica Cartwright, Wendy Crewson, Sandra Bowie, Greg Procaccino, Frank Barhydt, Waylon Jennings, Harry Anderson, John Considine, E. G. Marshall, Cleavon Little, Sen. Robert Dole, Sidney Blumenthal, G. David Hughes, Rev. Pat Robertson, Mary McGrory, Rep. Mickey Leland, James Davidson, Chris Mathews, Hodding Carter, Patt Derian, Peter Edelman, Aviel Ginzburg, Pamela Ginzburg, Ralph Nader, Studs Terkel, Lynn Russell, Kitty Dukakis, Rep. Ed Markey, Kirk O'Donnell, Bob Squier, Danny Darst, Gov. Bruce Babbitt, Joan Cushing, Rebecca De Mornay, Dorothy Sarnoff, Linda Ellerbee, Sandra J. Burud, Kim Cranston, Harlow, Gloria Steinem, Art Buchwald, Rep. Lee Hamilton. Zenith and Darkhorse Productions/Home Box Office.

Films directed by others

1947. *Christmas Eve.* D—Edwin L. Marin; P—Benedict Bogeaus; Story— **Robert Altman** (uncredited), Laurence Stallings, Richard H. Landau; S—Laurence Stallings; Ph—Gordon Avil; E—James Smith; M—Heinz Roemheld; C—George Raft, George Brent, Randolph Scott, Joan Blondell, Virginia Field, Ann Harding, Reginald Denny, Dolores Moran, Dennis Hoey, John Litel, Carl Harbord, Clarence Kolb, Joe Sawyer, Molly Lamont,

Douglass Dumbrille, Walter Sande, Holly Bane, Soledad Jimenez, Konstantin Shayne, Marie Blake. United Artists. 90 min. 35mm.

1948. *Bodyguard.* D—Richard Fleischer; P—Sid Rogell; S—Fred Niblo, Jr., Harry Essex; Story—**Robert Altman**, George W. George; Ph—Robert de Grasse; E—Elmo Williams; M—Paul Sawtell; C—Lawrence Tierney, Priscilla Lane, Philip Reed, June Clayworth, Steve Brodie, Frank Fenton, Elisabeth Risdon, Charles Cane. RKO. 62 min.

1951. *Corn's-a-Poppin'.* D, Ph—Robert Woodburn; S—**Robert Altman**, Robert Woodburn; M—John J. Thompson, Jr.; C—Jerry Wallace, Pat McReynolds, James Lantz, Dora Walls, Keith Painton, Noralee Benedict, Little Cora Weiss, Hobie Shepp and the Cowtown Wranglers. Crest. 62 min.

1970. *Events.* C—**Robert Altman.**

1976. *Welcome to L. A.* D, S—Alan Rudolph; P—**Robert Altman**; Ph—Dave Myers; M—Richard Baskin; C—Keith Carradine, Geraldine Chaplin, Sally Kellerman, Lauren Hutton, Harvey Keitel, Viveca Lindfors, Sissy Spacek, Denver Pyle. Lion's Gate/**Robert Altman.** 106 min.

1977. *The Late Show.* D, S—Robert Benton; P—**Robert Altman**; Ph—Chuck Rosher; E—Lou Lombardo, Peter Appleton; M—Ken Wannberg; C—Art Carney, Lily Tomlin, Eugene Roche, Bill Macy, Joanna Cassidy, John Considine, Ruth Nelson, Howard Duff. Warner. 93 min.

1978. *Remember My Name.* D, S—Alan Rudolph; P—**Robert Altman**; Ph—Tak Fujimoto; E—Thomas Walls, William A. Sawyer; M—Alberta Hunter; C—Geraldine Chaplin, Moses Gunn, Anthony Perkins, Berry Berenson, Jeff Goldblum. Columbia/Lion's Gate. 94 min.

1979. *Rich Kids.* D—Robert M. Young; Exec. P—**Robert Altman**; S—Judith Ross; Ph—Ralf D. Bode; M—Craig Doerge; C—Trini Alvarado, Jeremy Levy, Kathryn Walker, John Lithgow, Terry Kiser, David Selby. Lion's Gate/ UA. 96 min.

1981. *Endless Love.* D—Franco Zeffirelli; S—Judith Rascoe; Ph—David Watkin; M—Jonathan Tunick; C—Brooke Shields, Martin Hewitt, Shirley

Knight, Don Murray, Richard Kiley, Beatrice Straight, **Robert Altman.**
Polygram. 110 min.

1982. *Before the Nickelodeon: The Early Cinema of Edwin S. Porter.* D—Charles
Musser; S—Warren D. Leight, Charles Musser; C—**Robert Altman.** Film
for Thought. 60 min.

1985. *Lily in Love/Jatszani Kell.* D—Karoly Makk; Assoc. P—**Robert Altman**;
S—Frank Cucci; Ph—John Lindley; E—Norman Gay; M—Szaboks Fenyes;
C—Christopher Plummer, Maggie Smith, Elke Sommer, Adolph Green.
Robert Halmi. 103 min.

1988. *The Moderns.* D—Alan Rudolph; S—Alan Rudolph, Jon Bradshaw;
Ph—Toyomichoi Kurita; E—Debra T. Smith, Scott Brock; M—Mark Isham;
Assistance—**Robert Altman**; C—Keith Carradine, Geraldine Chaplin,
Linda Fiorentino, Wallace Shawn, Geneviève Bujold, John Lone, Kevin
O'Connor, Elsa Raven, Ali Giron. Rank/Alive Films/Nelson. 126 min.

1990. *Hollywood Mavericks.* C—**Robert Altman,** Alan Rudolph, Francis Ford
Coppola, Martin Scorsese, Peter Bogdanovich, Paul Schrader, David Lynch,
Dennis Hopper. 90 min.

ROBERT ALTMAN

INTERVIEWS

The 15th Man Who Was Asked to Direct
*M*A*S*H* (and Did) Makes a Peculiar Western

ALJEAN HARMETZ/1971

IT IS 4:30 ON a Friday afternoon in late December, and the Canadian darkness has fallen like a stone. Water pours down Robert Altman's Mephistophelean beard, and an incongruously thin string of love beads circles his massive neck. At 2 a.m. the preceding night he lurched to bed, a last glass of Scotch in one hand, a last joint of marijuana in the other. But the indulgences of the night have no claim over the day. He was the first man on the set in the winter darkness of 7 a.m. He will be the last man to leave in the slippery frozen twilight.

Standing in the rain with his 205 pounds zipped into a hooded, red nylon jumpsuit and the west coast of North America lying beyond his left shoulder, movie director Robert Altman looks a bit like a giant hawk, a bit more like Santa Claus, even more like Alan Hale as Little John to Errol Flynn's Robin Hood. But the overall impression is of a cheerful Old Nick. Only tail and pitchfork are missing.

Altman drinks hot buttered rum from a silver flask. He has had no breakfast, no lunch, but "the biggest problem in shooting a movie is time to go to the bathroom." In the few hours of daylight, he has completed 34 camera setups. He is pleased with himself, and he does not try to hide it. Later tonight, swacked on Scotch, grass, red and white wine, he will announce, "I was so good today it was fabulous. I embarrassed myself."

From *The New York Times Magazine* June 20, 1971: 10–11, 46–47, 49, 52–54. Reprinted by permission of Aljean Harmetz.

At 46, Robert Altman is Hollywood's newest 26-year-old genius. The extra 20 years are simply the time he had to spend, chained and toothless, in the anterooms of power—waiting for Hollywood to catch up with him.

While he was waiting, he made a million dollars as a television director and spent two million; fathered four children on three wives; gave up the last remnants of Catholicism for hedonism, and occasionally lost $2,000 in a single night in Las Vegas without losing half an hour's sleep over the money.

Eighteen months ago Hollywood caught up—with a vengeance. Robert Altman had waited 20 years for the historical accident of having 14 *more acceptable* directors turn down *M*A*S*H*. For *M*A*S*H* Altman won an Academy Award nomination. The film was chosen as best film of the Cannes Film Festival and also selected best film of 1970 by the National Society of Film Critics.

Later on this Friday in late December, Altman sits on the floor of his rented house in Vancouver, B. C.—a glass of red wine in one hand, a joint in the other—casually seducing men and women alike with the intensity of his interest. There are a dozen people in the room, almost all old friends, veterans of half a dozen Hollywood wars, now in Canada with him to work on his new film, *McCabe and Mrs. Miller*.

Round and round the circle goes the joint, sealing some mystical bargain. ("All of it is a love affair," says the screenwriter of *McCabe and Mrs. Miller,* Brian McKay. "Everyone on a Bob Altman movie is there because Bob needs them to make that film. If he doesn't need you anymore, goodbye. So wrapping your whole life in Bob Altman as some people do is dangerous. When he turns off the charisma, it hurts.") Altman will not let his 16-year-old son smoke marijuana. "He's too young. I do what I do. I get up in the morning and go to work. If he gets stoned in the evening, he's not committed to anything the next day."

By the time Altman lurches to his feet to take the circle out to dinner, he has consumed enough Scotch, wine and grass to put an army to sleep, but he shows no sign of wear. His energy level and his stamina are so high that he cannot easily blow out the light. (He does, however, have one other way of relaxing. He will sometimes take to his bed for a weekend, switching from television station to television station with his remote control in search of a roller derby. When he finds one, he will lie, half-hypnotized, for hours, watching the skaters go round and round.)

Halfway through dinner, he rests his elbows on the table, his eyes clos-ing, his head swaying. He is suddenly hostile. "I've found myself performing for you 16 times today," he tells a reporter—infuriated at even unintentional deceit in himself. He charges forward verbally—challenging, taunting—yet neither his crude language nor his massive self-confidence can mask or take away his considerable charm. More and more uncomfortable, his wife begs him to stop. He shrugs her off. Eventually she moves out of earshot to the other end of the long table.

The bill for dinner is $153.25. Altman pays it with an American Express card. He holds the plastic rectangle triumphantly. The card arrived that morning, proof that he is no longer a bad credit risk. He had been apply-ing for it for six years.

Altman insists on driving home. Each member of the party remon-strates, protests, begs, but he is too powerful to be stopped. Eventually they give in. He makes the wrong turn and there is a silent-movie chase around the restaurant.

Back at his house, Altman is handed a Scotch and soda as a matter of routine. Nobody tries to *handle* him. Nobody tells him he has had enough. After an hour of sipping Scotch and wine, he is completely recovered, in better condition than the others—most of whom have had far less to drink.

He is still on his feet when the house empties at 2 a.m.

Altman's staying power through the long Canadian nights is one thing. His staying power as a director is another. It is too early to make any sound appraisal of the range of Robert Altman's talent. Says director Blake Edwards, who has been there and back again, "It used to be that there were 10 direc-tors you were sure of. Now a guy has one great success and three failures and you look back and say, 'What did I ever see in him?'"

As a result of *M*A*S*H*, Hollywood—which rarely looks beyond imme-diate grosses—has chosen Robert Altman as its current *hot* director. In Matteo's Restaurant, the silken executives paw at his turtleneck sweater. At 20th Century-Fox, frightened men carry the grosses of *M*A*S*H* on the backs of torn envelopes. Four years ago the Mirisch company wouldn't allow him to direct a $5,000,000 picture. After *M*A*S*H*, they called and begged him to direct the film.

Offered the moon, Altman takes very small bites. "You can steal money in TV and movies. I could make $150,000 a year for the next two or three years without doing a thing. By making deals that never go through, by accepting money to develop projects that are never finished." He thinks that he has been "really lucky with the long gestation period—with failure. If I had had a hit, a major success, 15 years ago or even five years ago, it would have destroyed me." From years of gambling he has learned that "it takes only one minute to become totally irrational, to think that it's you who have done something, not the dice."

He hopes that he can remain moderately stable. It helps to have had "little minor successes, successes I can look back on and see they're nothing. You get caught up to the point you deceive yourself. You can't avoid the traps. There's too much money, too much adulation, too many people saying you're marvelous. You have to believe it."

He admires Ingmar Bergman, "who has avoided the traps by totally isolating himself." For Altman, who surrounds himself with people from the moment he gets up until the moment he is poured into bed, Bergman's way is admirable but impossible. Altman's own way of "avoiding the traps" is "to start out with material I think I can't handle. It keeps you honest. But that way, each thing you do eliminates that thing. Perhaps eventually you run out of things you can try."

M*A*S*H was Altman's second film. (If one doesn't count *Countdown,* a melodrama he was booted off in 1966, and two very early non-Hollywood films.) His first major film, *That Cold Day in the Park,* was a critical and financial disaster. His third film, *Brewster McCloud,* has shown up on half a dozen Best Films of 1970 lists, including those of Judith Crist and Andrew Sarris. It has also been dismissed by Pauline Kael ("no driving impulse and no internal consistency") and by Stanley Kauffmann. The movie is a fairy tale for adults, a myth about bird droppings and whether man really wants to fly or only wants the freedom that he thinks birds have. People who like the film like it very much. The rest detest it.

Altman, who has never gotten along well with bosses, started fighting with MGM after the first preview of *Brewster McCloud.* "The preview cards were better than *M*A*S*H* but afterward the hotel room was like a wake, because nobody had come out of the film laughing. If anybody came out of *Brewster McCloud* laughing, we didn't make the film we thought we were going to make."

The studio, eager to get rid of a peculiar film, dumped it with little preparation into vast, drafty theaters across the country. ("I wouldn't make a film at MGM today if they gave me 100 percent financing and 100 percent of the profits" is Altman's most printable comment.)

Since it cost only $1,500,000, *Brewster McCloud* will end up making a little money. Altman's newest film, *McCabe and Mrs. Miller,* may have equal difficulty turning a profit. Although it is, in one way, considerably more traditional, it is, in another, considerably more peculiar. And it cost slightly over $3,000,000. Warren Beatty is John McCabe. His real-life paramour, Julie Christie, is Mrs. Miller. *McCabe and Mrs. Miller* is a western in much the same strange way that *M*A*S*H* was a war film. It takes place in the northwestern United States in 1902, and it tells the story of "a fool, a poseur, a hero with a hole and it's that hole that makes him a hero."

The peculiarities of *McCabe and Mrs. Miller* begin with the look of the film. Of the many attempts by directors to use color to comment on the picture they are making (Antonioni's *Red Desert,* George Roy Hill's *Butch Cassidy and the Sundance Kid,* John Huston's *Moulin Rouge*), *McCabe and Mrs. Miller* is closest—both technically and emotionally—to Huston's grim use of color in *Moby Dick*. The faded quality of the color is Altman's deliberate attempt—by methods known as flashing and fogging—to create the archaic feel of an old photograph left for too many years in somebody's attic album.

Except for the snow sequence at the end of the film where he wanted to increase the reality of "the moment of truth" with as harsh a black-and-white effect as possible, Altman used fog filters throughout the picture. Then, before the negative was developed, the film was put on a printer and re-exposed to light. According to Altman, "adding more yellow than normal not only threw the print toward yellow but made the look of the film more extreme. Adding more blue did the same thing." Altman's intention was "to complement the period, the set, and the look of the people, to make the audience see the film as more real." To him the blue and yellow suggested the faded printed material of the period—old magazines and bottle labels, aging and yellowed newspapers.

Altman's desire to achieve reality has led him less to technical innovations than to the rejection of technical devices considered standard by other directors. Instead of ordinary, clear sound, he uses overlapping sound—characters' voices, even scenes, blend into and interrupt each other. "That's to give the audience the sense of the dialogue, the emotional feeling, rather than the literal word. That's the way sound is in real life."

On all his films he has used two cameras simultaneously and a zoom lens "to keep the actors honest, so that an actor cannot feel, 'I don't have to give very much in this scene because the camera is on my back.' They never know."

He built a real town for *McCabe and Mrs. Miller* without making any effort to leave room for his cameras; instead of trained animals, he used strays that wandered onto the Canadian set. "In a sense, we created problems for ourselves," he admits, "but a real town is not carefully constructed for cameras. And real animals don't always behave the way you want them to. We gained the advantage of environment—hopefully for the audience, definitely for ourselves."

Making his films "more real" is close to the core of Altman's work as a director. He wants to catch the accidents of life and fling them on the screen hard enough to knock the breath out of the audience. He wants to weigh the screen down with vulgarity, pleasure, pain, ugliness, and unexpected beauty. He wants, magically, to change two dimensions into three.

Altman is, of course, doomed to failure—which he admits in his rare morose moments: "Nobody has ever made a good movie. Some day someone will make half a good one." To Altman, a "good movie" is "taking the narrative out, taking the story out of it. The audience will sit and see the film and understand the movie's intention without being able to articulate it."

For his next film, *Images,* a modern Gothic horror story he wrote in one long, tormented weekend several years ago, Altman is already "trying in my head to take all the words out that make sense and to replace them with words that don't."

In *McCabe and Mrs. Miller,* the words that are there make sense, but in his attempt "to keep from being obvious, to keep the audience from seeing the devices," Altman has clipped several great chunks of plot out of the film. His concern for emotional rather than literal accuracy has left a number of puzzling and undefined characters to wander—mostly in long shot—in and out of the background.

Altman admits that this "will confuse the literal-minded," but he hopes that "the rest of the audience will sit back and accept the film rather than anticipate it, will simply let the film wash over them. In most films so much specific information is provided that the audience is allowed to be totally uninvolved. I try to make an audience do as much work as they would do reading a novel."

The result of this approach, with *M*A*S*H*, was that large numbers of people read Altman's antiwar film as a pro-war statement. He can only assume that "they are people who need to see children burning to think something is antiwar." He dismisses them as "people who want a political statement rather than an artistic one."

Altman does not like his films to make any verbal statements. He is interested in the look and feel of a film rather than in words and plot. He speaks often of himself as "an artist painting a picture." And adds, "It's not words we're dealing with in the films I make, not clever dialogue. I'm not interested in doing *A Man for All Seasons* or *The Lion in Winter.*"

As a result, most of the writers of Altman's films have ended up as his more-or-less-bitter enemies. By the time one of his films is finished there is nothing left of the original script except a couple of soup bones of plot and a few expletives. "Bob," says Brian McKay, "considers a script simply as an instrument, as the tool you sell the studio."

According to Bill Cannon, author of the original screenplay of *Brewster McCloud,* Altman "claimed I should take my name off the screen since, in fact, he, himself, had written most of the film."

Altman cheerfully admits that Ring Lardner Jr., who won an Academy Award for his script of *M*A*S*H*, "hated me. Lardner kept saying things like, 'That isn't a true Maine accent. You're being false.' Bull———. If I have an actor uncomfortable in a Maine accent, I let him use an accent he's comfortable in. I'm interested in the behavior pattern of the characters, not in what they say. In my films the actors can be creative. I don't think one person can write dialogue for 15 people. When I read Ring Lardner's script of *M*A*S*H,* I was thrilled with the idea of doing it. Yet if I had done his script the picture would have been a disaster."

Lardner is publicly quite circumspect in his opinion of Altman. (His private opinions are considerably more vitriolic.) "Mr. Altman does not treat a script very carefully. He contributed a great deal to *M*A*S*H* and not all of his contributions were good. He tried to do too much ad-libbing." Still, Lardner insists that "each scene came out on the screen more or less as it was intended by me on paper." Altman disagrees. "My main contribution to *M*A*S*H* was the basic concept, the philosophy, the style, the casting, and then making all those things work. Plus all the jokes, of course."

Brian McKay, who has worked with Altman more frequently than any other writer, says, "If you want me to get in line with the rest of the angry writers, I will, but it's more complicated than that. I think what Bob really wants is the European credit: 'A Film by Robert Altman.' And, often, he deserves it."

Seven years ago Altman told McKay, "Remember this. I take all the credit and most of the money when you work with me." Through several television series, *Brewster McCloud, McCabe and Mrs. Miller,* and a number of never-made films, McKay remembered. "Now I don't think I'll ever work with Bob again," McKay says, but he looks back on the association with affection. "I can't think of one person who was hurt from his association with Bob Altman—except emotionally."

Altman considers both *M*A*S*H* and *Brewster McCloud* "almost exclusively me—my films." For *McCabe and Mrs. Miller,* he is willing to share the credit—not with his writer but with his set designer, Leon Ericksen, and his star, Warren Beatty.

For *McCabe and Mrs. Miller,* Altman and Ericksen built the town of Presbyterian Church on a mountaintop in West Vancouver. The town cost $200,000. Everything in it was real. The town—all raw wood, foot-deep mud, and piles of manure that steamed in the freezing winter air—was created by carpenters who lived in the cabins they were building and got drunk at night on whisky from the still they had also built.

Life frozen upon a screen loses its spontaneity. The choices have been made forever. Altman tries harder than most directors to imply what lies below the two-dimensional surface of the screen. He stuffs his films with things that audiences cannot see yet of which he insists they are somehow aware. To pay for a quick call at Presbyterian Church's whorehouse, the actors held real money in hands that were never seen by the camera. "If someone's playing a scene and they look down and they've got some crappy paper in their hand, they just don't play the scene as well," says Altman. "I want to be able to go onto a set and open a drawer and find things in there although that drawer will never be opened in a scene. But it adds validity because the actor knows the things are there and so do I."

The organic relationship between Altman, his script, his actors, his sets and the final film can best be seen in the town of Presbyterian Church. He built the town because his film was partly about a community in the process of being built and changed. Presbyterian Church was constructed, building by building, as each new character entered *McCabe and Mrs. Miller.* By late last December, the town had reached its peak development—cabins, a sawmill, a whorehouse, a bathhouse, two saloons, and a barbershop.

"The town's been ruined," said René Auberjonois (the birdlike bird lecturer in *Brewster McCloud,* the Irish saloonkeeper in *McCabe and Mrs. Miller*), who came to Vancouver two weeks before the film started last October. "Only the guys building the town were living there. I felt like an outsider . It was their town. Then the actors started arriving, and we made it our town. We picked out houses to live in, and we had square dances at night in my saloon."

"The town grew as the script grew," says designer Ericksen. "Lots of things in the town changed because of the script; lots of things in the script changed because of the way the town was built. Everything happened organically."

"The film even changed because of the animals," says Altman's secretary, Anne Sidaris. "It changed because kittens were born in Presbyterian Church, dogs elected to live there, chickens hatched baby chicks." (To give some idea of the symbiotic relationship between the animals and the crew, less than a dozen of the chickens were left when the film was finished. It is assumed that the others were killed and eaten.)

Throughout the picture, it was rare for Altman to know on one morning exactly what he was going to be filming the next morning. Often, the next morning's scene had not yet been written. Late on a winter Thursday afternoon, Altman sloshed through the rain looking for a place to hold a funeral where the camera could see the church but not the housing development on the hillside across from Presbyterian Church. An offhand suggestion by his secretary of "Asleep in Jesus" as the epitaph for the dead man's gravestone led to a frantic search through old hymnbooks and, in Friday morning's cold mist, to a painfully affecting scene. The music was played on a fiddle by one of the actors. Altman had only given the lyrics to those townspeople—primarily the whores—who could be expected to know the hymn. The other actors shuffled their feet uneasily or tried to come in late on the unfamiliar words. It worked. And none of it had existed—even in Altman's head—24 hours earlier.

Later, referring to the funeral, Altman mused: "Had it been raining today, everything we did would have been different. I'm going to get accolades for *McCabe and Mrs. Miller,* and all it amounts to is being open to the possibilities—using what we have."

It is almost impossible to exaggerate the organic quality of an Altman film. Yet that quality does not result simply because one day there is rain instead of expected snow and a consequent change in the whole fabric of the film. It is agonizing for Altman to start a film. "You have to box him into a corner," says his assistant director, Tommy Thompson. "He knows that starting means two months of working seven days a week 24 hours a day." Once the film has begun, Altman moves cautiously, tentatively, finding out who the people are, assessing their relationships. "You can," says René Auberjonois, "almost see him get a sense of purpose."

There is nothing intellectual about this groping. It is done by hunch, instinct, intuition. Altman speaks of allowing some internal computer to take over, unrestricted by his brain. "I think you have to be careful in your old age," he says. "I think you mess up your computer, you get it so filled with cards. That's what makes you die."

Once the tone of his film is set to his satisfaction—which takes anywhere from three days to two weeks—he relaxes, open, within very broad limits, to whatever accidents of weather or actors' improvisations fate has chosen to bring him. (With *M*A*S*H,* he ended up shooting the rehearsals because there was so much interplay between Donald Sutherland and Elliott Gould. With *McCabe and Mrs. Miller,* he has discovered that "Warren Beatty, unlike most actors, gets better and better with each take, and he can't do it through rehearsals." Altman adapted himself to Beatty, shooting eight or nine takes of each of Beatty's scenes, despite what he calls his own "notorious past history of printing first takes.")

Before a birthday party was filmed in the whorehouse in *McCabe and Mrs. Miller,* the actresses playing the whores asked Altman if they could limit the guests to the actors they particularly liked. His first impulse was to refuse. A moment later, he reconsidered and told them to make out their guest list.

After six hours of shooting, neither Altman nor his actors displayed any signs of ill temper. Occasionally, Altman crooned, "Easy now, easy, settle down," as though he were calming nervous horses. In a heavy, black pullover and with his gray and black curly hair almost indistinguishable from his gray-and-black Russian wool hat, Altman looked like some bulky animal with a bald spot the size of a demitasse saucer in the center of its head.

At the suggestion of Julie Christie ("This is a festive occasion"), the cast had been drinking vodka instead of water since the first rehearsal. But it was not the vodka that freed them to improvise a cake-eating scene so wild and uninhibited that even Altman was doubled over with laughter. They had been given the freedom to—encouraged to—improvise by Altman.

A glob of cake fell on the bare breast of one of the actresses, and the others instinctively teased a shy, young actor with, "Lick it off, Jeremy, lick it off." Jeremy blinked, hesitated, was pushed forward. The young actors and actresses were, it was obvious, reacting to each other as people who had lived together for two months, not as actors in a formal scene. Even after Altman shouted, "Cut," they continued to squash cake in eyebrows, nostrils, ears.

In the final print of *McCabe and Mrs. Miller*, there is almost no trace of the wild finale to the birthday party. "It didn't seem necessary," Altman says simply. Yet he feels that the hours of shooting were in no sense a loss. "It brought the characters to a different relationship with each other. Without it, René Auberjonois wouldn't have ended up in the kitchen with that whore on his lap."

If Altman has any theory that can be phrased in a sentence, it is that "moviemaking is a collaborative art." Leon Ericksen says of Altman: "He can be satanic or angelic but he will always let you do anything you are willing to do. Being with Robert Altman is an awfully good place for any creative person to be."

The corollary is that being with Robert Altman can be unpleasant for less creative people. His intense anger at movie guilds and unions stems from their lack of participation in the collaboration. "The union art directors don't realize their job is to help make a picture, not to dress a set. The union sound men don't realize their job is to help make a picture, not to produce perfect sound. The unions are all the same. They degrade the people in them."

Ericksen, whom Donald Sutherland calls a genius, cannot get into an American union unless he serves eight years of apprenticeship as a draftsman. When Ericksen says tentatively, "We'll probably have to call the union to move that set," Altman answers. "Bull——. You move it yourself. We'll handle it with the union. We'll pay fines or something, but I don't want a bunch of guys trying to take it down who didn't see how it went up."

For Altman, the chief participants in the collaboration are his actors. He is proud that "I don't move my actors around. I allow them the artistic freedom to assist me."

Most of his actors reciprocate with adoration. Mike Murphy, who has been in all of Altman's Hollywood films and half a dozen of his television shows as well, says of Altman, "Most other directors treat you like a child. Bob spoils you. He never lets you down." As the hot-shot San Francisco detective, Murphy starred in *Brewster McCloud*. In *McCabe and Mrs. Miller*, he was offered one week's work. He never considered refusing Altman's offer.

Even Julie Christie was exhilarated by her work with Altman, although, at the beginning, she found it "most unnerving to work with a democratic director. Directors are little kings. Bob's a very kind man, and his kindness makes you comfy. He has a hedonistic streak which again is very different from most directors, who get so anguished by things. Bob wants to enjoy himself. He surrounds himself with people who won't spoil the experience as an enjoyable one."

There *are* actors who have reservations. "I got a telephone call from an old enemy last night," Altman chortles. The call was from Elliott Gould, who, according to Altman, "had just seen *Brewster McCloud* and who hated to call but hated more not to call." He has also applied the word "enemy" to Donald Sutherland. Yet Sutherland insists that he respects Altman completely. Sutherland's subtle reservations about Altman as a director concern the communication between the two. "Bob knows things totally rather than specifically. *M*A*S*H* was all in Robert Altman's head and I knew I'd never know what was in his head. He requires an actor to have absolute confidence in him and to give oneself over to him totally. I cannot totally give myself to anyone."

Warren Beatty also has reservations. Swigging Vichy water from a quart bottle, the picture half-finished, the constant rain beating against the walls of his trailer, Beatty says fastidiously that "my own particular taste is to know where I am from the beginning." Beatty found it hard to work without the comfort of a finished script. Altman found it hard to work with

"Warren's concern, his nit-picking, with the way he pushed me and bugged me." But Altman didn't try to make Beatty stop. "He drove me nuts, but he did it for the picture. His bugging kept me honest." Weekend after weekend, Beatty helped Altman rewrite the script, and now, the film finished and about to open in New York, Altman is willing to share the credit with his star. "Warren was involved in the picture."

Nothing in Altman's background could have been expected to lead him to his own mountaintop in Canada in the winter of 1970.

He was born in Kansas City Feb. 20, 1925. His mother's ancestors had sailed on the Mayflower. His father was one of the top life-insurance salesmen in the world—and one of the worst gamblers. "I learned a lot about losing from him: That losing is an identity; that you can be a good loser and a bad winner; that none of it—gambling, money, winning or losing—has any real value; that the value you thought came with winning $10,000 isn't there; that it's simply a way of killing time, like crossword puzzles."

He was raised by Jesuits, but he wriggled out of his Catholicism the day he joined the Army at the age of 18. At 19, he was a pilot with his own bomber crew. He flew 46 missions over Borneo and the Dutch East Indies, and it never occurred to him that he was killing people, "although I don't think it would have bothered me."

He was 22 when he came back from the war. He remembers himself as "an ass, wanting to be liked so much that I would agree with whoever I was talking to, really dishonest about myself, very anti-authority." He married, almost immediately, the last girl with whom he had had any contact before he went to the South Pacific. "It was never a marriage. I was a real chippie chaser." The results of the marriage were a daughter, Christine, now 23, a dozen separations, and, some time in 1950 or 1951, a divorce. His second marriage also went sour. With his second wife he had two sons— Michael, 16, who now lives with him, and Stephen, 13.

During those first postwar years he was learning his trade as a writer, producer, photographer, director, set designer, and film editor of industrial films for the Calvin Company in Kansas City. With Lou Lombardo, a cameraman for Calvin, Altman went to Hollywood in the early fifties. The silence was deafening. Leaving Lombardo to bang on closed doors, Altman retreated to Kansas City. Lombardo—who remembers Altman as "tall and thin, just as gregarious as he is today and just as prone to go out and charge $1,000 worth of clothes to cheer himself up whenever he is down and out"—is Altman's film editor on *McCabe and Mrs. Miller.*

A few years later Altman returned to Hollywood with a "deal" for a movie. The deal fell through. Again he retreated to Kansas City.

The third time he went to Hollywood was for keeps. He brought *The Delinquents,* a low-budget film he had written, produced, and directed. In 1957, he and George W. George made a documentary, *The James Dean Story.* For the next six years Altman wrote, produced, and/or directed for television. He was fired with regularity. "Because the star of *Combat,* Vic Morrow, couldn't be killed off, I'd take an actor, establish him as an important character in one segment, use him three or four times more, and then kill him early in the next script, offscreen, in a way that had nothing to do with the plot. That was unorthodox. It made them nervous. I used to get fired for it."

When he was making $125,000 a year with "my pick of anything, of everything," Altman quit television. He quit because he did not want to become "one of those hundreds of creative people who have just died in television." He was, as usual, in debt. Between 1965 and 1967 he did nothing but go deeper in debt. He continued to live in his big, four-bedroom house in Mandeville Canyon. Although neither the mortgage nor the milkman were paid, he continued to buy what he wanted when he wanted it.

"I finally begged the milkman to cut off our credit and stop delivering milk," says Kathryn Altman, his third wife. Kathryn is tall, redhaired, beautiful, and totally in command of herself. She is a woman with depth and mystery—strong, bright, witty, one of the few people Altman can't bully verbally. ("Bob has overpowered a lot of women," says actor Mike Murphy of their marriage. "He and Kathryn fight to a draw.") Altman finds her "exciting." She says of him that "he has driven me crazy but he has never bored me." She is the mother of his 10-year-old son, Bobby. They have also adopted a four-year-old half-Negro boy, Matthew. Matthew was Kathryn's decision. She felt she wanted another child.

Now, as a result of *M*A*S*H,* Altman is out of debt. His wife was able to go Christmas shopping last December with cash in her pocket. "The only way we had a Christmas the other ten years of our marriage," says Kathryn, "was because I had charge accounts in my previous name."

The money may disappear. (Altman's living expenses were five times as high as the $750 weekly allowance Warner Brothers provided during *McCabe and Mrs. Miller.* One week's rental of a yacht last October cost him $3,200.) But Altman can live artistically for years on the success of *M*A*S*H.*

All his pictures share a certain desire to show up the world's insanity, but there are also remarkable differences. *M*A*S*H* was crude and tough in its masculine viewpoint and in its use of women as sexual objects.

In *Brewster McCloud,* man the idealist is physically and emotionally seduced by women who are capable of saving, betraying, or destroying him. In *McCabe and Mrs. Miller,* the battle of the sexes is fought on more even grounds, although woman—the survivor—has the edge. ("Even though the women are all whores, I'm treating them nicely. I'm not portraying them as lascivious women, just as dumb girls. And that was a pretty good job for a girl, a better job than most honest women had.")

He explains the extreme differences in viewpoint with "I'm not making any of these films about myself. I'm exploring a situation, not expressing my own fears and feelings."

His own fears and feelings are expressed in his way of making movies themselves. "His film style," says Tommy Thompson, "is a continuation of his life style—or vice versa. Bob has to know everything that's going on. If somebody tells you that the milk didn't come for lunch yet, from halfway across the set he'll roar, 'What are you going to do about it?' "

Altman has intense loyalty to "my people." (The obverse is a suspicion of people who are not his.) Anybody who works on an Altman film—carpenter, prop man, electrician, actor—is welcome at his rushes.

Early that evening last December there were 72 people and two dogs sprawled on the floor of Altman's Vancouver screening room. During the rushes, Altman watched the people in the room as closely as he watched the screen. "I get a reaction, a feel about the film, even this early." In his pocket was a plastic bag of marijuana brownies baked for him by some admirer. On his lap was curled four-year-old Matthew, his adopted son. His eyes glittering, his shoulders thrust forward, Altman watched, sipping continuously from a plastic cup of Cutty Sark and soda. The moment the cup was empty, his secretary slipped from the room to refill it.

He has always been—at least in his work—more disciplined than he allows himself to appear. Now his life is more disciplined, too. His gambling has dwindled to football pools and friendly poker games. The big gambling simply doesn't seem necessary to him now.

The rushes over, the room almost empty but the images from the screening still imprinted in his head, Altman whispered — half-bravado, half-epitaph:

"If *they* should say to me, 'You'll never see your sons again or your wife unless you get out of the business of making movies,' I'd have to say, 'Sorry, Michael, Bobby, Matthew, Kathryn. It will hurt me not to see you again. But goodbye.'"

Nashville

CONNIE BYRNE AND
WILLIAM O. LOPEZ/1975

WITH *NASHVILLE* ALTMAN HAS expanded his own personal
style (Henry Gibson calls it Altmanscope), and at the same time he has
pushed the concept of collective film-making far beyond traditional limits
(we're talking about Hollywood movies). His actors write dialogue; they
re-form characters, incorporating aspects of their own lives; they are
encouraged to discuss, alter, challenge, and explore their personae with
the director and the company; they are plagued as little as possible with
tiny scenes shot out of sequence or with pick-up cover inserts; and they
are generally provided with a non-rigid creative environment which pro-
motes spontaneity and growth and which results in a number of remarkably
convincing performances often made even more exciting by the evident
intimacy between the actor, the character, and the director.

Because Altman does not Freudianize on the reasons "why" his characters get into certain situations, and because much of "how" they get there
lies on the cutting-room floor, the fact that the actors convey any sense of
characterization at all is fairly impressive. *Scenes From a Marriage* or *A
Woman Under the Influence* seem to probe deeper into the human condition
through the exploration of characters' backgrounds, the detailing of idio-
syncracies, and the discussion of events as they happen (the dialogue is
often the event itself); *Nashville* avoids these tendencies. *Nashville* does not
involve so much the exposition of character transformations as it involves

From *Film Quarterly* vol. 29, no. 2 (Winter 1975–76): 13–17, 23–25. © 1975 by The Regents of
the University of California. Reprinted by permission.

the observation of its consistently transparent characters as they circulate through a powerfully transformative environment.

Altman constructs his scenes and his overall narrative in a manner widely divergent from established film norms. In *Nashville*, the plot — the impulse toward suspense or resolution — is entirely subordinated to the moment. The story does not move toward any predictable denouement, rather it just meanders along. *Nashville* doesn't really lead up to the "assassination," nor does it end with it. The murder simply happens and people are already singing again by the final backwards zoom. This method of narrativity is closer to real life than a neatly tied-up package of moralized comeuppances or ritualized conclusions (although this latter element has climaxed most of Altman's previous works). In this sense, the Altman of *Nashville* can be called a realist.

The matrix of this non-story is comprised of extended panoramic zoom shots which sweep leisurely and relentlessly across wide, richly textured landscapes and eventually zoom slowly in on the main protagonists. The camera becomes a long, wide observer, less the usual intruding subject around which all actors, technicians, sets, lights, and so on must huddle. This style is documentary-like on a superficial level but manifestly works dramatically to enlarge the action rather than simply cover it. (More classical intensity could be achieved with montage, but conventional editing would diminish the sense of continuous, enveloping flow.)

With his "unobtrusive," low-key camera presence during the shooting, Altman achieves on the screen a Zen-like, detached omniscience which is rare in fiction films or documentaries.

Sid Levin, the editor of *Nashville*, reports on Altman's shooting methods in *Filmmaker's Newsletter* (Aug. 1975): He doesn't use a classic style. "By classic I mean the conventional use of master, medium and close-up shots. Instead, we often had what could probably be considered three or four different master angles of the same sequence, each with a slight variation in camera angle. However, because Altman wanted the actors to have as much flexibility as possible in the development of the characters, there were enormous variations in the dialogue and dramatic content of different takes of the same scene.

"There were, I think, about ten good scenes for every one that ended up in the finished film. We had about 70 hours of dailies (300,000 feet)."

Altman is justly famous for advancing the practice of film sound — not just technically, but in the service of a profoundly expansive vision of reality which captures an extraordinary fecundity of aural complexity and counterpoint. The sound itself is panoramic—the opposite, say, of Robert Bresson's sound, in which every visual detail is accompanied by a single precise sound effect, dubbed in afterwards. Altman's sound reaches out across the entire cityscape and records (with non-umbilical radio mikes) a symphony of direct, real, overlapping, synchronized, on-the-spot live sound: a glorious achievement which is guaranteed to thrill film-makers, technical buffs, and audiences alike, and which has increased the expressive potential of the cinema. (Other modern film-makers have achieved breakthroughs with sound. Federico Fellini and Jacques Tati, for example, are masters of orchestral complexity, but their sound is all post-dubbed. Jean-Luc Godard's crucial experiments crammed up a number of various levels of sound in the service of dialectical contrast rather than absorptive impressionism.)

Are there any particular things about Nashville *that you would like to start out talking about?*
ROBERT ALTMAN: I don't like the ads. And I can't criticize Paramount for them because they really like the picture and I think they just tried too hard. You can go through the grosses and look at the city and say Gee, I wonder why it isn't doing well there.... And you'll find that they are running the thing where you can't hear the sound, or the speakers are out, or they get reels mixed up. I mean the projection you just can't control. But those are just general industry complaints because unfortunately it is an industry.

Did Paramount send someone around to check out the sound?
They did it at all the key places we opened, but you know you can't suddenly do that to 10,000 places. And again, it's a unionization of the way those projectionists are and many of them...I mean you'll find a guy who cares and you'll find a guy who just really doesn't give a rat's fuck one way or the other.

What was wrong with the advertising?
What ad did they run where you are?

They had a bunch of critics' blurbs on them.
Then they were good. They like to settle in on one thing, and they just haven't been able to find it 'cause you can't find it in the picture. Com-

mercially the biggest problem with the film is that it doesn't have a shark. So nobody really knows except by word of mouth, and somebody says You ought to see it, it's really good. And you say What's it about? And, well, you can't answer that. So that's the problem every time you do a film that doesn't have an absolute, *one* focal point. That's what we run into. . . . You know I'm up here in Calgary and we can't get anybody into a theater to see this picture with dynamite. I've gone on radio and television here and they don't seem to care that we are up here making a movie. I mean it's weird. . . .

Do you feel misunderstood by the public? Don't you feel somewhat gratified by the critical response to the film?
Oh I'm thrilled, I'm thrilled with the whole thing *and* the public. I mean this picture is going to be the first picture in a long time that's going to go into profits for me. But what I really am probably trying to say is that it's a reflection of what the whole movie industry considers itself. We run in those two theaters in New York forever. In San Francisco we're doing terrific, and in every metropolitan city other than Los Angeles, and they don't know what films are about at all. . . . We are in the process of changing what movies are, I think. It isn't just buying a bag of popcorn and walking in at the middle, and if you like it you sit through to the part where you came in.

What about the process of getting down to the final cut? Was anyone pressuring you to cut it down to a particular length?
Well, there were a lot of people biting their tongues. Nobody really said anything. They were nervous that the film came out as long as it did.

How long was the first version?
Well, uh, we always knew it would end up three hours or under. When I cut a film I start showing it daily. I start responding myself to anybody's reaction to the film. I don't much pay attention to what they say, but you can tell by their reaction. The film that Pauline Kael saw is virtually the same film you saw. Your reaction to it, I dare say, would not be changed by the changes we made in it at all. Other than the fact that the sound track is mixed now and it wasn't before, and it was much rougher. We only cut it down by about ten minutes from that time and that was just removing a couple of songs.

What kind of material was removed from the longer versions?
Well, a lot of filler. A lot of just detailing the characters. It began and ended the same way. In fact, we are now starting to edit it back for eventual television release where it will be like four two-hour shows. It will begin and end the same way, it will just be fuller. And it will be specifically edited for television so that the commercial breaks will be at the end of each of the four episodes. This is three or four years away.

How long was the shooting schedule in Nashville?
Seven weeks.

Could you describe how you divide your energies during the principal photography amongst the various directorial demands such as organization, technical, rehearsing, etc.?
A lot of people made that picture. We used a lot of people. Actually, in *Nashville* more than any other film, what we did was sort of set up events and then just press the button and photograph them, pretty much like you would a documentary. In other words we didn't use the normal techniques of setting up a scene and then rehearsing it, and then saying, "OK, now let's set up a master shot," and getting what we wanted there, and then getting over-the-shoulders and close-ups. That's not to say we did it on the first take every time, but we basically shot each segment of the film as it was. We were covered because we knew we could cut from anything at any time, we weren't stuck with the length, we didn't have to worry about that. The best example I think is Barbara Baxley when she's doing her Kennedy speech to Geraldine Chaplin. Barbara wrote that, and I didn't know, I didn't even bother to listen to her material before we shot it. And she had rehearsed it and learned it. And we turned the camera on her till we ran out of film, and then we loaded it up again and ran another roll, so that it literally took 20 minutes. It was done once and that was it. Because I knew that I could pull out the pieces of it that I wanted, and I could get away from it at any time. I had a song going on and I had all those other characters that I had to deal with.

It is said that you like to keep the whole company around and have everybody watch everything....
I try to shoot in sequence and try to have all the actors available for the shoot, mainly so that we have the freedom to change our minds about what we are going to shoot.

You shot the film basically in sequence?
As much in sequence as you are going to find. I mean the opening scene
was the first time we shot and the ending was the last scene we shot.

*Could you talk about how your method of working with actors might differ from
the methods of other directors?*
I never have really watched anybody else direct a film, so I can just sur-
mise what they do. I have no idea. I find more and more that the less I do
the better the work comes out. So now my function is really to try and
stay out of the way, and make the conditions and circumstances as *con-
ducive* as I can for the actors to do what they do. . . . It really starts in the
casting. You try to get it so that they don't have to manufacture very
much—then they can draw on all their own particular things. And then
after we cast, we try to get them to switch the character around closer to
the actor. Originally, Susan Anspach was hired for the part of Barbara Jean.
She dropped out and we put Ronee Blakley in and Ronee Blakley happened
to have some rather severe burns on her body, from when she was a little
girl and her dress caught on fire from a sparkler at some sort of Fourth of
July thing. And she has gone through a series of skin grafts and those scars
on her chest still show. And so we just put that element into the character.

Was Joan Tewkesbury down on the shoot?
Sure, all the time.

You worked on the script throughout the shooting?
Yes.

Did you work out sketches or plans with the cinematographer the night before?
No, never. Half the time one assistant will be working with the background people, and I don't know what he's telling them or what they'll be
doing. He is making his own movie back there. Remember the scene when
the soldier gets off the elevator and sneaks down into Barbara Jean's room,
and the guard is standing there talking to the nurse about his gun and
how he never had to kill anybody with it? Well, I never heard that until
we got into editing because we hadn't pulled that track out. In editing I
said, Gee that's terrific. Well, that's just something Alan set up with the
guard. These aren't professional actors, and even if they were we like them

to be dealing with something that belongs to them rather than something that they don't understand or that's totally foreign to them.

Is there any time when you were shooting that you would just turn on the camera and people wouldn't know they were actually being photographed? Was it that loose?
No.

What about the sound?
We used an eight-track system and it's really unmixing rather than mixing sound. We'd just put microphones on all the principals and hang them out the window and stick them in the clock and under the doorbell and wherever we want a live sound. And they all go down on different tracks, pretty much the way music is done today. And in our musical sequences we had an additional 16 tracks. We didn't have to come back later and put in dead sound effects.

For instance, when Elliot Gould drives up and we hear him talking in the back seat of the car before it stops and before he gets out....
The microphone is on him inside the car. They are all hidden, they are really built into the wardrobe.

There's a psychological reality that you captured that could never be achieved with dubbed sound....
No way. And the thing that people in our industry don't understand is that once you free one area, once you don't have the mike boom hanging overhead, and you don't have to worry about shadows and lights and all that, it gives you such freedom with your camera. You can put it wherever you want, you can get back as far as you want, it just compounds its qualities.

At the beginning of the Parthenon rally sequence when Michael Murphy comes out of the car and walks up to Beatty: Were they radio miked?
Yes.

You could hear the transmission and the mike rubbing up against their clothes.
Yes, that's what it is.

What about the sound truck and the crowd noises and other effects?
We added those later, but they were done down there. Thomas Hal Phillips went down to a recording studio and made his speech. . . .

I read that the public down there didn't actually know that the Phillips campaign was unreal. Is that true?
A lot of people didn't.

And people called up to volunteer their services to the Replacement Party?
I don't know if that specifically happened. But I know people would stop and ask about it. We had those bumper stickers on our own cars. My wife would wear a button around town. People would ask her, "Who is this guy?"

So you would drive the sound truck around without any sound actually blaring?
Yeah. There was no sound. Well, sometimes there was sound coming out of the truck when we were shooting it silent. We were equipped, we could play the speech or music or whatever we wanted to through those horns. And sometimes we'd do that just to get crowd reactions.

Speaking of crowd reactions, was there a unified reaction from the people of Nashville about your film? I read that the Nashville Banner *ran a big front-page headline saying "Altman's* Nashville *Down on Nashville."*
What happened was that the *Banner* sent a reporter up to New York and sneaked him into one of our initial screenings, which they didn't have to do, but they did. Then he went back and gave us the headline. The editor of the other paper, *The Tennesseean,* came up and we showed it to him. He went back and gave us a headline saying it was the best picture he had seen and absolutely authentic. So for about four days in a row we had a nice argument going on the front pages of the two Nashville papers. And we took the film down there and showed it to the people—it hasn't opened in Nashville yet, but we had a screening before we opened in New York for the people in Nashville who contributed to the film. They had a lot of press down there, but it didn't amount to very much. The musicians like it. Some people thought it was too long. Some people thought that the music was not authentic, and some thought it was. It was kind of a bore.

You were quoted in an AP article as saying that the "people at Opryland aren't interested in the truth, they are interested in their corporate image." Did you actually say that?

Probably. They run that place like a church. Those people come in, they aren't there to be entertained nor *are* they entertained. That audience you saw in the film is the audience that's in the Grand Ole Opry. That was a legitimate audience. I mean we put up signs and advertised and those people came in. The only thing was that they didn't have to pay for it.

They came in to see "Connie White"?

They came in to see Lily Tomlin and Henry Gibson and to see a movie being made. And they brought their Instamatic cameras and they took pictures. At one point when Henry Gibson was on he said, "Now, Barbara Jean, she's in Vanderbilt Hospital," and he gave that address. In the film you'll see a woman take out a piece of paper and write it down.

What did the musicians who appeared in the film think of the music?

Some of them liked it, some didn't. But all of the musicians we used— except for Baskin and one bass player we brought in to play with the trio—were Nashville sidemen. So when they came in to work it was like a regular session. So they've played better music than that and worse.

Baskin commented that the people down there were pissed off because these Californians came in and knocked off a lot of good music and made a big movie and had a lots of fun and then just split, and they were still stuck in Nashville.

That's true.

Do you think that you've turned off whole segments of the population in the South with this film?

No, no. I think the people who feel that way haven't seen the picture. I mean anybody who would read Rex Reed and believe him. . . . It's just those kind of people who will respond in that manner.

Which were the most sensitive articles about your film?

It's hard to say. . . . I like the good ones and don't like the bad ones. But people look at it in different ways. I just got a review sent to me from the *Kansas City Star* that I think is probably the best review of the film. Because

I think the critic did what a critic is supposed to do. In the body of the review he said, Don't go in expecting *this,* but if you look at it in *this* manner you will have one hell of a time. So he's helping to lead the audience toward really enjoying the film. Whereas somebody like Rex Reed is just absolutely infuriated because the other critics have liked it. He got on the *Merv Griffin Show* and said, "Well, all I can tell you is it's false advertising and false publicity and everybody is lying because people are staying away from that picture by the millions." That's true because nobody in China or India has seen the film. But Rex Reed has a personal problem with me. I had a hotel room next to him in Cannes in 1970. And he left his door open. . . . I don't want to go into it, but anyway he's gone after me on every picture.

Robert Altman, age 50, grew up in Kansas City. He attended Wentworth Military Academy, dropped out of college, piloted B-24s in World War II. Stationed at a base near Los Angeles, he attempted to sell stories in Hollywood but had little luck. Finally he sold some treatments, but the studios wouldn't hire him as a screenwriter. Giles Fowler, in an outstanding article in the *Kansas City Star,* reports that Altman was determined to "try his luck in New York. On the way, stopping off to visit his family, he ran into a friend who was working for the Calvin Company, an industrial moviemaking outfit. Altman was persuaded to try for a job, was hired, and remained with Calvin for six years as a writer, director, photographer and editor." He made an independent feature, *The Delinquents,* in 1955, and later codirected a documentary feature, *The James Dean Story.* On the strength of these films, Alfred Hitchcock gave Altman the opportunity to direct TV mysteries. From there he moved into a solid career as a television writer-director, working on such series as *Bonanza, Combat, Kraft Mystery Theatre,* and *Whirlybirds.* According to one source he clocked 300 hours of television. Moving up to his first big studio feature, *Countdown,* Altman was fired for letting his actors overlap their dialogue. Unwilling to go back to television, he struggled for two years until he got a job directing the underwhelming *That Cold Day in the Park.* Altman was the 15th choice to direct *MASH* (one source says 17th or 18th). Since the release of that film (1970) he has been a director of international renown, and has produced an impressively varied body of work conveying an original and distinctive vision: *Brewster McCloud, McCabe and Mrs. Miller, Images, The Long Goodbye,*

Thieves Like Us, California Split, and *Nashville.* Altman has been highly praised by critics, who have compared him to Joyce, Renoir, Faulkner, and Whitman.

You're resented around Hollywood to some degree for being a "darling of the crit-ics." We were talking to some film-makers who said they wished they'd taken their film to New York and "romanced" the critics....
ROBERT ALTMAN: That kind of talk is petulant. A friend of mine from New York who worked on the press for *Nashville* spent a week in Hollywood and she came back to New York and said, "My God, it's true! I thought you were exaggerating but nine out of ten people I met out there said the pic-ture's not doing well, it's hyped, it's not as good a picture as they said it is. Altman loves critics, he's just the darling of the critics." And they really resent it. And I've never had dinner... Again Rex Reed on that show said that I go back and I buy and dine and drink. I just don't do that.

Pauline Kael is probably not going to be easily seduced by that stuff anyway.
I don't think so. I don't even know her that well anyhow. The whole rea-son for her being invited to that screening along with Judith Crist and Bruce Williamson and Charles Michener was that they had all been down on the location and they had all seen dailies at various times. And they knew about it in some detail. So when I had the film virtually finished I took it back and I showed it to Paul Newman, I showed it to a lot of friends of mine, and a lot of people I know just to get the thing opened up. The only reason Pauline wrote about it early was that she was going into her six-month period off *The New Yorker*. She said she just literally *had* to write about it. And Hollis Alpert, who wrote the same things about it, probably saw more of it than anybody because he just happened to be in California with a friend of his and dropped by for a drink one night when we ran about four or five hours of film. So that's just ridiculousness.

Tom Wicker quoted you as saying that you don't have any philosophies, you don't believe in propaganda, you don't have "anything to say," but in a Village Voice *article about Joan Tewkesbury she says that you were responsible for most of the political content. And during the whole opening sequence the sound truck says, Like it or not, everything is political. Could you talk about that?*
I put it in, but I didn't write that speech and I didn't direct the man who did. I didn't give him any guidelines whatsoever. I took Thomas Hal

Phillips, who is a novelist from Mississippi and who's politically oriented (his brother ran for governor down there and he managed the campaign) and is a man I respect. All these comparisons to George Wallace are just pigeonholing. I told Phillips to invent a candidate. The only requirements I gave him were that he be a third party candidate. I didn't want a Democrat or a Republican. And I told him to invent a man who he would like to see elected, and who he thought *could* be elected.

Howard K. Smith. Did you just call him and ask him if he wanted to be in your movie?

Yeah. We gave him Walker's main speech, which is played throughout the picture. We told Smith where Walker came from, what his background was, and asked Smith just to do a commentary on him. We don't care whether it is pro, con, or what. In other words, we dealt with it like we were doing an actual thing. Because we weren't trying to put forward any political philosophy. Thomas Hal Phillips probably was, but I wasn't.

You dissolved a blimp over Howard K. Smith....

Well, a Goodyear blimp was down there. And Tommy Thompson, our production manager, said there was an electric newspaper under it. So we went out and got the blimp and we went out and photographed it.

Are there any political movements or figures that you identify with or sympathize with?

I'm a Democrat, if anything. I supported McCarthy, McGovern, Kennedy. I was very, very angry from the beginning about people like Richard Nixon. I don't like Reagan or Wallace. Probably right now my prime choice for a candidate would be Sargent Shriver, and if he runs, which I suppose he will, I would probably support him actively. But this doesn't have anything to do with the films I make.

With the society breaking down the way it is now, isn't there a call for a redefinition of politics?

I think there will be. I think you have to realize that we are a very young culture, we're 200 years old and you can throw out the first 75 years because everybody was chopping down trees then. I think that we've done very well and we're recovering well. I have great hope, great faith.... I think change is going to come through social pressure. The anti-materialism movement that took place in the sixties is certainly an expression of that. I think the black revolution being literally bloodless is a fantastic social step. It's all based on communication. I think television stopped the war in Asia. I have high hopes, great expectations.

Why do you think the American public is so blind to the possibility of liberalizing society?
It's the Death of a Salesman syndrome. The majority of the people are quote Good, and they have done what they have been told they were supposed to do. And now we are saying, "Oh, that's not right," and when you take somebody, and they've worked for their new Chevrolet every two years and they've got their house and their barbecue and they've sent their kids to college and done this and this, and then say, "Wait a minute, this has all been wrong," it's kind of hard for them to take. Willy Loman went out and killed himself.... It's a slow evolution. I mean it's just a matter of consciousness. Nobody knew when they threw a tin can in the river or took a leak in the lake that they were polluting. But now people do.

But hasn't there always been a tradition in the US—you can see it in Bob Hope, for example—of hating politicians, and sort of joking about them and making fun of the president, and yet we still have a horrible situation. People still are cynical, like Michael Murphy said, "They're all a little crazy." But the public lets it go on....
That's what the picture is about, really. The whole point of making the political analogies to the country-western stars is the fact that people don't listen...it's a popularity contest. You take somebody and put them in a voting booth and what the hell are they supposed to know? How do you know if Gene McCarthy is for real or if he's a jerk? So what you really have is the majority of people constantly voting *against* something, even if it's just a new idea. I mean people voted for Nixon. I don't think anybody liked Nixon, but they thought, "I'm not gonna have a bunch of goddam hippies telling me what to do." And with the Kennedys we were looking for Royalty. It's the easiest way....

Like people are looking for a song at the end to make them feel better after the senseless killing....

I think most killing is senseless. And that song is double-edged. I think it's both a negative and a positive comment. In one way you can say, Jesus, those people are sittin' there singing right after this terrible thing happened; that shows their insensitivity. And on the other hand, no matter how bad things get, there's always a positive hope for the future. And we went on to mostly children; you can't expect them to understand the under-compounds of an assassination like that when the adults don't understand it. . . . You ever watch an automobile accident? People'll sit there and gawk, then get back in their car, turn the radio on and finish their Pepsi-Cola. A friend of mine was shot in a parking lot in California a couple of days ago and killed. There's not one single reason in the world why that person was killed, because whatever the people who killed her wanted, she would have given them, had it been money, or . . . she was raped about three months before in Philadelphia. . . . So what you really have to wonder about is the reason for it or the lack of reason for it. We sit and demand such great answers in our drama but in our lives we'll accept anything.

Right. Because we have no choice. We'll even accept death.
Woody Allen says, "I'm not afraid of death, I just don't want to be around when it happens."

So you don't consider yourself a bleak cynic or a nihilist as you've occasionally been painted?
Not at all. Journalists tend to have this great requirement to make you colorful. They have to explain why all these things happen. The truth of the matter doesn't satisfy them.

Do you see many current films?
No.

Has the feminist movement affected you?
I just wish they'd hurry up with it so I could be a little freer. That has never been a particular problem with me. I've probably got as many females that I work with as males. We don't share the same bathrooms yet, though. . . .

In Newsweek *and other publications it was said that your favorite pastimes are going to parties and smoking dope. How do you feel about that?*
I'm gregarious. I like to smoke dope. I like to drink. I like to be with the people I like. I don't mind what anybody says about me.

Pauline Kael says that journalists tend to take you too literally....
No, she said that I'm not very expressive and that if somebody asks me what my films are about that I'll sound silly....

There seems to be some confusion about who the assassin in the film was actually after.
I don't know any more than you know. People who ask, "Why did he kill her instead of the politician?" have answered the question when they asked it. That means we condone political assassination but anything else is senseless. We do accept and condone and consequently create political assassinations. I mean, it's OK. We've got three assassins incarcerated in this country right now, and we have the psychiatric and technical capabilities to send a man to the moon and go to bed at night and not even worry about whether he's gonna get back or not because we know he is. And yet there's not any person on earth who can tell you why these men committed the assassinations they committed.

Do you actually believe in the lone nut theory?
Sure. Sure do. And whether it's true or not doesn't make any difference. We didn't say this guy was alone. Maybe Connie White hired him, I don't know. And I think the reason that we don't believe in the lone nut theory and the reason we look for plots and collusions is that we are looking for a *reason* that *computes*. We're all just human animals. We invented money, we invented values—none of them ever existed on any other layer— we've invented this society, we've invented the buildings, we've invented the murders, we've invented the elite, we've done the whole thing. And we demand logic but it doesn't necessarily have to be there.

Robert Altman

BRUCE WILLIAMSON/1976

WITH BUFFALO BILL AND *the Indians* — his ninth movie since 1970, when *M*A*S*H* became the most successful antiwar comedy in film history — Robert Altman seems virtually certain to rekindle the controversy that raged after *Nashville*. Sparked by Paul Newman's startling performance in the title role, *Buffalo Bill* is also apt to be hailed as another myth-shattering masterwork when the more vehement Altman addicts take the floor. All the stylistic hallmarks that make an Altman film unique are there in abundance: the spontaneous, seemingly improvised acting; the breezy, ballsy throwaway humor; the indifference toward traditional storytelling structure; and the eight-track overlapping sound, judged either inaudible or boldly innovative, depending on where one stands in that debate.

No director since Sam Peckinpah has provoked such passionate disputes; perhaps no director ever has taken such undisguised delight in watching himself become a cult figure and quasilegend under the very noses of the incumbent Hollywood moguls, who still consider him a freewheeling maverick with an erratic track record.

Actually, *M*A*S*H* was not only Altman's first but, to date, his only financial blockbuster; his subsequent movies, hits and flops alike, have been less memorable for making money than for making waves. But he has built a formidable reputation as the American director whose vigorous, uncompromisingly personal films have put him in the superstar pantheon with Stanley Kubrick, Ingmar Bergman, and Federico Fellini.

Last year's *Nashville* was widely touted in advance as a breakthrough work that would both captivate critics and achieve a huge commercial success. But though it won the Best Film and Best Director awards from the New York Film Critics Circle and earned five Oscar nominations, *Nashville* failed to break box-office records. No one remained indifferent to Altman's aggressively funny, colorful collage—a kind of grassroots *Grand Hotel* about two dozen oddly assorted characters who while away five days in America's country-music capital before destiny brings them together at the moment of an inexplicable assassination. Music critics, book critics, political commentators, columnists, and composers were seemingly compelled to take a position on *Nashville*. As *New York Times* book editor John Leonard noted: "Writing articles about *Nashville* and writing articles about the articles that have been written about *Nashville* is almost a light industry."

Altman, born 51 years ago in Kansas City, Missouri, is a product of America's heartland and a renegade Roman Catholic from the Bible Belt. He sprang from English-Irish-German stock. "The usual mélange," Altman calls it. "When my grandfather opened a jewelry store in K.C., he dropped one N from Altman because they told him the sign would be cheaper." His father is still a practicing insurance broker back home. The first and feistiest of three children, Robert used to sneak out of bed to see such seminal epics as *King Kong*. After a stretch in a military academy, he piloted a B-24 bomber through World War II, chalking up 45 missions over the Dutch East Indies before going home to Kansas City and joining an industrial film outfit to learn about making movies. When he decided he knew how, he flew a few sorties into Hollywood armed with radio scripts, short stories, and screenplays. In 1957, he coproduced a documentary, *The James Dean Story*, which impressed Alfred Hitchcock. For the next six years, Altman was the whiz kid of TV, directing episodes of *Alfred Hitchcock Presents, Combat, Bonanza, Whirlybirds*, and their ilk, earning—and recklessly spending or gambling away—up to $125,000 per annum.

Altman quit TV in 1963 to direct *Countdown*, a melodrama starring newcomer James Caan. He was fired from that job, prophetically, for letting two actors talk at the same time because he thought it would sound more natural. It was 1968 before he got another feature, *That Cold Day in the Park*, a muddled suspense drama starring Sandy Dennis.

Then came *M*A*S*H,* which 15 directors had rejected before Altman claimed it by default. The rest is history—but hardly one of financial triumph. *Brewster McCloud* (1971), an anarchic comedy about a boy who longs to be a bird and crash-dives into the Houston Astrodome, itself took a header. *McCabe and Mrs. Miller* (1971) costarred Warren Beatty and Julie Christie as a plucky pair of American free-enterprisers in a frontier town and got the director's bandwagon rolling again. *Images,* made in Ireland, was generally ignored, despite a 1973 Best Actress award at Cannes for Susannah York's performance, and *The Long Goodbye* (1973), with Elliott Gould, brought private-eye Philip Marlowe into the seventies. *Thieves Like Us* (1974), a warmly vital social drama of the Depression era, was followed by *California Split* (1974), which was a moderate success and teamed Gould and George Segal as a pair of compulsive gamblers.

Through the highs and lows of his prolific output, Altman has remained a loner. His list of sworn enemies, fast friends, and those who haven't made up their minds is impressive, even for Hollywood. His friends include a tight floating repertory company: Shelley Duvall, Michael Murphy, Bert Remsen, and Keenan Wynn are among those who would rather work for Altman than eat. Nowadays, it's relatively easy to manage both. Lion's Gate Films, his bustling production headquarters, occupies a two-story California-Tudor warren of cubbyholes and cutting rooms on Westwood Boulevard in L.A.

While he makes no secret of his fondness for booze and pot, Altman has been too busy of late to indulge his vices to capacity. But he does little to dispel his reputation as a hard-living, high-rolling roustabout, and once when an inquisitive lady journalist gingerly broached the subject of his three marriages, he twitted her by jovially responding: "I've had many, many mistresses. Keep 'em coming. I just giggle and give in!" Giggles aside, he has been married for 17 years to his third wife, Kathryn—a former Earl Carroll showgirl and a bright, witty, unstoppable redhead who appears more than capable of fighting the battle of the sexes to a draw. Altman has three children by his former wives; he and Kathryn have a son, Bobby, 15, and have adopted a black boy named Matthew, aged nine. When one tries to picture Altman simultaneously as devoted family man, all-American hedonist, savage social realist, veteran Hollywood rebel, and major influence on the films we'll be seeing today, tomorrow, and three years from now, the images tend to blur, not unlike the voice track in one of his own movies. To find out how the man keeps it all together, *Playboy* movie critic and contributing editor Bruce Williamson headed west toward Lion's Gate with a sheaf of questions. Williamson reports:

"During a casual acquaintanceship dating back several years—drinking with Altman in Cannes, getting stoned with him in New York—I believe I have seen the best and worst of him as a private person who is convivial, erratic, difficult, generous, funny, vulnerable, and incredibly, sometimes bitingly, perceptive about people. In physical appearance, he has been compared to Santa Claus, Mephistopheles, and a benevolent Captain Bligh, and he fits all three descriptions.

"The day I arrived at his Lion's Gate inner office, a homey baronial den with a pinball machine twinkling just outside, Altman spent the first hour or so rapping with Cleavon Little about his role in the film version of Kurt Vonnegut, Jr.'s *Breakfast of Champions,* an Altman project they wouldn't be ready to begin shooting for at least a year. What Altman didn't want to do was get on with our interview. It would be better to start talking after I'd seen *Buffalo Bill and the Indians,* Altman decided. If I loathed it, of course, all bets were off. We marked time until Paul Newman arrived, clean-shaven, along with 40 or 50 other people who were visibly itching to see a rough cut of the movie. Later, Altman collared at least half of them to ask point-blank how they had liked it. A mind-blower, nearly everyone, myself included, agreed.

"Altman's reluctance to begin our taping lessened the next day, as a series of phone calls reaffirmed the good vibes about the unveiling of *Buffalo Bill.* Finally, Altman settled down to talk. 'At first,' he said, 'I thought, well, I could probably thwart you, but that would be a waste of time.' He would just give straight stuff, no performances, he promised, maybe fill a couple of tapes . . . then we'd have a drink or two and go on with it the next day. That sounded like the best offer I'd be getting."

PLAYBOY: *Isn't there a natural link between your two latest pictures,* Buffalo Bill and the Indians *and* Nashville, *in what they say about our passion for celebrities in America? Is it true, as one critic observed, that we're a nation of groupies?*

ALTMAN: You people—critics and writers—always pigeonhole these things. Me, I just take a subject and say, Hey, this could be fun; let's make a movie out of it. *Buffalo Bill,* in many ways, is closer to *McCabe and Mrs.*

Miller than to *Nashville*, though, like *Nashville*, it is about show business. Buffalo Bill Cody was the first movie star, in one sense, the first totally manufactured American hero. That's why we needed a movie star, Paul Newman, to play the title role. I don't think we could have made it with a nonstar, someone like, say, Gene Hackman.

PLAYBOY: *Hackman, who is asking $1 million or more a picture, isn't a star?*
ALTMAN: Not in the terms that Newman and Robert Redford and Steve McQueen are. In any picture where he can be Steve McQueen, McQueen is worth his $3 million, because his pictures can be booked around the world and earn back the tab. Hackman is a fine actor, but I don't believe he's worth paying that kind of money, unless he's in a very good picture. In a bad picture, he just goes down with the whole crew. McQueen can over-come that handicap. The same thing might be true of Redford, who's next in line, then maybe Newman. Jack Nicholson, with an Academy Award now, is probably in their league, and certainly Marlon Brando.

PLAYBOY: *What's the real difference in the star quality these actors project?*
ALTMAN: It's something that happens, there's no telling why. It happens with politicians, singers . . . they've got to have a certain amount of ability. But primarily they hit on a kind of heroism a mass audience likes to iden-tify with. You can't judge simply by the U.S. and Canada, because it's a worldwide market. For Europe and Japan, you put McQueen in some kind of action picture and they'll flock to see him . . . or Charles Bronson or Alain Delon, or even Terence Hill, whom most people here have never heard of. *The Drowning Pool*, which was just a little Lew Archer detective story that didn't do well at all in the U.S., did terrific business in Europe because it had Paul Newman. European audiences are about 20 years behind us. They're still not judging films as art but as entertainment.

PLAYBOY: *Were you required by your backers to cast a major star as Buffalo Bill?*
ALTMAN: Yes, because there's $6 million or $7 million tied up in the pic-ture; it's the most expensive picture I've ever made. But we wanted a major star, anyway, as I said, because stardom is part of what we're talking about in *Buffalo Bill*. Before we knew quite which way we intended to go, I talked to Brando on the phone because of his interest in the Indian thing. I talked a long, long time to Nicholson. But Newman was our first choice.

PLAYBOY: *Was Newman aware that your approach to Buffalo Bill had him spoofing his own golden-boy image to some extent?*

ALTMAN: Oh, sure. That's why I wanted him and the reason he wanted to do it. He was very consciously deflating not only Buffalo Bill but Paul Newman, Movie Star. Nobody can live up to that kind of image.

PLAYBOY: *In fact, aren't most of your films exercises in debunking, if not of specific historical characters, at least of classic genres?* M*A*S*H *was a spoof of war movies;* McCabe and Mrs. Miller, *of the cliché western;* The Long Goodbye, *of detective yarns; and so on.*

ALTMAN: Apparently, it's something that attracts me. But I see it only after the fact, and then I say to myself, Well, there I go again. I think what happens is that I research these subjects and discover so much bullshit that it just comes out that way. I have a lot of sympathy for these characters, however; they're the victims of their own publicity.

PLAYBOY: *You had a lot of fun depicting Buffalo Bill Cody as a frontier dandy with a weakness for opera singers. Is the film historically accurate?*

ALTMAN: It's based on fact, though we took off from there. Cody was a very handsome guy, very impressionable, a ladies' man. When he started moving into the social whirl, he got mixed up with a bunch of Italian actresses; we used the idiom of opera as typical of the kind of cultural thing he was reaching for and really couldn't grasp. I feel a great deal of sympathy for Buffalo Bill. He was pure, I think. My intention was just to take a more honest look—satirical or not—at some of our myths, to see what they are. It's no accident that the picture is subtitled *Sitting Bull's History Lesson.* We like to think of Cody as a brave man, a great buffalo hunter, an Indian scout. Well, he shot a lot of buffaloes. But lots of guys who lived in the West at that time got jobs as scouts; that's like saying you worked on the railroad. Cody was a very sad character. I'd equate him with Willy Loman in *Death of a Salesman.*

PLAYBOY: *Is* Buffalo Bill and the Indians *intended to be your Bicentennial valentine to America?*

ALTMAN: Nope. When I first got the call from David Susskind about doing *Buffalo Bill*, I didn't know there was a Bicentennial. We're making a statement about a culture that happens to be American; you can probably make the same statement about France or Italy or England. I don't know what aboriginal tribes were chased out of Europe by the Europeans, but I'm quite sure they were treated pretty much the same way we treated the Indians we found here. My attitudes and my political statements, however, aren't nearly as harsh as people seem to think. When *Nashville* came out, there was this wild reaction: Oh, what a terrible view of America! It's a view of America, all right, but I don't agree that it's terrible. I'm not condemning America. I'm condemning the corruption of ideas, condemning complacency, the feeling that any way we do things must be the right way.

All my films deal with the same thing: striving, socially and culturally, to stay alive. And once any system succeeds, it becomes its own worst enemy. The good things we create soon create bad things. So nothing is ever going to be utopian, and when I make films like *Nashville* and *Buffalo Bill*, it's not to say we're the worst country in the world, or God, what awful people these are. I'm just saying we're at this point and it's sad.

PLAYBOY: *Do you feel as sad about the country's future as you do about its past and present?*

ALTMAN: If I were to make a real judgment about this country, I would say I'm optimistic. I think that parts of the system no longer work, but we're very young; there's a good chance we'll survive all this. It's probably the best place to live that I know. I mean, if you're rich, you can go anywhere. But if you're poor—well, I'd rather be poor here than poor in India. There's always a sense that you can rise above your trappings in this country, whereas even in England, for example, you don't feel the same hope—unless you can become a rock star.

PLAYBOY: *Behind the laughs in* Buffalo Bill, *there's an implication that that kind of manufactured hero still walks among us. Can you spot any on the current political scene?*

ALTMAN: Yes, all of them. Any person who develops a public and packaged personality is the same as a movie star, unfortunately. They can't be real, regular people. You take a Teddy Kennedy or a Jerry Brown: He has to maintain the public's image of him, and he finally becomes that image, at which point he's lost a lot of freedom. No way is Teddy Kennedy going to walk around your kitchen with his shoes off and level with you; he's not going to be loose, because he can't afford to be. There's no such thing as a private life anymore. The media are so vast, you're caught up and made an eccentric. It's just like this interview or any interview done with someone like me, to be printed in so many words: The words you guys pick may not give a true picture of an individual, whether it's to sell magazines or political candidates.

PLAYBOY: *Is that why you have been so reluctant to do this interview?*
ALTMAN: No, I'm just afraid I'll start listening to myself. I wonder how much bullshit an interview will be, because I have nothing to say about anything. I'm not interested in analyzing myself. What I'm doing right now is a very dangerous thing for an artist to do.

PLAYBOY: *Why?*
ALTMAN: Because when you start trying to explain what you do . . . well, once you find out, you probably won't be able to do it again. Things come out of me only when I relax and let them come as an unconscious, emotional expression rather than an intellectual expression.

I tend to say a lot of arbitrary, contradictory things, and if I don't like a person, I'll get very hostile and say, Aw, fuck it, and purposely try to antagonize him. Yet there's usually some truth in everything anyone says. Again, it's a question of freeing your subconscious.

PLAYBOY: *Do you or don't you use booze to free your subconscious? In a Newsweek cover story, you were quoted as saying, "I work a lot when I'm drunk and trust that all of it will eventually appear in my films." On other occasions, you have insisted you never drink on the job. What's the truth?*
ALTMAN: The fact is, I don't drink while I'm working. But I work a lot while I'm drinking. No matter what you read or hear, I never get drunk on a film set.

PLAYBOY: *But when aren't you working? You've made nine movies in the past six years, virtually without taking a vacation. Don't you ever have to stop and catch a breath or recharge your creative batteries?*
ALTMAN: Perhaps I should stay home on the beach, but all I say is, I can't remember a time when I haven't been working on a project. I come in every day, whether there's anything to do or not. If I don't have something to do, I create it. This is the life, man. I can be here in the office, get

drunk, go next door and edit out a piece of film. It's terrific, like owning the world's biggest erector set.

PLAYBOY: *Someone has suggested that with Lion's Gate you're founding a mini-MGM. Are you?*

ALTMAN: If I am, it's in self-defense. Most of my money goes into the place; it costs about $600,000 a year just to keep the doors open. But I'm trying to keep a group of people together who are very important to me. I'm producing films for them to write or direct, to keep them available to me as need arises. All of them could get better jobs. They could improve their incomes, their status by working somewhere else.

PLAYBOY: *Are you referring to their having to buck the anti-Altman sentiment among members of the Hollywood establishment?*

ALTMAN: Yes, but that sentiment is understandable. I've never been very nice to the establishment, either. I've always been very outspoken in the press; my tendency is always to be a little loud. I'm a little arrogant and they're a little afraid.

PLAYBOY: *Do you believe your maverick status in Hollywood had anything to do with* Nashville's *relatively poor showing in the Oscar awards?*

ALTMAN: I was thrilled that we got as far as we did with recognition for the film, which had been turned down by all the major studios; Paramount merely picked it up for distribution. But *One Flew over the Cuckoo's Nest* wasn't a major Hollywood production, either—the money was put up by a record company—and Milos Forman is not a Hollywood director. Even *Dog Day Afternoon* was a New York picture, so maybe what it really shows is that there's a lack of good product coming from the major studios. The main value of these awards, anyway, other than to rub your ego a little bit, is that they may open the door a crack wider for people with ideas that aren't run of the mill.

PLAYBOY: *But with five nominations for* Nashville, *didn't you expect to win more than Keith Carradine's prize for Best Song?*

ALTMAN: Well, the Academy is a private club, so its members can do whatever they want with it, I guess. They declared *Nashville* ineligible for an editing award. *Nashville* was more edited than directed, for Christ's sake. They ruled us out on costume design, art direction, and camera, and even disqualified our musical score on a technical point. Johnny Green and Jeff Alexander, the old men who run that Academy section, are determined to keep it all to themselves. When Green did a score made up of standard songs of his for *They Shoot Horses, Don't They?* they had to change the rules that year so he could qualify and be nominated for an Oscar.

PLAYBOY: *In the categories in which* Nashville *was qualified, did you do any active campaigning?*

ALTMAN: Paramount did a little, not much. I wouldn't have wanted them to do any more. I don't know what United Artists spent promoting *Cuckoo's Nest*, but I'll guarantee you it was over $80,000. That's the trouble, the whole thing becomes like a national election, with primaries. I won the New York primary, *Cuckoo's Nest* won the foreign primary—six Golden Globe awards—and so on. But nobody knows who votes. I think if a magazine took photographs of each of those Academy members—the ones who actually cast the ballots—and published them all and said who they were, you'd be able to make a pretty good evaluation of what an Academy Award is really worth and how it's arrived at.

PLAYBOY: *Louise Fletcher, who took the Best Actress award for* Cuckoo's Nest, *was originally supposed to play the role that got Lily Tomlin a Best Supporting Actress nomination for* Nashville. *Some follow-up stories, commenting on this behind-the-scenes irony, hinted that you had given the role to Lily because she had a bigger name. Is there some misunderstanding?*

ALTMAN: Not on my part. That role as the mother of the deaf-mute children was written for Louise, whose parents are deaf. But her husband, Jerry Bick, who was my producer on *Thieves Like Us*, came to me and said he didn't see how Louise would be able to leave her kids and go off on location in Nashville for eight or ten weeks . . . and what was he supposed to do during that time? I felt very guilty then, because there was no money in the part . . . we felt all the actors in *Nashville* were doing us a great big favor, and it seemed to me we were just asking a little too much of Louise. I'm not sure Jerry went back and told her that he had indicated she shouldn't take the part, since they have to live together. But that's when I started considering Lily. In any case, Louise is a deserving actress. I coaxed her out of retirement for *Thieves Like Us* and we showed film on her to Forman and Mike Douglas to help convince them she should get *Cuckoo's Nest*.

PLAYBOY: *Is it true that Robert Duvall was supposed to play the Henry Gibson role in* Nashville?

ALTMAN: The part was written for Duvall. It was one of the last characters added and turned out to be one of the most important. Duvall came down here and said he wanted to be in the picture and could sing country-and-western. So I said, "Fine, you can write your own songs." Then I guess we broke over money.

PLAYBOY: *In view of everything you said a moment ago about the Academy, how would you have felt if you had won an Oscar?*

ALTMAN: Surprised. And I'd be very pleased. Going in as an underdog and winning an uphill battle makes anybody feel good. But, my God, people get crazy; they call you up and say how sorry they are, they were so sure you'd win. It's not a foot race; one doesn't set out to make a movie with that goal in mind. Or maybe some do. Recently, I saw an interview in the *L.A. Times* with Billy Friedkin, talking about his new picture, a remake of *Wages of Fear*, apparently meant to top *The Exorcist*. Mr. Friedkin, who has some kind of chronic diarrhea of the mouth, was very humble, as usual; for the $10 million he's been given to spend, he said, "Well, to be frank — I'm going for a classic." But nobody really cares what he intends to do or what I intend to do; it's what we end up doing that counts.

PLAYBOY: *But a lot of the controversy about* Nashville *centered on exactly that question: What did you intend to do? How would you sum up the central metaphor of* Nashville?

ALTMAN: If you take all those 24 characters in the film, you can break each one down into an archetype. We carefully picked those archetypes to represent a cross section of the whole culture, heightened by the country-music scene and extreme nationalism, or regionalism, of a city like Nashville. When you say Nashville, you immediately focus on an image of great wealth and instant popular success. It's like Hollywood 40 years ago. Kids still get off buses with guitars; two years later they can own a guitar-shaped swimming pool.

Another thing *Nashville* signifies is that we don't listen to words anymore. The words of a country song are as predictable as the words of a politician's speech. When President Ford announces that the state of the Union is that we're solving problems in the Middle East, we don't listen; we don't read or pay attention to what he says. It becomes rhythm and music rather than meaningful words. No one can quote one thing Ford has said since he's been in office.

Nashville is merely suggesting that you think about these things, allowing you room to think. Many people, I guess, want to know exactly what it is they're supposed to think. They want to know what your message is. Well, my message is that I am not going to do their work for them.

PLAYBOY: Nashville *never became the commercial blockbuster that you and many pro-Altman critics anticipated. Why?*
ALTMAN: Well, I can only think it's because we didn't have King Kong or a shark. I don't mean to take anything away from *Jaws*, but *Nashville* was not a one-focus thing like that. Also, maybe there was too much critical response; the word "masterpiece" frightens people away. It's still been more profitable for me personally than any film I've ever made; it's grossed about $8 million and may go to $10 million. I think *Buffalo Bill* is going to be easier for audiences than *Nashville*, because it doesn't pose a threat: The indictment is in history, so we can always put that blame somewhere else. *Nashville*'s indictment made too many people nervous. The whole community of Nashville disowned it; the country-music people said it was no good, it was a lie; and that kept a lot of those fans away.

PLAYBOY: *Wasn't the specific charge they leveled against you that the music was phony, wouldn't pass muster at the Grand Ole Opry?*
ALTMAN: This crap about a Nashville sound is mainly a matter of opinion. I wasn't making records, goddamn it, I was making a movie. Take any song in there, I can point out a current hit or failure that's better and worse—musically, lyrically, and every other way. The main reason for that criticism was that they saw the names of actors, not professional songwriters, on the songs; and Richard Baskin, who did all the arrangements, was not a country-and-western guy. It's my contention that anybody can write a song. The Nashville people have to claim they're more professional; otherwise, how are they going to justify the $1 million a year they make?

PLAYBOY: *One last question about* Nashville. *In the assassination scene at the end—*

ALTMAN: I know what's coming. When I go around to the universities—where quite a number of kids don't understand my pictures and don't especially like them—they always want to know: Why'd he kill her?

PLAYBOY: *Well, why did he?*

ALTMAN: When you ask why he killed the singer instead of the politician, you've already answered your question—and discovered my motive. The point is that we can accept the assassination of the politician but not that of the girl. Because we condone political assassination in our culture. We say that's all right, we understand that. Assassination has become acceptable in this society and it's going to spread, the way hijacking did. I think we're in a very dangerous situation. And now, with the Patricia Hearst trial and all its implications, it's becoming almost nightmarish.

PLAYBOY: *What implications do you see in the Patty Hearst trial?*

ALTMAN: I mean that the Patty Hearst case was not about her at all, and it's the worst thing that's happened in this country since the Julius and Ethel Rosenberg trial. You knew she would be found guilty, she had to be found guilty; there was no way that judge and jury could not convict Patty Hearst, because they're afraid, afraid of Hearst power; so now they've stripped that away to prove that money can't protect her. They're afraid of revolution.

PLAYBOY: *You suggest that society as a whole demanded her conviction?*

ALTMAN: Absolutely. And I think we're going to see that girl's mother, Catherine Hearst, become so radicalized that I would not be surprised at any act she might perform in the next year or so. It turns out that Cinque, or DeFreeze, was a prophet. "If you go back there," he told Patty, "they'll put you in jail." And, by God, that's what happened. We're now in the full swing of the Nixon-Kissinger heritage, with all their philosophy coming down to us. We're even beginning to look at Gerald Ford as if he were a nice guy and pretty smart.

Patty Hearst had to be convicted for not being a well-trained soldier. She shouldn't have gone on trial in the first place. Jesus Christ, she was 19 years old, thrown into the trunk of a car, locked in a closet, absolutely terrorized; and I think from that point on you've got to discount every single thing she has done. I have spoken to several people who are very strong in the ACLU, real liberals, people who suffered through the McCarthy era, the Hollywood Ten and all that. And when they said they thought this kid should be convicted, I couldn't believe it.

The Hearst case deals with exactly the same kind of collective fear the Rosenberg trial did. The fear then was of communism, that Russia might get the bomb. Now there's terrorism and anarchy throughout the world and everyone is panicky. We're afraid of Patty Hearst because she lived with a guy willingly and wrote letters, made statements. What society is actually reacting to is its fear of hippies, and of sexual freedom, and of revolutionaries, people with beards and long hair who don't keep their pants pressed or wear neckties.

PLAYBOY: *Would you consider making a film that dealt directly with this kind of volatile social problem?*

ALTMAN: Funny you should ask, because I'm just concluding a deal with Ed [E. L.] Doctorow to coproduce a movie based on his novel *The Book of Daniel*; he'll write the script and I'll direct. It's a fictionalized story about the children of the Rosenbergs, about the hysteria of an era when people are frightened and people get sacrificed.

PLAYBOY: *You and Doctorow are thick as thieves since he presented your New York Film Critics award and introduced himself as "Altman's new best friend." You're also making the movie version of his novel* Ragtime *together. When will that be?*

ALTMAN: Not for a while. I've got a first-draft screenplay from Doctorow that is about 340 pages long and brilliant; I'm thrilled with it. The son of a bitch is uncanny, really an artist, and I just like him a lot. I mean, we don't hug or anything, but we talk on the phone almost every day. He came up to Calgary while we were on location and was pressed into service; he makes his screen debut as a Presidential assistant in *Buffalo Bill.*

PLAYBOY: *Isn't 340 pages pretty long for a screenplay?*

ALTMAN: I think we'll make two films out of it, of about two and a half hours each, then expand that into ten hours of television. This will not be just another movie. It'll be an event.

PLAYBOY: *Didn't you once have similar plans for* Nashville?

ALTMAN: That's already done and reedited as two two-hour television programs, which will probably air on two Sunday nights to start the 1977 fall television season. Eventually, we're going to do the same thing with *Buffalo Bill*; we've already made the deal.

PLAYBOY: *Do these projected films for TV indicate that you feel some dissatisfaction with the shorter original versions?*

ALTMAN: No, but there are really good sequences from *Nashville*, for example, that weren't in the movie because you cannot ask people to sit that long in a theater. Some movie buffs will gladly sit for five hours, but people generally won't do it. On television, that's not offensive. You've got breaks. You can eat, stretch, go to the bathroom.

PLAYBOY: *You're working with heavyweights now, between Doctorow's* Ragtime *and your plans to film Kurt Vonnegut, Jr.'s* Breakfast of Champions. *Is it intimidating for you to tackle movies based on two such famous novels?*

ALTMAN: Well, it's no worse than making a movie about something like the Civil War.

PLAYBOY: *Have you considered making an epic nonfiction film, as it were? Something like* All the President's Men?

ALTMAN: To me, doing that movie would be like making an illustrated lecture, because you're not able to deviate from the facts much. I understand the success of it, because everyone knows who the bad guys and good guys are, and you've got that big face of Nixon's looming over all of it. The majority of people in this country—61 percent of them, remember—are exactly like Nixon. They chose him, he betrayed them, and those are the cats who respond to *President's Men* as much as you and I and the liberals who say, "Aw, shit, I told you so." They've got to love it because it's real, it's revenge. Nixon was the perfect President for this country, but he dumped on them and they're still feeling hurt.

PLAYBOY: *Could you work up greater enthusiasm for making a movie based on Woodward and Bernstein's sequel,* The Final Days?

ALTMAN: Well, long before Watergate, we thought about a movie of that kind from a book—not a very good book—called *A Night at Camp David*.

It's about a President who goes insane. We were flirting with buying it, then I suddenly realized it was all actually happening. The book was almost prophetic, but it was not for me.

PLAYBOY: *Are you an activist in politics?*

ALTMAN: I get involved. I mean, I give money and support. I supported Gene McCarthy, I supported George McGovern. Right now there's nobody to get passionate about. Intellectually, Morris Udall seemed the best. Jerry Brown is attractive to me; I think he's getting set up for four years from now. But the rest offer nothing fresh.

Actually, I don't think it makes a lot of difference who gets elected in 1976. I doubt that we're going to have a President of any value this term. Probably the next time around will be better. In fact, maybe we shouldn't care who's President. Maybe it should be someone like the chief executive of AT&T, a board chairman whose name we don't even know. Because government today is only a firm that builds highways, maintains a system of courts to keep people from infringing on other people's rights. As for genuine leadership and philosophy...well, I think we're past that.

PLAYBOY: *Some feminists have tried to make your films a political issue. What do you say when your work is attacked for projecting—and we quote— "an adolescent view of women as sex objects"?*

ALTMAN: I simply don't understand that. Again, let's look at the films. Women had most of the major roles in *Nashville*. I did *Images* with Susannah York, which was certainly a sympathetic treatment of women. I think Julie Christie as Mrs. Miller is a very accurate portrait of a woman's role in the West if she wanted to survive in that era. Maybe the accusation harks back to Hot Lips in *M*A*S*H*, but the precise point of that character was that women were treated and are treated as sex objects. They can't blame me for the condition because I report it. We're dealing with a society in which most of the significant activity until now has been initiated by males. If you make a western or a sports story or a story about big business or gangsters, it's automatically going to reflect the secondary positions women hold.

PLAYBOY: *You retain complete control over your movies, as Francis Ford Coppola, Stanley Kubrick, and a few other privileged directors do. Is there never any pressure brought to bear to make you change a film?*

ALTMAN: Oh, sure. But nobody has ever cut a film on me. There was a lot of pressure up front from Barry Diller at Paramount, who wanted me to cut one sequence in *Nashville* so we'd get a PG rating rather than an R. The Motion Picture Association's ratings board said it would make a deal with us: It would let us keep the striptease scene with Gwen Welles if we would cut the word "fucker" somewhere else.

PLAYBOY: *Did you give up the "fucker"?*

ALTMAN: No, I didn't. We finally took an R. The word itself didn't make much difference to me one way or the other, but I felt I couldn't cut it because that would put the ratings board in a position in which it's not supposed to be. The ratings people are supposed to be advisors, not censors. If they are what they say they are, there shouldn't be any appeal from their rulings. They should just give you an R or a P or an X or a Q or whatever and make it stick.

This whole MPAA thing is so unwieldy, and also corrupt—though by corrupt I don't mean you can buy them off. But they represent a privileged group of industry people, and if you belong to that group, you get slightly different treatment. More money has gone into some pictures, so they're considered more important and handled accordingly; but there's no way anybody can show me the justification for *Papillon's* getting a PG rating while *Thieves Like Us* got an R. There's no consistency. I took an R for *California Split* because we had 12 "fucks" and a couple of "cocksuckers." But the minute they say they want to trade me a "tit" for a "fucker," that proves to me they're corrupt.

PLAYBOY: *If you are so often at odds with the Hollywood establishment, why do you continue to live and work in the enemy camp, so to speak?*

ALTMAN: Well, it's a big town, and I've got an awful lot of people I depend on who also depend on me. It doesn't make a bit of difference where you are, anyway. *Nashville* was made in Nashville. *Buffalo Bill* and *McCabe* were made in Canada. *Thieves Like Us* was made in Mississippi. My feeling about Hollywood is that all of that has nothing to do with the pictures I make. I'm the catalyst, I guess, for a kind of East Coast-West Coast cultural separation, the Great Divide, which drives the studio people crazy. Because they want money-making pictures, sure, but they also want the snob appeal of critical acceptance and prestige—meaning films that get good reviews.

PLAYBOY: *The New York critics love you, but do you get much support from the press here in Los Angeles?*

ALTMAN: I always get a kind of left-handed criticism out here, except from a few people. Charles Champlin on the *Times* practically runs ads predicting who will win the Oscars and who he believes should win. He never misses. The people who vote read Champlin and think: Oh, Champlin's right, because he's not one of those East Coast people who are always pushing us around.

At the Academy Awards, I ran into Ruth Batchelor, whoever she is; she's a chairman of the Los Angeles critics' group, which was just formed to give out prizes the way the New York critics do. She came up to me and said, "You know, on the first ballot, *Nashville* won everything, but we use a point system and had to keep revoting." And I told her, "You had to keep revoting until you didn't coincide with the New York film critics." She said, "Well, uh . . . yes, that's right." It's all pretty silly.

PLAYBOY: *Is it just that they want to be different from their New York colleagues?*

ALTMAN: No, I think it reflects the quality of the critics. The same division exists between France and England. They love me at Cannes, while in England they say, "Well, he was just lucky." Generally, I think the Eastern critics are more appreciative of art and exploration in films. I think the California people are more interested in preserving their traditions. I'm not charging that Champlin is a bad critic. But this town responds to him because it feels he represents the industry. It's chauvinistic, like people who live in Chicago rooting for the Cubs or the White Sox. But we shouldn't discuss only New York versus Hollywood. Seattle is a terrific movie town, much closer in taste to the New York anti-Hollywood attitude; and Denver's the same way. I think we're talking about Hollywood versus the rest of the country, not just the East.

PLAYBOY: *How closely do you follow what critics write about you?*

ALTMAN: The main function of critics, for me, is that they furnish some sort of guidelines. You don't go to a king, you don't go before a jury of 12 citizens picked at random to judge a film. I don't go to the guys at my dad's country club in Kansas City, because they would be bored to death watching one of my movies. I'm trying to reach the several millions of people in the country, or the world, who are film oriented. The critics, who see virtually all films, are in touch with that audience, so I read what they say. There are certain critics I tend to agree with almost straight down the line.

PLAYBOY: *Do you want to name them?*

ALTMAN: I'd rather not, because it might seem to alienate or discredit anyone who's left out. And if I say Rex Reed is my favorite critic, Rex will get intimidated and start writing bad things about me.

PLAYBOY: *We could probably guess that Reed isn't your favorite critic, since he is one of those who have called you a lazy artist, a sloppy worker who improvises too much with too little control. How about Jay Cocks of* Time, *who has suggested that you should take your work more seriously than you do?*

ALTMAN: Jay Cocks has always made personal comments about me; he can't seem to separate me as an individual from my films. I've never met him and can't answer his assumptions.

I probably am a lazy artist and probably don't control things as much as some people would like—but that's my business. And if my style is too loose or improvised for some people's taste, that's their problem—totally. The fact is, I'm not the greatest Hollywood director and all that bullshit, but I'm not the opposite, either. And I am not careless. I may be irresponsible, I may strive for things and not always succeed, but that's never the result of sloppiness. Maybe it's lack of judgment.

PLAYBOY: *Stephen Farber, who recently became* New West's *film critic, described you as one of the New Has-beens a couple of years ago, just before your reputation started to soar. How did that grab you?*

ALTMAN: Well, Farber ought to have his typewriter taken away from him or go get a job working for the oil companies. He is not a critic, he doesn't qualify as a critic. He's a hatchet man and paid assassin, a guy *The New York Times* knows it can go to if it wants an "anti" piece because there's been too much praise of something. I'm sure Clay Felker hired Farber for the same reason he hired John Simon as *New York's* critic—because he wanted somebody to really get the shiv out and sell magazines. I don't like Simon at all, but at least I give him credit for being a critic. I can't give that much to Rex Reed, who's basically a gossip columnist, but Farber's worse than any of those guys.

PLAYBOY: *The loudest member of the pro-Altman critical claque has been* The New Yorker'*s Pauline Kael, who created a stir when she wrote an ecstatic review of* Nashville *based on an unfinished early version. This year, Kael reportedly claimed that she's qualified to review Altman movies in this manner because she knows your work so well she can tell in advance what's going to be left in and taken out. Is that true?*

ALTMAN: Did she say that? Well, I suppose she can. Pauline is such a student of film, she probably knows pretty well in which direction a movie is likely to go. In general, I don't mind who sees a film in rough cut. I show them to lots of people without fear of reprisals, though I wouldn't let Rex Reed see one of my films in finished form. He'll have to buy his own ticket.

PLAYBOY: *Is it true that you threw Barbra Streisand out of your office after one such screening?*

ALTMAN: Yes, because she was rude.

PLAYBOY: *Do you want to tell us about it?*

ALTMAN: She came as a guest of mine with her boyfriend, Jon Peters— to see *Nashville*, at her request, as a matter of fact—because Peters was planning to direct a rock *Star Is Born* or something. So we screened the picture for them and for 20 or 30 other people, including some of the actors in the film. Then we came back here to the office; Barbra sat down and all her conversation was about "Jon and I." "Listen," she said, "Jon and I want to know how you did this, how you did that." Finally, I said, "Don't you think you owe a comment to a few of the people in this room?" She had nothing to say. She was so completely wrapped up in herself, she didn't even know what I was talking about. I just asked them to leave.

PLAYBOY: *Aren't there pitfalls in your practice of screening rough cuts of your films for friends, colleagues, sometimes even for critics?*

ALTMAN: Well, sure, a little masochism is part of it, you can't delude yourself. But we don't just pull people off the street. I have to be very careful not to load a preview with people I know are duck soup, who will just go for the film no matter what. I'm also arrogant enough to invite people who I'm sure will want not to like it, who really hope to see it fail. I love to make them commit themselves up front, then turn it around on them later. You see, the way I edit films is to start showing them as I'm pulling them together. I don't actually pay much attention to what people say, but I make decisions while looking at the backs of their heads, seeing the movie through someone else's eyes. If I get embarrassed by a certain sequence, that tells me something.

PLAYBOY: *How did you arrive at your free-and-easy approach to filmmaking?*
ALTMAN: Well, I don't like to rehearse a scene before we're actually ready to shoot it. If I do, the freshness is gone for me when we go back to it later; everything seems set and kind of dry.

PLAYBOY: *Your unorthodox methods must be a little unnerving for some actors. How did it go with Newman?*
ALTMAN: Oh, Paul was sensational. He had no problem at all. Donald Sutherland in *M*A*S*H* loved working that way and his improvisation was profound; he's a hell of an actor. Warren Beatty in *McCabe* probably had the toughest time. But Warren was already a star, dealing with an unknown director and properly nervous about it. And Warren doesn't trust anybody very much.

My work is not really as loose and frenetic and unorthodox as everyone seems to think and it's not nearly as improvisational as I get credit for. I suspect that some actors see my films and sense a certain kind of freedom or fantasize about it. But most of the actors who have worked for me don't work for anybody else. Shelley Duvall has given absolutely marvelous performances in four or five of my films; her work in *Thieves Like Us* is as good as any performance I can imagine. I'm always amazed that other directors don't pick up on her, but nobody has; she can't get a job . . . I guess because she doesn't have big tits. Ronee Blakley was looking for an agent, so I had a few of them down here to see film on her while we were cutting *Nashville*. I showed them her hospital scene, her breakdown scene, and they said, "Gee, she's terrific, but . . . you know, she's a country-and-western singer." I said, "No, there's nothing country-and-western about her. If anything, she's a hip West Coast girl." They could not get it through their heads that she was acting. They finally said to me, "Well, uh, you've got a way of making real people look like actors." And I told them, "Well, I hope I have a way of making actors look like real people."

PLAYBOY: *Have you done any casting for* Ragtime *or* Breakfast of Champions?

ALTMAN: We have no cast in mind for *Ragtime*, but *Breakfast* seems pretty well set. Peter Falk will play Dwayne Hoover; Sterling Hayden will play Kilgore Trout; Cleavon Little will play Wayne Hoobler; Alice Cooper will play Bunny Hoover; and Ruth Gordon will play Eliott Rosewater, the richest man in the world.

PLAYBOY: *Ruth Gordon will play a male part?*
ALTMAN: Sure; she's an actor, why not? All the feminists say we shouldn't discriminate. We're using Alice Cooper as the fag piano player, and Ruth Gordon can certainly look like an old man. Our sexual differences tend to disappear with age, anyway; all she has to do is cut her hair and sit in a wheelchair.

PLAYBOY: *You once indicated that* Breakfast *would be a breakthrough movie sexually, in which you'd let it all hang out. Is that still the plan?*
ALTMAN: No, that was one of those early ideas that just didn't develop. I was going to deal primarily with the Kilgore Trout section of the story, where his books were being turned into pornographic movies, but we've abandoned that whole concept.

PLAYBOY: *Which films will you do next?*
ALTMAN: I'll be starting with *Yig Epoxy*, based on a book by Robert Grossbach called *Easy and Hard Ways Out*. It'll be a studio picture for Warner Bros. all shot on a sound stage, with Falk and Hayden again, Henry Gibson and a big, big cast. The whole thing takes place in one of those huge engineering-firm think tanks. It's a flat-out comedy, a cross between *Dr. Strangelove* and *M*A*S*H*, a really funny situation; and I'm going to see if I can make the audience wet their pants.

PLAYBOY: *What does* Yig Epoxy *mean?*
ALTMAN: Epoxy, of course, is glue. A YIG is a sort of radar device, and there's a YIG filter, which is used in aircraft for evasive action with ground-air missiles. They can't find the right glue to hold this thing together; consequently, all these planes crash....

PLAYBOY: *Sounds like a million laughs. What else is on your calendar?*
ALTMAN: I produced a film that's coming in, an original by Robert Benton, called *The Late Show*, with Art Carney and Lily Tomlin. Then there's

Alan Rudolph's film *Welcome to L.A.*, which I'm producing, and another thing we're working on for Lily, *The Extra*, which is about the life of a Hollywood extra, an exploration of people who believe the publicity of their own defeat.

PLAYBOY: *Haven't you had some difficulties with extras?*
ALTMAN: I will not tolerate the Screen Extras Guild. If I rent the shoemaker's shop next door to shoot a scene in front of it, I'm supposed to take out the two guys in there who know how to run all the machines and replace them with two extras who try to act like they know what they're doing. There's no way I can get the same effect. So who am I putting out of work—a couple of unskilled people. I haven't used the Extras Guild since *M*A*S*H*.

PLAYBOY: *Do you draw any royalties from the* M*A*S*H *television series?*
ALTMAN: None whatsoever. The TV show is still using the *M*A*S*H* theme song, "Suicide Is Painless," for which my son Michael wrote the lyrics when he was 14 years old, and he's made a lot of money out of it. I didn't get a fucking dime out of *M*A*S*H*, except for my director's fee. Ingo Preminger, who produced it, personally made at least $5 million, and God knows how much Fox collected. Yet I can't even get an audience at Fox. They don't want to talk to me.

I sometimes think that if we were all paid less money and nobody could make a big killing, most of these clever manipulators who are in this business strictly for the money would stay away from the movies and leave them to the artists—to people who really love what they're doing.

PLAYBOY: *Let's be realistic. Isn't one of the reasons backers balk at putting money into your pictures the fact that, with more than one person talking at the same time, they find your sound tracks unintelligible?*
ALTMAN: I could go back and show you some of Howard Hawks's early pictures and you'd find exactly the same effect. Somebody picked up on it in my films after *McCabe* because it irritated a lot of people; yet I've got a file of reviews and letters saying the sound track was the best thing in the picture.

PLAYBOY: *Wasn't Warren Beatty, the star of* McCabe, *one of those who were irritated?*

ALTMAN: Warren was infuriated, he is still infuriated and he'll just have to stay infuriated.

Sometimes, though, I'm afraid audiences have a legitimate reason to complain, because we record dialog under ideal circumstances. In theaters where the speakers aren't working properly, you get a muddled version of the sound track. But that can happen to any director on any film.

PLAYBOY: *Are there any directors on the scene now whom you especially admire?*
ALTMAN: I admire anybody who can get a film finished. Kurosawa's films impress me. I was very impressed with Fellini's *La Dolce Vita*. I like Bergman, who has always gone his own way and never had a success, really.

PLAYBOY: *You've been called an American Fellini, though John Simon recently hinted that Fellini might learn a lot from Lina Wertmuller.*
ALTMAN: Well, Simon has finally found someone to fall in love with and I'm glad for him.

When I first saw Bertolucci's *Last Tango in Paris,* I was about ready to quit. He dealt with certain sexual attitudes that are usually kept under wraps and I thought it was a great step. I admire Kubrick, but I can't say I like him. I mean, I don't know him personally. What he does is terrific and the opposite of what I do. He supervises every little detail of his films down to the last inch. But I leave a gap so wide that anything between A and X may be acceptable. With Kubrick, it's between A and A 1.

PLAYBOY: *Whom would you single out from the ranks of the younger directors?*
ALTMAN: Well, I think Martin Scorsese's going to endure. I think Steven Spielberg will endure, though it's tough when a picture like *Jaws* brings you a lot of success and money overnight that may not strictly be related to the merit of your work. I am not knocking *Jaws*, which was a magnificent accomplishment for a kid that age. But will he now be able to go off and make a small personal film? There's too much coming at you. It's the same with actors. Keith Carradine's suddenly hotter than a pistol since *Nashville*; they keep telling him, "We've got this great part for a street singer." He doesn't want to do those things.

Ivan Passer is a brilliant director; his *Intimate Lighting* I consider one of the best films ever made, though he, again, gets caught up on subjects he's not really familiar with and, consequently, fails. Coppola, of course, is a good producer-director. I get bored, as an audience, with John Cassavetes; though John is terrific, I always have the feeling that if he ever made a movie that was generally accepted and successful, it would really worry him. Paul Mazursky at least makes films that are recognizable as Mazursky films, though I personally don't like them; and I can get by pretty well without Peter Bogdanovich. Like Friedkin, he's constantly talking about his movies; he seems to know too much, and I've never seen a film of his that I thought was even passable.

But my idea of total mediocrity is Richard Brooks's last Gene Hackman thing, *Bite the Bullet,* which is about the worst kind of obvious, commercially inspired movie I can imagine. I guess people like it. I am not acquainted with Brooks, who's done some fine films, but that certainly isn't one of them.

PLAYBOY: *You must be buttonholed by many aspiring young filmmakers. What do you say to them?*

ALTMAN: I tell them that the only advice I can give is never to take advice from anybody. I've had a lot of experience doing industrial films, documentary films, films I hated doing. I've plugged in the lights, cleaned up, cooked the lunches, learned where to waste time and where to spend it. I also tell them they'd better be lucky. You don't need a lot of money to be a painter or to write a song, but it costs minimally $1 million to make a movie and nobody's going to hand you $1 million. There probably should be a system of apprenticeships.

PLAYBOY: *Do you hire apprentices?*

ALTMAN: Sure, all the time. I don't care whether they come out of schools or off the street. We take a lot of people if they can serve us and we think we can serve them, but many fall by the wayside because they discover it isn't as much fun as they'd thought. They expect they're going to sit around listening in on heavyweight discussions about art; they soon find out that what they're doing is driving 300 miles a day getting film to the airport.

PLAYBOY: *One of the least celebrated chapters of your professional life, before you broke into television, was a period you spent tattooing dogs. Where did you do that?*

ALTMAN: Inside the groin of the right front leg. We'd tattoo their state and county license numbers.

PLAYBOY: *Fascinating—but we meant where geographically.*
ALTMAN: It started here. After the war, in 1947, I bought a bull terrier from a guy named H. Graham Connar. He had this idea for dog tattooing, which he called Identi-Code. I was writing then with a friend, Jim Rickard; we'd decided to become press agents. Then we got the idea of setting up this whole scam on a national basis. We invented our own tattooing machine, developed a numbering system, and moved to New York and Washington. I was the tattooer.

PLAYBOY: *How did you make out?*
ALTMAN: Pretty well, for a while. I tattooed Truman's dog while he was still in the White House. We were lobbying in Washington and on the verge of being bought out by National Dog Week—which is a corporation owned by four major dog-food companies—when we went broke.

PLAYBOY: *A couple of years ago, you claimed you were practically broke again. Isn't your financial picture today on an upswing?*
ALTMAN: My percentages are bigger, but I seldom see any of the money. I have no wealth of any kind that would allow me to take three months or a year off. It's nice to be able to borrow from the bank now, because they think I can work, but there's never been a time I wasn't in debt. My personal take from *Nashville* will be a few hundred thousand, which is terrific. But the government grabs half of it right off the bat and the rest goes to support this Lion's Gate operation.

PLAYBOY: *Aren't you a pretty big spender?*
ALTMAN: I'm not an extravagant person, no. I have to travel quite a bit. I live reasonably well. I buy a lot of whiskey and a lot of dinners.

PLAYBOY: *How's your luck at cards? Do you still have a passion for gambling?*
ALTMAN: It's not quite a passion, but it's something I really like. I like to play poker, like going to the races, but I can't allocate any time to it. I love betting on football.

PLAYBOY: *Are you a heavy bettor?*

ALTMAN: Yeah, within limits. I have good years and bad years. Year before last, I won about $26,000; but I never stop while I'm winning. I may bet $500 or $1000 on a game, but you always lose in the long run because of the percentages. I never bet on the Dallas Cowboys. There's just something about that team I don't like. I'm not sure what it is, though Texas is not my favorite place.

PLAYBOY: *Do you suppose there's a connection between your gambling instincts and your career?*

ALTMAN: Only in the sense that if you've experienced life as a gambler, you realize you can get along without great security. Consequently, it doesn't bother me when there's no money in the bank. I have this optimistic attitude that nobody's going to starve.

PLAYBOY: *Maybe having grown up during the Depression helps. What was your childhood like?*

ALTMAN: I probably had the most normal, uneventful upbringing possible. My parents were stricter with me than with my two younger sisters. As a youngster, I was not a good student, but I just loved movies. I saw them all, went all the time. I got into a lot of trouble once because I sat through Wallace Beery's *Viva Villa!* about four times, until my parents came looking for me. I went to military school for a couple of years and lost my virginity, neither of which made me unhappy. It was generally just a regular childhood.

PLAYBOY: *Hasn't your son Michael written a book about your life and work?*

ALTMAN: Oh, yes. It's a slender volume, and he even got some of the facts wrong. He came up to Calgary to talk about it during the filming of *Buffalo Bill*, and I almost threw him off the set, though I sort of admired him for going ahead anyway.

PLAYBOY: *What's the title?*

ALTMAN: *The World of Robert Altman.* Just a nothing book, with a little synopsis of each picture, quotes, interviews, condensed reviews—oh, God, it was awful. I read the proofs in about four and a half seconds, and I think now it's going to be shelved. If ever I did a service to my son Michael, it was to keep that tome from being published.

PLAYBOY: *You mean you've killed it?*

ALTMAN: Well, he had some material in there he didn't have rights to, so we just intimated that we might sue Simon and Schuster, who were supposed to release it. Michael seemed to analyze all my films as being failures in terms that were rather interesting, and they had a whole horoscope in there, with an astrological chart that tried to explain why I am the way I am. There's another unauthorized biography being written by some guy who called and asked if I'd assist him.

PLAYBOY: *And did you?*

ALTMAN: Jesus, no. Let them wait and write a book about me when I'm dead, if anyone's still interested.

PLAYBOY: *You're now on your third marriage, but that has lasted 17 years. What do you think makes it work?*

ALTMAN: Well, I suppose it's a matter of growth. And Kathryn is terrific. If I were married to someone who tried to influence me or push her personal feelings into my films, it probably wouldn't last. Yet Kathryn is the one who brought *Breakfast of Champions* to my attention. She'd read it first and just said casually, "You could probably make a movie out of this." She's around, she goes to screenings, she sets up a home with Matthew and Bobby wherever I happen to be shooting, she entertains; but she never intrudes intellectually into what I'm doing. We really live quite separate lives, but we live them together.

PLAYBOY: *Before we wind this up, can you tell us which Robert Altman film is your own personal favorite?*

ALTMAN: *Brewster McCloud.* I wouldn't say it's my best film; it's flawed, not nearly as finished as some work I've done since, but it's my favorite, because I took more chances then. It was my boldest work, by far my most ambitious. I went way out on a limb to reach for it. After a while, you become more cautious. People keep telling you you've got to be careful, you shouldn't do that. Nevertheless, I don't think there's a question in the world that the films we'll be making and seeing 20 years from now will be films that none of us would understand today. Music's the same way; if you had put a Bob Dylan song on the radio back in 1941, they would have thought you were crazy, closed the station. And I feel it's the obligation of the artist to keep pushing ahead, to stay within range of his audience but to keep pushing and educating them one step at a time.

PLAYBOY: *When you look into your own future, what do you want to have accomplished?*

ALTMAN: I can't imagine getting up in the morning without the same frustrations, the same fears, and the same elation I experience every day. All I want is to do what I'm doing. What else would I do?

PLAYBOY: *Then you don't think, as some have claimed, that the ultimate Altman movie has already been made?*

ALTMAN: I certainly hope not. I'm just warming up.

The Artist and the Multitude are Natural Enemies

F. ANTHONY MACKLIN/1976

ROBERT ALTMAN HAS DIRECTED many provocative movies, including *M*A*S*H, McCabe and Mrs. Miller, Nashville,* and *Buffalo Bill and the Indians*. He presently is producing his first three movies—*Welcome to L.A.,* directed by Alan Rudolph, *The Late Show,* directed by Robert Benton, and his own *3 Women,* with Sissy Spacek, Shelley Duvall, and Janice Rule. Altman's company, Lion's Gate Films, Inc., is located in Westwood, California. This interview took place in Palm Springs, California, where Altman was preparing *3 Women.*

INTERVIEWER: *Would you give me a short history of Lion's Gate?*
ALTMAN: It originally started not under that name. Ray Wagner and I formed a partnership to do television and films. We moved into those offices over there [Westwood], the first two offices.

INTERVIEWER: *How long ago was that?*
ALTMAN: About 12, 13 years ago. We did a couple of pilot films out of there, and we developed a film called *Petulia* which Ray and I had originally paid for and I developed with a writer named Barbara Turner. Then a thing that I prepared with Roald Dahl called *Oh Death Where Is Thy Sting a Ling a Ling?* We did a pilot for CBS called *Night Watch* that looked like it

From *Film Heritage* vol. 12, no. 2 (Winter 1976–77): 1–23. Reprinted by permission of F. Anthony Macklin.

was going to go. We couldn't get the two film projects done with me directing. Nobody wanted me directing those two shows. Ray finally came to me and said he had a way of getting it done with another director, and would I let him off the hook and he'd give me the television. So I had no choice but to do that. It just worked out that way.

INTERVIEWER: *Both properties?*
ALTMAN: Just the *Petulia*.

INTERVIEWER: *Which Richard Lester made.*
ALTMAN: Yes, he took it to Lester and they got it made.

INTERVIEWER: *Did Wagner produce that?*
ALTMAN: Yes. And then I sold *Death Where Is Thy Sting a Ling a Ling?* under pressure because Pat Neal was very ill with her aneurism problem. Dahl needed the money and everybody said, "You're holding him up. They won't make it with you." So I sold that, and they went ahead. They started with Gregory Peck and David Miller, and then they shut it down after about 32 days of shooting.

INTERVIEWER: *David Miller directing it?*
ALTMAN: Yes. And they closed the thing down. Then I brought Don Factor in. (He's one of the Max Factor heirs.) He came in as kind of a partner, and we developed a thing called *That Cold Day in the Park* and I wrote a script called *Images*. Factor financed *Cold Day in the Park*, half of it, and Commonwealth financed the other half. We made that film and then Don, because it cost him quite a bit of money to do that, kind of phased out of the thing. Then I was cutting that film and Preminger came to me to do *M*A*S*H*.

INTERVIEWER: *Otto or Ingo?*
ALTMAN: Ingo. I took that, and the next film was *Brewster McCloud*. And I just kept operating out of that office. Eventually the corporation was formed, and it sort of grew like Topsy. We kept it there as a defense outpost to stay out of the major studios, in both office space and everything else. We really have that feeling of independence so that we're not influenced by the way they do things primarily.

INTERVIEWER: *What was the key moment when you suddenly flew, when you suddenly had your wings?*

ALTMAN: There's always been a parachute dragging behind someplace. I don't know of any particular time when it became easy. It's probably at its most fruitful right now with these three films [*Welcome to L.A., The Late Show,* and *3 Women*], but it's also in the most jeopardy because we've suddenly become really a large company. Our financial responsibilities are large. It's become a big, roaring mouth that has to be fed constantly. A couple of disasters and some idle time, and we'd be wiped out.

INTERVIEWER: *But you have three films that are budgeted under two million dollars. Now if even one of those takes off, you'll be set, right?*

ALTMAN: Yes. We figured out our nut is $660,000 a year roughly. Fifty thousand a month is what we have to generate in income to keep the thing going. We feed back through the machine just on our own equipment rentals and things like that, the money that comes back through the company, where we compete with other companies, in other words, where we do our own sound transfer work and we have our own editing equipment and our own sound equipment and things like that. So about $100,000 to $130,000 a picture comes back into us. That doesn't come into us profit, but it keeps us cycling. The money pays people's salaries that are working on those pictures. If I could keep four pictures a year coming out of there...

INTERVIEWER: *With relatively low budgets?*

ALTMAN: Yes...we wouldn't need to make any profits. In other words, it would sustain itself.

INTERVIEWER: *The evil is the big budget.*

ALTMAN: Yes, but I've never gotten involved in that. Like with Dino's [De Laurentiis] *Buffalo Bill* film, we were not involved in that, in any financial jeopardy. We took money; we had a pretty good income from it. It serviced us very well.

INTERVIEWER: *Isn't the natural end of an operation such as yours bigness?*

ALTMAN: I'm afraid it kind of is, but I also think there's a way to keep it down. I'm starting to cut back now. I would like to do four pictures a year, one of which is my own and then do three others. But it's hard to find the people who can execute them. I don't want to just make films for the sake of making films.

INTERVIEWER: *You have to trust a person before...*
ALTMAN: Oh yes, right. They're doing it. It's also got to be a film that I think will push the edges a little bit.

INTERVIEWER: *Does Lion's Gate have clout in the film community or not?*
ALTMAN: We have clout in the business end of the film community just because of our record of production. I can go to most of the production people at most of the major studios, heads of production. They know when we get them the budget and we say we can do this picture for this, that it'll be brought in for this. Of course, we now back that up with the completion. So it's very comfortable for them if they suspect a project is all right when they look at it.

INTERVIEWER: *What do you mean you "back it up with a completion"?*
ALTMAN: I can now guarantee completion of these films. Like I'll get a flat figure. I say I'm delivering *3 Women* for a million seven.

INTERVIEWER: *And that's in your contract?*
ALTMAN: That's it. That's all they're ever exposed. And if the picture costs a million nine, it costs me $200,000. If it costs a million four to make, which we hope we can make it for, then we've made $300,000 profit—but then that's for an original screenplay, directing and producing, and completion. So that's really a lower fee than I get normally. If I would go and do one of their projects, I would end up making more money.

INTERVIEWER: *The feeling that I get is that Lion's Gate is very insulated. It's almost insulated from the outside world.*
ALTMAN: Yes, it is. It is insulated, I guess, rather than isolated. Its geographical position is a lie. In other words, the fact that it's in Los Angeles has no meaning whatsoever. It could be just as well in Dayton. The only thing is its access to laboratories, equipment rentals, and things like that. But as far as our being part of the Hollywood community, we are not. And we've made some kind of interesting alliances. We have, for instance, Dan Perri who does our titles and most of our ad things. He has his own com-

pany, and he does this for many, many others. I tried to buy his company. I tried to have him become part of Lion's Gate, and he couldn't, and for really a good reason as he pointed out. He's in the business of dealing with a lot of other directors; he does a lot of pictures, and if suddenly Mike Nichols knows that he's working for me, he's not going to go to Dan Perri. I wouldn't. So what I did is I rent him space over there because nobody comes to his place. It's just a place where he works. So he runs his own company, and yet he's there in the same building with us. He's in and out of the office, and he's in on every project that we do from beginning to end. It's not like we call him in for one day. He's there saturated with it all the time. We get the advantage of his thinking and advice and trying out things free because he knows that ultimately he's going to end up getting our business anyway. So it works in a very good way.

For our dubbing room we go to Goldwyn's Dick Portman, who has probably the best dubbing facility in the world for print finish dubbing work. We do so much work over there—our eight track—and they like the way we do the things so that we have first call in that place. We've kept it locked up now that I've gone from *Buffalo Bill* to *Welcome to L.A.* to this [*3 Women*]. I could have damn near kept that place open for a year. We could almost occupy their full schedule. They have other rooms than that big room. But we know that before they'll take on some big job they'll call us and say, "When do you think you're going to come back in?" We'll say maybe, "Block out February for me," and they'll do that.

INTERVIEWER: *I get a very good feeling from being in Lion's Gate. However, from talking to some people on the business end of it, the conventional wisdom is that Robert Altman may not be commercial. Does that affect these relationships with anybody?*

ALTMAN: No, because commercial to them, any of these other people, they don't care whether a picture is a success or a failure other than their own ego because it doesn't affect their money, their income in any way. It's just my constant struggle with the distribution. But again, we're talking two million dollars on a picture, a million eight. They're not going to give them much trouble because they've got a television sell-off, the picture's going to do a certain amount of money, and in the case of *Welcome to L.A.* it's going to cost under a million dollars. That's what U.A. put up, $900,000. It's costing me about maybe $60,000 or $70,000. Yet none of us took any fees out of it, Richard [Baskin] or Alan [Rudolph] or myself. So U.A. isn't worried about that film. If the film is an absolute, total failure, they're going to lose $300,000 maximum, and that's not a loss for that company. When I start going into three million for a picture, three million and half, then it's different.

INTERVIEWER: *You never want to get into the distribution end yourself, do you?*

ALTMAN: I do, but it's very difficult. Part of the reason Mike [Kaplan] is with us is to head toward that end. He covers us on the publicity that's required, the P.R. that's required on the pictures and getting the stuff together, also on following through on how the pictures are booked, advertising. He acts almost as a producer's representative, and hopefully if the right project comes along at the right price, we're looking for one where we can say, "Here, let's just do this ourselves," and we'll handle it.

INTERVIEWER: *To my way of thinking* Buffalo Bill *was horribly marketed, the teaser ads in* TV Guide *for instance. Did you have anything to do with the marketing end of it?*

ALTMAN: I did with the ads.

INTERVIEWER: *For instance that "Sitting Bull Says Bull"?*

ALTMAN: That was my idea.

INTERVIEWER: *It didn't work, did it?*

ALTMAN: I guess not. The idea was to try to let people know what the tone of the picture was.

INTERVIEWER: *The tone really isn't "Sitting Bull Says Bull," like the ads say, is it?*

ALTMAN: I wanted the idea that it was something to make you laugh at and that Buffalo Bill was full of shit.

INTERVIEWER: *There was no mention of* Buffalo Bill, *the picture — those were teaser ads.*

ALTMAN: Yes, those were teaser ads. Buffalo Bill says, "If God didn't want the whites to win, he wouldn't put us here to take the Indians' land."

INTERVIEWER: *It seems like so many of the marketing things that have been concerned with your pictures have not been as good as the pictures, for instance the showing of* Brewster McCloud *in the Astrodome. What's your feeling about that?*

ALTMAN: That was a terrible, terrible mistake. We all knew that. But that was the deal we had to make to get in the Astrodome. They insisted on that in front. [M-G-M had to pay a $50,000–$70,000 penalty if they didn't do it.]

INTERVIEWER: *But it's legend how abysmal it was. Doesn't that hurt, when the critics are put off not so much by the picture but by the environment of the picture? I think many of the people in New York were put off by the environment of* Buffalo Bill*'s press screening rather than giving the picture a chance to evolve into what it finally evolved into.*

ALTMAN: See, the problem we were sitting with is that normally we would have called that press conference off or postponed it. I didn't want to show the film in that condition. I got forced into it by Dino. He said, "You must take this and preview it." That didn't give us time to change it, and we had already set up that press conference. So I had no choice but to show it under those circumstances. And I didn't want to show it in a show of indecision.

I had done two pictures before *Brewster McCloud* really. I had come off of *M*A*S*H*, and I had nothing to do with the marketing of that. I didn't know a thing about any of this. My whole attitude at that time was to make the picture and that's all. Let them do all that. Plus the fact I was already up shooting on *McCabe* when that was opening. But that's when I started to realize that you can't stay out of those things. You may come down to simply the matter of there isn't a good way or an easy way to market the pictures, and they look for one all the time. I talked to someone yesterday about this. He had seen *Welcome to L.A.* at U.A. and commented to them, "You know, we look at these films in the wrong way. We don't sit down at the film and try to see what the film does to us as an audience. We're sitting there all saying, 'How are we going to sell this? How are we going to get them to do so-and-so?' " And the trouble with my film is the trouble with *Welcome to L.A.*—I don't think the same thing exists in *The Late Show*—is that what do you tell people it is? How do you tell them about *Nashville*? There's no shark in it. There's no way to tell them. How do you tell them about *Buffalo Bill*? They have no frame of comparison. Pauline Kael, a long time ago, said, "You should never even preview one of your films because your preview can't even be a success. People have to be put in the position where the audience that wants it can discover it. But you can't shove it down anybody's throat because the minute you do that they're bound to be disappointed. There's no way they can expect what they're going to see."

INTERVIEWER: *Yes, right. But when what they think they're promised is what they are delivered, then they're happy.*

ALTMAN: But it's hard to find out what it is. What do you say about *Nashville*? Is it about country western music? Who's the star? Who's the star of *Welcome to L.A.*? That's the problem we've got even around Academy Award time. It doesn't fit. There's no cards in there with holes punched in that it'll go and match it.

INTERVIEWER: *Is a film that stars Paul Newman not as Paul Newman but as something else doomed to failure from the start?*

ALTMAN: No, I don't think so. I think there were many things that caused *Buffalo Bill* to fail. The most marked thing about it is that people stayed away; an uncommon percentage of people did not even expose themselves to that film. They just didn't go. There is some reason they didn't go. They knew it was something that they didn't want to deal with. "I don't want to hear that shit, whatever it is." I think the bicentennial year literally back-fired on us. The history of the bicentennial is going to be rather interesting to look at one day because there were no big government things. There were just a lot of little things. A lot of people went out in the streets, out-doors. There was no big thing; they had their own little things. They didn't want some asshole like me coming along telling them that it was wrong. Watergate had them up to the point where they knew not to make it a march down the street with elephants, and big speeches. But they didn't want to deal with that attack, and they knew it was going to be that some-how. I'm just winging all this because I'm guessing, but there were a lot of things that deal with temperament. You see I believe that everything has its natural enemy. There are natural enemies, in which case neither can be blamed. You can't blame the minnow for being the natural enemy of the bass. The fish is going to eat him. The artist and the multitude are natural enemies. They always will be, both ways. The artist is an enemy of the multitude, and the multitude is the enemy of the artist. And when the disguise comes off and they're both standing facing one another, they're just there at odds ends.

INTERVIEWER: *Do you admit that you're an elitist?*
ALTMAN: I admit that I'm an artist. But I think that's a trade.

INTERVIEWER: *You're discriminating and...*
ALTMAN: But I have no choice. I mean I can't do things any different than I do them. There's no way I can do that. I could go out and kid myself and try, and end up being the same thing. I've seen the process happen too many times. And what it is, is it's not the elitism. It has to do with... "multitude" is the only word I know, "masses."

INTERVIEWER: *But isn't the artist an elitist by his very nature in that he's an explorer, he's an individual?*
ALTMAN: Yes, but an elitist is someone who places himself in a group. It's like a party. "Let's have so-and-so. He'll be terrific together." That's elitism. I don't think the artist does that. I think the artist says, "This is the way a palm tree looks to me; this is what the desert feels like to me," and he paints it and shows it to them. When you start dealing with people and cultures, as is the easiest road for film to deal with, which is the way I deal with it, in terms of culture, you're trying to carry people into areas they don't want to go into. But I don't think you have any choice. I could tell you right now I could invite 500 people to see a film, and I could invite 500 people who are just going to absolutely love that film.

INTERVIEWER: *How many of them would be sycophants?*
ALTMAN: Most of them, but they're people who are already in tune and probably ahead of me. In other words, once you learn, it's art appreciation, once you learn that you can enjoy something. Mainly it's taking away the fear that the multitudes have—"What kind of shit is that?" They're inhibited because they think maybe it's something they think they're not going to understand. And if you don't understand it...

INTERVIEWER: *You can't like what you don't understand.*

ALTMAN: Then you can't like it, and you feel, "How come that guy's laughing? I don't think that's funny." And whap, you're through. That person is through. You're not going to get to him.

INTERVIEWER: *Did you know this before* Buffalo Bill?

ALTMAN: Yes. I always try to deal...I mean I'm shocked. There was one point where I looked at *Buffalo Bill*, say two-thirds of the way through the cutting process. One night I went and looked at some cut footage, and I was really by myself except for the people I worked with. I looked at that; I just got that flash you get where you see something differently for a change. I looked at it for what it really was, I guess, and I thought, "I'm crazy. Jesus!" I thought I was doing something really simple and entertaining and funny and not very particularly probing, something that anybody could sit down and really like. If anything when I'm doing something, I'm trying to simplify it, simplify it, to make it accessible to the most amount of people. We use that word "accessible" making a film constantly.

INTERVIEWER: *The film is not that difficult if you get the key. But people just don't get the key.*

ALTMAN: That's what I mean. We're fixing it with this picture we're doing right now. I'm constantly trying to find a way to do what I want to do or what I'm going to do and not inhibit. And I think I've got a shot with this because I'm dealing really with two people primarily that you'll obviously get involved with. And I'm going to deal with a great deal of mystery as such. So that there will be inexplicable things, but they will be done in a manner that you'll say, "Oh that's weird." I mean you can attach those words.

INTERVIEWER: *Can the general audience relate to Shelley Duvall externally? Won't the general audience back in Dayton, Ohio, think she's kind of freaky and kind of spacey and kind of weirdo?*

ALTMAN: I don't think they will in this film. In *Nashville* she was a cartoon. That's what she was supposed to be. In *Thieves Like Us* I think people loved her in that. She was just heartbreaking.

INTERVIEWER: *We've not talking about the general audience now, are we? Because the general audience didn't see* Thieves.

ALTMAN: Well, I know that. But I think had they seen it, I don't think that Shelley would have been their point of . . .

INTERVIEWER: *Shelley is not a Faye Dunaway, for instance. They can relate to a Faye Dunaway.*
ALTMAN: Why? Because she's not real. Faye Dunaway's not real. There's no such thing as Faye Dunaway.

INTERVIEWER: *There are three specific scenes that I would like you to talk about. It seems to me that there's sometimes at war in your work the implicit with the explicit. There are three scenes that are to my mind explicit in three different films that I would like you to talk about. The first is in* Nashville. *When she goes to that smoker, could a thing like that really happen?*
ALTMAN: Oh yes.

INTERVIEWER: *Wouldn't they want her to do more sexually? It was a very tame smoker. Is there such a thing as a tame smoker?*
ALTMAN: Yes, I think so. I don't think there is in film, but you see I believe that another problem that we have is that we'll accept anything in our own lives in terms of reality. I mean we will accept anything. You look around yourself, which you don't do. But consequently, in our fantasies we demand a great deal of order; we demand reasons for people's behaviors in our dramas and in our comedies. But in our own lives we will accept many things. We will look out and say, "Jesus, what's that elephant doing walking down the street? That's really weird." We'd say, "It probably is in the circus. That's really funny." But if I had an elephant walking in the street and made no comment in the picture, they'd say I was crazy. We went in and we shot a scene in *The Long Goodbye* that is not in the film. It was cut. It was the guy Jack Riley singing the song "The Long Goodbye" at the piano bar, and this big, fat woman is sitting next to him. She's crying, just tears. She's sitting there all by herself; she's trying to sing along the lyrics with him and she doesn't really know . . . she's just in tears. She finishes and she takes a dollar out and she puts it in the kitty and she says, "Oh Riley, do it to me again. Come on, Riley. 'There's a long goodbye.'" It was terrific, and we threw it out because it just didn't work right. Last night we went to dinner in a little Italian restaurant here [Palm Springs, California], Shelley and Sissy and Scotty and Alan and myself. We sat

down at a piano bar. Guy's playing the piano. Big, heavy-set woman came in. She sat down, profile to us like this. He started singing; she started crying. Tears were running down her face in cascades. She said, "Oh," just in ecstasy-agony. He sang about three songs, and she just bawled all the way through. And I just sat there and. . . . This was much more extreme than what we had done. What we had done had a little bit of a purpose to it. The people in *Nashville*, the way people dressed, if you very carefully look at that film you will see that everybody's wardrobe is very, very specific to tell you who they are. But they're also in solid colors, and they're rather conservative in their extremity. If you look at any of those people and then you look at the people who are standing behind them, almost any of the people behind them are so much more bizarre and extreme than the people you're laughing at. But those are real people and you don't see them. Nobody has ever said, "What are all those guys wearing Shriner hats for in that audience?" Had I put Shriner hats on people and said, "Oh, this is what I'll do—I'll put Shriner hats on and put them in the audience," it would have been a disaster. But the fact is that they really had Shriner hats on, and they weren't funny to them. And the way they behaved, those people were right because those people were real and you accept that. But if I put a Shriner hat on Keenan Wynn, you wouldn't have accepted it.

INTERVIEWER: *But do you think her humiliation visually was strong enough? A lot of people talked about that scene as a great, great scene, and it just rang false to me because I thought the men would demand that she straddle the chair or something.*

ALTMAN: You could be right. It could happen any of many ways. I've seen stripteasers that are much more mild than that. The type of man that we had there was not hard-core. It wasn't the real thing. A lot of them would have been very embarrassed if something really had gone on. That's why when they lined her up our rationalization was that they just wanted a girl so that they got what they wanted delivered but it didn't put them in any sense of jeopardy. Actually the way we got that crowd of them in there is we said, "If you want to be in a film, come down to the interviews. Wear your good dress. You've got to be there two days. We're going to raffle off two tickets to Hollywood and a side trip to Disneyland." And those are the people that showed up. And the people who showed up are the same people that would have been at that affair. They behaved pretty much in that manner. When she was doing that scene those guys were saying things like, "Let's see the tits, baby." The minute she got through and actually did that strip and walked off stage one of the guys said, "I think that we ought to give her a hand." And they all stood up and gave her an applause. " 'Cause it's quite a thing that little lady did." And they felt sorry for her. But usually in a film situation, that same situation, it would be carried to much more of an extreme.

INTERVIEWER: *One of the other things is in* Buffalo Bill *when Bull's human dignity silences that crowd. Have you ever seen that happen?*
ALTMAN: I don't think so.

INTERVIEWER: *Could it happen?*
ALTMAN: Yes, I think so. I don't know whether it's. . . . You say it's dignity to them. It may just be the fact that nothing's happening.

INTERVIEWER: *They applaud, don't they? Why would they applaud nothingness?*
ALTMAN: That's a difficult scene for me to . . . I was dealing with it from Cody's point of view rather than from any sense of reality. I think that could happen. I don't think it ever would happen the way we did it. I think we manipulated it quite a lot. That is not one of my favorite scenes.

INTERVIEWER: *How about the* Romeo and Juliet-*on-the-radio scene from* Thieves Like Us?
ALTMAN: That is one of my favorite scenes.

INTERVIEWER: *Why?*
ALTMAN: I don't know. I just really like it. Gwen's striptease is not one of my favorite scenes either. The *Romeo and Juliet* thing I knew full well that I was going to get punched all over the place for doing that, and a lot of my own confidants begged me to take it out. I just enjoyed it, and I saw no reason not to do it. It was never done as a sense of reality, except those programs were played in those days. It was a period program that actually was done in 1937 or whatever. I didn't write it to happen, but in our research in pulling together all these old tapes we found that. It's one of those excesses that I just absolutely cannot pass up. If that picture had been a

smashing success and made four million dollars or 20 million dollars, that 20 million dollars and that success would have been eventually some day dissipated and that *Romeo and Juliet*, reading the sound of that over those two kids in that bed, to me was worth more.

INTERVIEWER: *Was that film hurt by* Bonnie and Clyde*? If* Bonnie and Clyde *hadn't been before it, wouldn't it have been appreciated much more?*
ALTMAN: I don't know. I would have thought not. I think it was a depressing film. It came out at a time when there were three other films kind of like it—*Badlands*; [*The*] *Sugarland* [*Express*] came out, which wasn't in the same mood that *Badlands* was; *Bad Company* came out. There were a lot of those kind of . . . you didn't walk out whistling the tune.

INTERVIEWER: *You've had kind words to say about both Marty Scorsese and Francis Ford Coppola. In their work the roots of their Catholicism, or the vestiges of their Catholicism, are very evident. Are they evident at all in yours?*
ALTMAN: I don't know. See, they both are more Italian than Catholic, and that's more in their culture. It's more part of family and neighbor culture, that whole Catholic ethic. With me it was just in my own family and the school, and I never paid too much attention to it.

INTERVIEWER: *At what time did you stop practicing?*
ALTMAN: When I was 18 I went into the Army, and I left it.

INTERVIEWER: *One would think, though, that those first 18 years would be a part of you as an artist.*
ALTMAN: It's the kind of thing that comes out in my work. It's very easy for me to deal with, with the behavior that I remember seeing around me. I mean if I had been brought up in Judaism, it would have been a different thing. It's an immediate contact that I have. But as I say, I never was an extremist about anything at all.

INTERVIEWER: *Do you think it influenced your shattering forms at all?*
ALTMAN: Catholicism?

INTERVIEWER: *Yes, because that's a very stable and strong form.*
ALTMAN: Well, my fights against that establishment went on as far as I can remember. So that's quite possible. Everything that formed me is part

of my shape. It gives me shape. And everything that I do in film, all that material passes through me, so it must have my shape, more or less. And I can't do anything about that.

INTERVIEWER: *Peckinpah always relates back to his past and the judge and his father. Coppola and certainly Scorsese do. Most American artists, be they film artists or literary artists, are always at war with or trying to make order out of their pasts. And we don't see that explicitly in your work. Do we see it implicitly? is what I wonder. It would seem to be almost a certainty.*

ALTMAN: I always possessed that as far as I can remember, although it was never a big deal. I never went along with any of that. It was the situation I was in, and I had to deal with it until I got out of it. The first time I was sent to school it was a pre-school—I was like three—this is a family story. It was a girls' school run by French nuns. They took boys in in the pre-school. The first time I went to school they went through all the new students, and they came to me and they said, "Are you a Catholic?" And I said, "No, I'm an American." They had a big fuss about that, those French nuns.

INTERVIEWER: *They didn't think it was funny?*

ALTMAN: No, they thought that perhaps I wasn't a Catholic. They called my mother. I never had any traumatic experiences. Catholicism to me was school. It was restrictions; it was things you had to do. It was your parents. It was Mass on Sunday and fish on Friday. And then when I got out of that, I got into the Army. It was the same thing—you had to have a pass to get out. You had to wear this kind of clothes, and you had to address them so-and-so. I just turned it to that. Then when I got out of the Army, why then it was you've got to wear a tie to get into this restaurant or you've got to have a suit if you're going to the party. Or you don't try to fuck a girl on the first date if she comes from a good family. All of those things. And I just...I was never a revolutionary. Those were just some of the things in life that you had to do.

INTERVIEWER: *Who do you relate to personally in* California Split, *and how? When I saw that film, I related myself to it and a friend of mine. Are you standing detached from the two?*

ALTMAN: Yes. I don't relate to either of them. I understand Elliott's character much more.

INTERVIEWER: *Another thing, have you ever seen that happen to a guy that wins and then says, "I can't take it"? You've seen that happen?*

ALTMAN: It's just exhaustion. It wears you out because it's the realization that it isn't anything. It was forced—that was set up that way. That was the only story in the whole picture, that point. All I was trying to do was create the atmosphere of gambling and not the details of it—just the feeling, the feelings of it. And the mistaken feeling that winning... you can't spend that money; you don't go out and pay the milk bill with it unless you're about to go to jail. It just means that you can play that much longer. "For $41,000," Elliott says, "Jesus, let's go to Florida. We'll go to a track. We can spend six weeks there. We can buy a car. We can get around. We can sell the car if we get in trouble." In other words, it's passes. It's more tickets to the amusement park—that's all it is. Because you don't go spend it anywhere else. You don't change your life style. I find that's true—I was talking with Shelley last night about it—I find that's true of me now. I'm now in a position where I don't have to worry about spending. I mean, if I want to go spend $5,000, I can go do it. If I want to walk across the street and go into a clothing store and buy 28 shirts like this, I can go in there and do it and say, "Send them over." And yet I'm sitting over there in the room. I've got three shirts and they're all dirty. And I'm wondering whether I should drive down and get one. I don't want to send somebody out to get one for me because that seems kind of... I don't use my money for those things that I would have thought I would use it for because now that I've got it and can do it, I don't have any... I don't really care anymore. The most pleasure I have is if Kathryn says, "Oh gee, I'd like to buy a new couch," or "I want to do this." I say, "Fine, go ahead and do it." Twenty years ago down here, have an apartment building at my disposal, a thousand dollars, be able to go to the liquor store, buy steaks and come back—that was just more fucking fun that I could dream of.

INTERVIEWER: *Twenty years ago.*

ALTMAN: Yes, and now it's just, well, I've got to have dinner tonight. It's going to be as easy to cook dinner as it is to go out. It gets down to the real joy is the company of people you're with.

INTERVIEWER: *That's what Lion's Gate is.*

ALTMAN: In a way, yes. It's a controlled chaos. It has to be. If it goes too far. . . . One of the editors there has been with us for years. During I guess it was *Buffalo Bill*, he started feeling guilty because he wasn't doing really anything. I came in one night and everybody was sitting around there drinking beer and they were smoking grass. I said, "Jesus Christ! You guys, we're paying all this fucking money," and I was shouting at something. "You didn't get this done and that didn't get done." I wasn't even talking to Dennis; I was talking to somebody else. And I was totally unjust in all my accusations. I was the one that was having problems. Next morning Dennis came to me, and rather than say whose fault he thought it was, he said, "I'd like to leave." And I said, "OK." He said, "And I'd like to leave right now if I can and I don't want any...." I said, "Leave right now." I knew that he wanted me to say, "Why do you want to leave?" and I wasn't going to do that. I was pissed off. And he quit and he left. He was gone maybe three months and then he came back. He came in smiling a couple times and would hang around. I didn't say anything. One day he came in and he said, "Listen, I want to go to work," and I said, "Fine, go to work." He said, "What do you want me to do? Where do you want me to work?" And I said, "Dennis, you do exactly what you did when you were leaving. Find something to do." And it worked out. But I mean that's the danger of it, that a guy can sit around and wonder about his own identity, because we don't give those editors . . . they don't have total control of a film. They all work on the films there. So I think there's a little insecurity. Not knowing where you are or not having a regimented place to be is difficult for people.

INTERVIEWER: *Are you paternalistic? I get the feeling with Lion's Gate and some of the people there, and with the two girls [Shelley Duvall and Sissy Spacek], you seemed to have that role.*
ALTMAN: With the two girls I have to be paternalistic because I'm setting up a relationship that has to work in the future. This is "necking"; it's "foreplay." Because we have to get to a relationship where they can understand enough to become free enough to really contribute to this thing [*3 Women*], but that I will always have control of. Yes, I think I'm paternalistic.

INTERVIEWER: *And it works.*
ALTMAN: I don't think there's any way you can do this thing and not be. I don't like the position sometimes. I find that I'm left out of things. There's a lot of things that go on that I'm kind of shocked—they get together and

nobody invites me. I'll say, "How come I wasn't invited?" and they'll say, "Gee, we didn't know that you wanted to...." I've had a lot of those kind of deals. Somebody called it a "benevolent monarchy" because it's certainly not a democracy.

INTERVIEWER: *Mike Kaplan called you a "commander" yesterday. I said, "Is he a dictator?" and he said, "No, a commander."*
ALTMAN: That kind of thing could not exist in any other way. And it's no different than shooting the film. I find that the more I do, the less I do. That's why I do so much of this kind of stuff ahead of time, of trying to set little ground rules and desires and things that I expect and want from the cameramen. We talk too much. When the film starts, work on the film, nobody talks to anybody. We're working and getting the thing done. But I'm getting to the point that all I really have to do is that if I establish that I am the silent censor...

INTERVIEWER: *S-e-n-s-o-r?*
ALTMAN: Both...all I have to do is go in in the morning and turn the switch on to GO. And all these people will come in and do their thing. I don't have to say, "Do that and do that," or "Do this," because they're thinking, "Oh, he wouldn't want me to do that, but he'd want me to do this." So they're living out...I mean my control is still on, yet I don't have to do anything. Then at the end of the day I turn the switch to OFF and go home. There're big scenes and the work is done. Yet had I not been there, nothing would have gotten done. My presence is necessary, but eventually as it gets purer or better, all that is necessary is the presence.

INTERVIEWER: *What exactly is the eight-track system?*
ALTMAN: The eight-track system is simply a way of recording the sound as you shoot it on the set on separate tracks. So it gives you the control to change the balance the way you want it when you finish. It's much the same way that music is done—it's exactly the same.

INTERVIEWER: *What's the most people you've had miked?*
ALTMAN: In *Nashville* we had as many as 40 tracks, most of them with music, but we've had maybe 11, 12 mikes out going onto seven channels. You only have seven channels on the eight-track. One track has to carry

the synch posts. So it gives us seven. We make combinations at times, sometimes because we want to and sometimes because we're forced to.

INTERVIEWER: *Do you find that the general audience is more agreeable to your experiments with sound than they were earlier with* McCabe, *etc.?*

ALTMAN: Yes, because I'm doing better. It's not as noticeable.

INTERVIEWER: *Can you give me an example of one of the times that you really had a challenge that you conquered with sound?*

ALTMAN: I think all of *California Split.* There's a shot in *Buffalo Bill* back-stage where Cody is behind those spears. He's putting his make-up on, and Annie Oakley and Frank Butler are back there. She's saying, "How do I look?" Or he's saying, "How do I look?" or something like that. The kid comes up, Johnny Baker, and says, "You're on in five minutes, Mr. Cody." He says loudly, "I heard ya!" But there's actual dialogue pertinent to the thing in the background between Geraldine and John. Now if we were doing that in a single-track system, all you would have gotten on that track would have been, "I heard ya!"—the prime dialogue. You would have seen them talking back there, but you never would have heard what they said, but it didn't make any difference too much. But suddenly by having that track there live—although it's not anything that we strove for, it was just there—we were able to put their lines in, and it just gave that sense of reality to the thing that otherwise it wouldn't have had. So it's bonus material more than anything else.

INTERVIEWER: *But in a sense it's your signature, isn't it?*

ALTMAN: I don't think so. People have to find signatures to pin on you. That's one that's been talked about a lot. It's easier. But I'm certainly not an innovator in that. It's a technique that I use. I abhor looped sound, post sound. I think sound is an integral part of the motion picture process. In *Images* it was a situation where we literally eliminated sound and replaced it with music totally rather than even put the two together, but it still is the use of sound whether it's a negative or a positive use. This picture I'm doing now I think is going to have a very...I don't know quite what it is yet, but I'm starting to come to understand what the sounds are going to be like. It's going to have a very specific, clean, direct, simple sound track. I'm really going to try to capture that whole desert.

INTERVIEWER: *What is the difference between a producer and a presenter—Dino De Laurentiis, David Susskind, and yourself were all credited on* Buffalo Bill.

ALTMAN: That's just a way of getting your name on the picture if you have anything to do with it, and we divide those titles up. The term "producer," there are as many shadings and gradations as there are from white to black on the gray scale. You can be producer that is a totally creative producer, that controls the whole project, that hires a director, that looks at the dailies and says, "Go back and reshoot that. I don't like the way so-and-so played that. I don't like the way it was lit." The director can sometimes get in an argument and get fired for it. There is the producer that is the guy who went out and got hold of the rights for *Moby Dick* and goes to somebody to do it, and he's called the producer and all he does is he had that to contribute. Just every gradation—where they have no involvement to total involvement.

INTERVIEWER: *Susskind had the rights to the play?*

ALTMAN: Susskind had the rights to the play, and that is all. So we called him the executive producer.

INTERVIEWER: *Now what is a presenter?*

ALTMAN: That's the title Dino wanted.

INTERVIEWER: *That's the guy who puts up the money.*

ALTMAN: Yes. And in Alan Rudolph's case in *Welcome to L.A.* the screen credit goes to my name. It says, "Robert Altman presents a film by Alan Rudolph, *Welcome to L.A.*," because I am presenting his first film.

INTERVIEWER: *So when one sees "present" that's usually the bankroll?*

ALTMAN: Yes, or it's somebody that's involved in the thing and you've got to have his name in the thing some way, so they say, "You be the executive producer, and then I'll present a production of." It gets ridiculous. A director is a director, a writer is a writer, the cameraman is the cameraman, the actor is the actor. The rest of those things can mean anything.

INTERVIEWER: *Jerry Bick produced two of your films [*The Long Goodbye *and* Thieves Like Us*].*

ALTMAN: Jerry Bick had the rights to both of those.

INTERVIEWER: *What does that mean?*

ALTMAN: That means that he owned the screen rights. He had purchased options on the material, and he actively worked with me on the pictures. He was in Mississippi when we made that picture. He did administrative work on the thing.

INTERVIEWER: *In fact he gave his wife [Louise Fletcher] to the project.*

ALTMAN: Yes, we took her. He worked on the thing, but there were no creative discussions.

INTERVIEWER: *On* The Long Goodbye *how did he operate then?*

ALTMAN: He worked in his office in Westwood and did administrative things.

INTERVIEWER: *But he didn't have the property.*

ALTMAN: No, Elliott Kastner did, and he was working for Kastner at the time.

INTERVIEWER: *Lion's Gate is still an experiment, though?*

ALTMAN: Yes. The roots are getting stronger and stronger.

INTERVIEWER: *Don't you get inundated with scripts?*

ALTMAN: Yes. It's not so much the script as it is the people involved. In both the other films the writer and director have been the same. It's always been the guy's directing his own materials. I know that there's a vision there. If I found a really good script that I thought could be interesting, I might say, "Let's find a director for it," but that would mean a lot more work on my part. I wouldn't just do a film and say, "OK, I'll just put my name on it and have it done in Europe or something." That doesn't mean anything. If I don't have a contribution, a legitimate contribution, even if it's just protecting someone else, it isn't worth doing.

Robert Altman

CHARLES MICHENER/1978

THE FIRST TIME I met Robert Altman I unthinkingly took my shoes off. That was five years ago; Altman had just finished directing *Thieves Like Us,* and I had gone up to his suite at the Sherry-Netherland hotel in New York for an interview. As anyone who has ever worked on an Altman movie will tell you, he runs the most relaxed of sets ("creative playpens," I once called them) and his actors are inclined to reveal more of themselves than they usually do—just as I was inclined to kick off my loafers while we talked over scotch-and-sodas at the Sherry.

Since then I've written about Altman many times—once as a cover story for *Newsweek.* I've watched him shoot three or four movies. And I've even jumped into the playpen myself, playing a reporter during the climactic assassination sequence in *Nashville.* ("How did I do?" I asked Altman after the shot. "You stuck out," he said. "But I was the only person up there who was *real,*" I protested. "That's why you stuck out," he said.) The following interview took place in Altman's Park Avenue apartment in midtown Manhattan after he had finished a casting session with director Robert Young for *Rich Kids,* a movie Altman is producing. Again, we talked over scotch-and-sodas. And again I kicked my shoes off.

Where did the idea for A Wedding *come from?*
When we were shooting *3 Women,* a journalist—from *Mother Jones,* I think—came onto the set just as we were about to film a particularly diffi-

From *Film Comment* vol. 14, no. 5 (September–October 1978): 15–18. Copyright © 1992 by the Film Society of Lincoln Center. Reprinted by permission of *Film Comment.*

cult scene. She ran up to me and said, "Hi! What's your next movie going to be?" It was a tough day, and I wasn't in a good mood; and I was so enraged at the stupidity of that question at that time, that I just said, "I'm going to shoot a wedding next. I'm going to stop all *this* silliness and hire myself out to photograph a wedding."

We broke for lunch, and it occurred to me that it was a pretty good idea. A wedding would provide a device to explore the foibles of a society. After all, people behave differently when they're placed in formal situations. At a wedding or a funeral, unless you're an out-and-out rebel, you follow the amenities of the culture. You don't act the way you normally act; you're putting on a front. You're not comfortable, you're not dressed the way you dress at any other occasion. So we had the arena for a multicast, cultural, comedy situation.

A situation like that of Nashville.

I never would have done *A Wedding* directly after *Nashville*. But having the "breather" of *3 Women*—a small film, at least in terms of wheels moving—I thought it was time to carry the *Nashville* experiment a little further. For example, we doubled the number of characters, from 24 in *Nashville* to 48 in *A Wedding*. And to give the picture a focus, the action would all take place in one location in one day. And so it evolved.

I wanted to deal with rich people: *very* rich, very conservative, very old, deep money—so old and deep that hardly anybody can remember where it originally came from. A matriarchy. I drew a lot of it from the women in my family back in Kansas City: All my aunts sang, or played the harp, and they'd all gone to Europe, and spoke French. I named the Lillian Gish character "Nettie," after my father's mother, who was the matriarch of the family. We wanted to play the border-Southern *nouveau riche* family against the decadence of this matriarchy, a family that had had almost no connection with the outside world.

How did the script evolve? Why did you choose John Considine, the actor, to write the script with you?

John and I had talked about a number of projects before. I knew he'd been working on his writing, and I knew I needed someone with whom I could freely talk the thing out. So I called Considine, and he liked the idea. We made an outline of character sketches, rather than a dialogue script. Then we determined which situations we needed. We just followed the protocol of a wedding. You have the ceremony; then what's the first thing people do when they get back to the house? Well, they've been sitting in church for two hours, then in a limousine for an hour—so they all have to go to the bathroom. And we used the bathroom scenes to bring some of the characters together. And so on. We blocked all of this out on index cards.

The film begins on a rather farcical basis, and then goes through different turns: melodrama at one point, bittersweet romance at another. Was all this in the script?

As it evolved, it was pretty much there in the plot outline, on the cards. But we were vague on some of the characters until they were cast; then, based on the casting, we'd flesh out the character. All the actors took these parts without really knowing much of anything about their characters. The minute we had the picture cast, I put Allan Nicholls and Patricia Resnick on the film as writers. All of the actors were free to go to any of us to work on their characters' background stories—as with *Nashville,* I had the actors write out their characters' histories—and so, by the time we began shooting, each actor had a lot of information to work with. And we did encourage the actors to use as much of themselves and their personalities as they would allow themselves to do.

But the tone and even the plot of the film evolved as actors came into—and occasionally dropped out of—the various roles.

Right. Originally, Shelley Duvall was going to play the girl next door, the lady on the horse; and Sissy Spacek was going to play the sister of the bride—the part taken by Mia Farrow. We first thought of Ben Gazzara to play the father of the groom, an Italian-American who's thought to have some Mafia connections. But we couldn't afford Ben, or he couldn't afford to work with us, and so we thought of an Italian actor who'd lived in America for some time: Vittorio Gassman, who had made films in Hollywood in the mid-fifties. The first person I wanted to play the mother of the bride was Dinah Shore. But that didn't work out, and when I heard that Carol Burnett wanted to do a movie with me, I realized she'd be perfect for the part.

When I saw the movie in rough-cut, I thought Carol Burnett's style stuck out. As a comedienne specializing in television skits, she'd go for the clearest registration of character possible—and she's superb at that—but it seemed that that approach jarred both with the other actors and with the oblique, off-the-nose kind of acting you've developed in your films. In the final cut, it's smoother, but there's still a difference in tone.

But in *M*A*S*H,* and even somewhat in *Nashville,* a lot of the actors were dealing in different styles of comedy: Some people were underplayed and subtle, some were absolutely pratfall stick-outs. I see no reason not to do that. In *A Wedding,* sometimes the situations are broad, sometimes the performances are broad. I was always really pleased with Carol's interpretation and her performance.

Of course, Carol was playing a character that was further removed from her experience than the ones played by, say, Dina Merrill—who's been around an upper-class society all her life, so you never had to worry that she wouldn't know exactly what to do and how to act—or even Lillian Gish. To me, Nettie's death is the death of a silent screen star.

What about Nina Van Pallandt, who was so striking—and, as an actress, so raw—in The Long Goodbye?

Nina had got married after *The Long Goodbye,* and moved back to Europe. One day, while we were casting *A Wedding,* she dropped in our office and said she wanted to get back to work. We said, "Well, if you want to work here, you're the mother of the groom." She has that really beautiful look....

The look of a beautiful victim?

Nina's character is a victim of narcotic addiction—morphine, since the birth of the children. She'd been put on it, and became addicted. I grew up with a friend whose mother had that problem. There are a lot of rich people with that habit—Main Line mainliners. We created the doctor [Howard Duff] for that reason. Originally, there was a line in the movie where the doctor is asked about his practice, and he waves at the family and says, "Madam, *this* is my practice."

You told me once that you saw the people of McCabe and Mrs. Miller *as ancestors—that you could imagine futures for individual characters: that the bartender played by René Auberjonois might become the governor of the state, for example. Is* A Wedding *the next generation of* McCabe?

No, what I call the next generation is *Thieves Like Us*—when the adventurousness of the early pioneer days was snuffed out by the poverty of the

Depression. To me, *A Wedding* doesn't have the sense of a past or a future. It's just: *a* wedding. Which is why I was so particular about the title. Not: The *Wedding*.

How long did it take you to shoot the film?
Eight weeks—45 days.

Eight weeks on virtually the same set.
Three days in the church, and the rest in the house. It was the Armour mansion in Lake Bluff, Ill., owned by Mrs. Aleka Armour. It's a great house—designed by David Adler. It has its own place in the cultural history of the area. Mrs. Armour was terrific; she knew about my other films, and was completely helpful. We had no art director on the picture. She left all her furniture there, and we changed nothing. The house is as you see it, except for the Italian grotto we built in the basement.

We chose the wardrobe, but we sent our cast to some wedding people we'd hired as consultants. And *they* told us the protocol; *they* did the flowers; *they* dressed the church; *they* chose the cake; *they* picked the menu; *they* put the tent up; *they* selected the presents. We let the people who would actually stage a wedding for one of those rich families stage our wedding.

You worked with a huge company of powerful actors—and striking actresses. How was the working ambiance?
A Wedding was the easiest, the least troubled picture I'd worked on. The temperament was good. Everybody got along.

In its final form, A Wedding *makes its satirical points less insistently than* Nashville *did. It's not necessarily a less serious film, but it's got a lighter feeling.* It's not as much an indictment. It should prove easier for audiences to take. They'll see themselves and their families and culture in the film, but they're unlikely to see themselves as the target for the film's satire.

But, having known you well during Nashville, *I sense a lessening of passion, of intensity, about this film in its birth—a less nervous father presiding.*
Well, I've had more children!

I'll say! Right now, A Wedding *is ready for release; you're editing* Quintet; *you've just completed shooting* A Perfect Couple *[formerly* A Romance*]; you're*

about to shoot Health; *you're developing the script of* Martha; *and, on top of all this, you've produced Alan Rudolph's* Remember My Name, *and are producing his next picture as well as Robert Young's* Rich Kids. *There can't be another American director—at least since the end of the studio system—who has directed, and even produced, so many overlapping pictures. Does this stimulate you?*
It does. I was interested to see that Vincent Canby, in his review of the new Woody Allen picture, said that the real film artists are those who are the most prolific. Then again, Peter Rainer in *Mademoiselle,* who reviewed *A Wedding* unfavorably, said I'm probably the most prolific filmmaker in America—and maybe I should stop and take a breath. I don't know why it's all right for Woody, but not for me!

I think it's fine in principle. But I wonder about the editing process. Isn't there a chance that you're so involved in so many projects that it becomes difficult to do the fine tuning in the editing of a film that by now is three or four projects away?
It's not a problem. I think my work is better when I'm really busy. When I'm not totally absorbed in one thing I can make decisions quicker. I can see it fresher, make it less precious. The film can speak to me.

Is there a danger in making so many films that you lose touch with life?
I don't know. I know that once I've made a film, I can't make the same kind of film right away. So I try always to be in over my head. When the subject for a film presents itself, I say, "God, if I stop long enough to think about this, I'd better pass on it." It's better for me not to know exactly what I'm getting into. It keeps the flow going. It makes me listen to other people, see other things, approach it with a little trepidation. It's come to the point where I now do this consciously. It doesn't scare me any more, because I know I'm going to learn something. There's a sense of discovery that, I hope, the audience will be able to share.

You used to say that you wanted your movies to be like life itself, and that the making of movies was like a lifetime in itself. Would you say that today?
Yes. It's like a complete life experience.

But where you were once involved in overlapping dialogue, now you're involved in overlapping lifetimes.
That's true. But partly it's because I'm able to do that now.

A lot of people wonder how you are able to do it — how Robert Altman can keep making so many movies when he's had only one commercial success, Nashville, *since* M*A*S*H.

You got me. I really don't know.

Is this partly due to the goodwill of Twentieth Century-Fox — that you're a prestige director?

My working relationship with Fox is good: In the creative aspect it's terrific, though there are some problems in the sales aspect. I've done *3 Women* and *A Wedding* for Fox, and they'll distribute *Quintet* and *A Perfect Couple.* I consider myself morally obliged to offer them my own pictures first. But I don't think any corporation in history has ever given a damn about prestige.

Or is it that the crap-shoot is moving so fast that they keep saying yes just to stay in the game?

Sometimes I feel like little Eva, running across the ice cubes with the dogs yapping at my ass. Maybe the reason I'm doing all this is so I can get a lot done before they catch up with me.

Is there another explanation for the studios' continuing to finance your films? Is it because although your pictures rarely make a lot of money, they're made so inexpensively that they also rarely lose a lot of money? Only Buffalo Bill and the Indians *cost much more than $2–3-million.*

Well, *Quintet* is as expensive as *Buffalo Bill* — about $7 million.

Is that because Paul Newman is the star?

Partly. Paul Newman and Vittorio Gassman, Bibi Andersson, Fernando Rey, Brigitte Fossey, Nina Van Pallandt. And the magnitude of the sets, and the difficulties in location shooting — in Montreal, and in the Arctic Circle.

What's it about?

I guess you could call it a grim Grimm's fairy tale. When I first had the germ of the idea — and at that time I wanted somebody else, Walter Hill, to actually write and direct it — I saw it as a melodrama. But as it developed it became more about death and life, and how you can't have one without the other. It deals with the death of a culture.

It's set in the present?
It's set probably in the future, or else in the present in a parallel world. It's as if there were a mirror planet to ours—one in which life developed in a way roughly similar to ours. It's of no known culture. The international cast—with all the different accents and mannerisms—was chosen to suggest the weird meld in this society, and the sense of rootlessness and disorientation.

As I understand it, these people play a kind of death game.
There is a game, called Quinet, which is the game of the culture—just as the Chinese and other nationalities have had a cultural game. Just as Backgammon is the cultural game of. . . .

Of Elaine's.
Of the East. In this culture, Quintet is their art, their war, their literature. It's the only thing—the only remaining thing in the culture. The game is elaborate. And as the tournaments continue, it becomes violent. Paul Newman, our tour guide, or Everyman, is forced to defend himself like a bull in a bullfight: acting admirably, with grace and guts, as the victim in a stupid, deadly game.

Is it a parallel Rollerball?
Not at all. The violence in the film is not for the sake of violence, or for the sake of those people in the audience who enjoy watching violence.

Where did this idea come from?
I don't know. My father was dying of cancer at the time, and I'm sure that event and the experience had a great deal to do with the ultimate drift of the film, influenced the color of it. It's one dark film. And yet it has to do with the life force. One character tells Newman at the end that he's going off to almost certain death. And Newman says, "*You* know that. But *I* don't."

What was it like shooting your finale in the Arctic Circle?
Cold. Sixty below zero. But we needed that expanse above the tree line, that bleakness. We wanted to show a frozen world. You were talking before about a lessening of passion. Well, I hope the intensity of my ardor matches

the material of *Quintet*. Even *A Perfect Couple,* which seems lighter and funnier, has its dark, serious, even intense side.

What's it about?
It's about two people of radically different backgrounds. Paul Dooley plays a middle-aged divorcé from a conservative Greek-American patriarchy, who's involved with classical music; Marta Heflin is backup singer with a rock group. They meet through a videocomputer dating service. It's kind of a musical. By that I mean I'm going to use musical numbers as punctuation.

The way Ozu would use clothes hanging on a line as. . . .
As an idea, or a connection, or a chapter heading, or ending. It's hard to say how the picture will come out—I haven't started to edit it yet—and it may turn out to be more conventional. But I have a feeling it'll take me into an entirely different format: more theatrical, less naturalistic.

Maybe we can see—or hear—that already in A Wedding. *There seems to be less overlapping dialogue.*
There's more overlapping dialogue in *A Wedding* than in any picture I've done!

Maybe we've gotten used to you.
Maybe we're doing our sound a little better.

So you're not giving up on the famous Altman trademark.
No, there'll be quite a bit in the picture I start shooting in February, in St. Petersburg, Fla.: *Health*. It stars Glenda Jackson, Lauren Bacall, Carol Burnett, and Jim Garner. Frank Barhydt, who wrote *Quintet* with me, is writing the script. It's set at a healthfood convention, and the main characters are the national officers.

You smile.
Well, it's another *Nashville-Wedding-M*A*S*H* kind of large-arena film. One location, a capsule time span—but we're trying something different with it.

And yet the movies you've produced—Robert Benton's The Late Show, *and Alan Rudolph's* Welcome to L.A. *and* Remember My Name—*are closer to chamber pieces.*

I like that. And I like being a producer. I like looking in from the outside. And I like helping people make movies that might otherwise not have been made. I think Benton's career was helped by *The Late Show*. And Alan Rudolph, I firmly believe, will soon be recognized as a formidable film artist.

So you're a benign, non-Mafia godfather.
It's not all that altruistic. Producing these films allows me to keep a unit of technicians together, a continuity of personnel.

Have you made money on your own films as producer or director?
We haven't made any money, but we've been able to keep a cash flow, to keep everybody working, to pay salaries. I couldn't tell you what my net debt is; I know there's very little net worth. But that's the way all businesses are run!

Your studio is in Hollywood, but you're not part of the Hollywood community. In fact, you've had an apartment here in New York for the past few years. Has spending a lot of time in New York nourished you?
Sure. I see more people. I see more things. I'm in a town where not *everybody* talks only about movies. At the moment, I'm here as a producer—of *Rich Kids*—and I'm learning about the problems of making a film here. It's a valuable experience, because I think I'm going to shoot *Martha* here next summer.

What's Martha *about?*
I don't want to say that it's a female *Marty*, but that's probably why I named the character Martha. She's a woman in her late thirties who's a New York construction worker. She's not "pretty" like a model, but she has all the sexual and emotional needs that a Lauren Hutton has. The needs are fed by all the be-beautiful advertising, but it's hard for her to satisfy them. She's a lonely person. I want the film to see through her eyes—through the eyes of Margery Bond, who's going to play her. She's had small parts in *A Wedding* and *A Perfect Couple,* and I think she's a great comic find.

You've been the favorite of a lot of critics. Do you have favorite critics?
I tend to value most highly the ones who like my latest movie!

Do you fare better with the European critics?
Sure. But that's true of almost anybody: You have rougher going in your own place and time. Jesus of Nazareth found that out. If you ask American critics who the great directors are, they'd say Fellini, Bergman, Truffaut. And in France, it'd be Fellini, Bergman, and Altman. And in Sweden, Altman but not Bergman. It's easier to make it in a strange place. If you're close to the situation, it's hard to bring that awe to the work of an artist.

Do you ever look at your old movies? And what do you think of them?
I look at them. And there's nothing I'd change in any one of them. They're finished works, reflecting a specific film experience. To change them would be like doing plastic surgery.

And, honestly, I like 'em better than I did at the time. I looked at *That Cold Day in the Park* recently, and I wanna tell you, that's one hell of a movie!

Robert Altman on Video

ANDREW SARRIS/1980

ROBERT ALTMAN HAS CHANGED the course of the
American cinema since he first burst into prominence with
M*A*S*H in 1970. Such innovative works as *That Cold Day In The
Park, Brewster McCloud, McCabe and Mrs. Miller, Images, The Long
Goodbye, Thieves Like Us, California Split,* and *Nashville* broadened
the options for imagery and sound in American film. Altman has
also added new dimensions to the use of multichannel sound
systems in movies and has become identified with a restlessness
in technological experimentation that has often left both audiences and critics lagging far behind.

A culture hero to some, a self-indulgent maverick to others,
Altman has gone his own way with a highly eccentric vision
of the world, its lives, its rhythms, and its sounds. It is fitting
that he should be the first major film director to produce and
direct programs especially for the home video marketplace,
as he will through a new deal with ABC and the Shubert
Organization.

Video Review had contributing editor Andrew Sarris conduct
the first interview with Altman on his home-video plans during
a lag in the production of his new film *Popeye,* being shot in
Malta.

From *Video Review* (May 1980): 31, 33–34, 93. Reprinted by permission of Andrew Sarris.

ANDREW SARRIS: *I'd like to ask you about this video deal you made with ABC and the Shubert Organization. First of all, have you firmed up any specific projects with them yet?*

ROBERT ALTMAN: We have several, of course, although nothing's going to happen till I finish shooting *Popeye* in Malta, which will be in May. We plan to shoot at least two or three this year, but the idea is to produce any property that normally would not make a film. For instance, things like *Wings, Colored Girls*, Pat Carroll as Gertrude Stein, *Letters Home*, things that would never make a film and we feel should be recorded. I don't mean that we'll shoot them on stage in a proscenium situation. What we're trying to do is really find a new form, where we could use all we know about cameras and backstage visions, in other words a non-front-row look, and, say, take that and elevate it—move it to a style that isn't a movie, isn't a play, isn't television. It offers a chance for a lot of impressionism, abstraction because you don't have to appeal to a mass audience—like poetry. And that's kind of the plan. I have no specific idea what the form will be, but I suspect that the easiest things I'll start out with are the things that will probably be the most obvious.

SARRIS: *How do you feel about this in terms of your career? Do you feel that this is kind of a parallel track or a new direction? Somewhere you've been working toward? For several years now, many of your projects have been very personal, very idiosyncratic. They seem to have reached somewhat smaller audiences than the normal financing situation or the normal distribution patterns indicate.*

ALTMAN: I got interested in it for many of the reasons that you said. But I don't plan to direct all of these. In the case of *Wings*, I would never direct that if the original director were available to do it. Like *Colored Girls*, I would never deal with that without talking to the author. But there's also a lot of failed plays, nice marvelous material that didn't succeed because it wasn't commercial.

SARRIS: *How do you perceive the audience in this new form, videocassettes?*

ALTMAN: It's like publishing—like going for an elite audience, if the word elite isn't misinterpreted. But we can do these inexpensively, reasonably. The great thing about the infusion of ABC's money and the Shuberts and what I want to do is that we're not in any hurry to get that return. We don't have to show that our effort makes profit immediately.

SARRIS: *Has that been a problem for you in the theatrical field?*

ALTMAN: Well, we are allowed to stack these. These wouldn't be released anywhere until we have whatever a volume or set of volumes consists of. So it allows us to get rid of the time element, where a thing has to be two hours long for a movie. We could do a 15-minute thing and an 18-minute thing. We could do an album. If Carol Burnett didn't want to go on the air to do her specials, we could bring Carol Burnett in and say, "Hey, how'd you like to do one hour?" It's like making a record. And then she could just knock herself silly for a week rehearsing, come in and we could do things like a comedy hour.

SARRIS: *How do you feel the home-video revolution is going to affect the traditional area of theatrical film distribution?*

ALTMAN: I don't think it's going to change it at all. I think that theatrical film distribution exhibitors have got down to such a point that you have to go for the lowest common denominator, including cost of advertising, everything. I'm not really particularly interested in making any more movies. But it is what I do and I don't want to face the day when I wake up and start making cane furniture.

SARRIS: *Many people feel that home video will be a way for artists to escape the trap of the lowest common denominator. Do you agree with that? Will video be a new way out?*

ALTMAN: Well, it will offer a way out until it becomes instantly successful, then it will become the lowest common denominator again. It's like the history of television. Consider the growth of television and you'll see that the quality disappears as the economics change. And the same thing will happen with home video.

But I would assume that this thing isn't going to go quite that fast in my lifetime. Even if I only get five good years in, at least there's a chance to do things that will eventually change the patterns.

I think it is much like publishing. There will always be best-sellers, there will always be Harold Robbins and there will always be some early Edgar Doctorows.

SARRIS: *To go back to your specific intentions for a moment. If you were to produce* Wings, *for example, for videocassette. It's not what anyone would*

remotely call cinematic, but it does have that great Constance Cummings perfor-
mance. How would you handle it? Which do you think would be more appealing
to the audience—a record of the play or a kind of reworking of that into film?
ALTMAN: I think a reworking is mandatory. But I think that reworking it
is just changing the position of where you and the audience sit. Obviously
a new art comes into this because someone is changing your focus, they're
changing your distance. But are we changing the play? I don't believe so.
When you sit in the theater with 300, 400 people, and when you sit at home
with five people or alone, the goal of the medium is still to get that same
message or that same song through.

I'm talking very arrogantly like I'm going to improve these things, and I
don't mean that at all. Also, we're talking about one small aspect of it. I
think that a cooking lesson on how to make an omelet could be terrific.

I think eventually what home video will do is allow you to view programs like you read a book. You can say, "I'm gonna see *The Godfather*
tonight," and you put it on. Then suddenly the phone would ring and
you'd say, "Oh shit." You can stop it and you go back, and then go to the
phone again and you go back and think, "Oh I don't feel like seeing it."
And you can start all over again. You can back it up to so-and-so, you can
use it, you can get sleepy and you can put the "book" down and you can
pick it back up and you can go back and your memory still has the rest of
it. As a director, I now have to deal with those kinds of things, not with
the totally concentrated audience of longtime things.

SARRIS: *You also have to deal with longtime exposure to a production and the*
challenge of making it to wear well.
ALTMAN: Well first of all, the color's not going to last, so in 40 years you're
not going to be able to see them anyway. And when they transfer films to
cassettes or the color changes, it's like getting a print of a print of a print.
But I don't think any of that is important anyway. I don't think my work
or anybody else's work in film is important other than its technical aspects—
when we find out that technically we can emotionally motivate somebody
or an audience with film.

SARRIS: *Are you saying that you don't find your work that important histori-*
cally, as an indicator where you were at a certain time?
ALTMAN: The color is important to my films today with contemporaries
because the elite audience is saying "Oh!" So they see that color and it

means something to them. But that color won't mean anything 100 years from now.

SARRIS: *You seem to remain resolutely a modernist. You're always looking forward, you're not looking back. Is it because you feel that you are changing or growing, or that the world changes and that this is a medium that is always reflecting the new reality of the world and has to keep going in that way?*

ALTMAN: Well, I have a job, and I love all my films. I look back at them and I run them quite often. I go over here and we run everything because we have nothing else to do. And I sit and look at them with this new audience every time, and they're all terrific. But I don't think they mean a goddam thing.

SARRIS: *If you were suddenly out of the theatrical field altogether, and began working exclusively in video, would you become a different type of artist, perhaps less freewheeling, more precise?*

ALTMAN: Probably quite the opposite. I think the whole thing that interests me is that suddenly I've got an area that nobody's ever been allowed to go into before. And I can listen to some fool who'll say, "Why don't we shoot his thing in a curved mirror?" It's exciting.

SARRIS: *Whom do you see in your ultimate audience? Do you see a crowded theater, a small theater, two people sitting in front of a TV set playing a cassette?*

ALTMAN: The only audience to me is the people who worked on the project that day who sit and look at the dailies the next day or whenever they can, and cheer for each other. That's the full movie to me.

SARRIS: *And the rest of the audience is sort of incidental to that?*

ALTMAN: I love it when they like it, and I'm disappointed when they don't. As for the video venture, I'm excited about it or I wouldn't do it. I hope it is very successful.

Altman Talking

RICHARD COMBS AND
TOM MILNE/1981

I REALLY ASKED TO do *Popeye* because . . . why not? A movie is just a fantasy anyway. And it occurred to me that this was a chance to create my own environment, which I'd done in *Quintet* but it didn't work with audiences or critics. Popeye was never really a favorite of mine. I mean, I was certainly aware of him when I was very young. I was a sort of frustrated cartoonist myself, and it was easy to draw Popeye, easy to copy him. But I didn't really understand what I consider to be the social impact Popeye had until I decided I was going to do the picture, then went back and read a lot of the original comic strips.

What I think we're doing in both *Quintet* and *Popeye* is creating a culture that has its own restrictions and boundaries. I dare say that if I took you to some Sherpa village in Tibet, the way people live there and their customs would be as strange to you as the people in Sweethaven. *Quintet* was a lot more allegorical, because we only dealt with the principal characters, and everyone else was almost zombie-like. But of course that was part of the particular environment. What I'm trying to say is that the environment, the look of the place, the costumes, the fact of the dogs in *Quintet* or the absence of animals in Sweethaven . . . all those things, whatever the rules I set up, are not anything you can immediately identify with. With *Popeye*, of course, I had the cartoon history to back me up. Had I invented the whole thing myself, and said okay, this is a fairy tale I'm going to show you, the picture would probably be a failure.

From *Sight and Sound* (Summer 1981): 184–86. Reprinted by permission of *Sight and Sound* and the British Film Institute.

It's not possible, but I would love to be able to show *Popeye* to a broad audience of people who had absolutely no reference to the cartoons or the comic strips, cutting out the Max Fleischer extract and starting with the storm at sea. What would they think? I haven't the slightest idea. A few might say, My God, this is genius; 99 out of a hundred would probably say this is the silliest thing I've ever seen in my life and get very angry. So the pre-knowledge people have of Popeye is on the one hand a help, and on the other a hindrance, because everyone has his own image, and if I don't live up to that, I'm either falling short or I've gone too far.

I don't want to get glib about this, but what I was trying to do in creating the *Quintet* environment was to show that life itself can come down to an ethnic game. Most cultures have games that are indigenous, they grow out of people playing polo or whatever; but what we were saying in *Quintet* was that there was nothing else, there was no diversion, and eventually it came down to where the game itself was life. And the only people who really had the sense of life were those who played the game. After all, interchange in life is just . . . it's like when children play, they're practicing being adults, they're imitating, like animals do when they're taught to hunt or birds when they learn to fly. But we're showing the destruction of what I consider *human*, when everything gets down to the smallest set of rules and emotions disappear; and then I bring the alien in, the man who messes the directions up. I don't think *Quintet* necessarily took place on this planet. I consider it a parallel society rather than necessarily an extension of *this* society. Or it could be either. And I didn't care to tell about that . . . which was one of the criticisms levelled against the film.

You may be right that in *Quintet* I doubly exclude the audience, in that not only is the setting very strange, but the rules of the game on which everything depends are not explained. That's true, but you can't teach anybody a game. I've been playing backgammon for thirty years, and my wife knows the rules, but I could never teach her backgammon because she just doesn't want to learn. So, in a film, so long as I know there's a reality, then I don't feel I have to teach it to anybody. If I know it's real, then I can confidently go ahead and show it, and assume my confidence will spill over to the audience, that they'll realize it really is a game. I don't think they have to know how to play it.

Actually, the game in *Quintet* is one I invented, and it's a very good game. The problem is that it takes too many players, and in today's society games have to be two-handed rather than family games. However, I got a letter recently from a girl in Chicago. She and her boyfriend had found a set of the rules for Quintet which we printed up for the original press kit, and she sent me pictures of elaborate inlaid leather boards she'd made and taken to these science fiction clubs that meet around the country. And now they're having tournaments....

Unlike *Popeye* or *A Wedding*, the characters in *Quintet* are simply pieces on the board. So the film gets back to the idea of hope and what is a human view of things. That is why we harped so much on memory with the Bibi Andersson character. She says, 'I don't trust my memories,' and Essex says, 'Memory's all you can trust.' In other words, we're really talking about a dead world, in which there was no hope, absolutely no hope of survival. And in the end, when Essex is challenged as he's leaving, he says, 'I'm going north' because that's where he saw the wild goose going. Told he'll be dead in a day and a half, he says, 'You may know that, but I don't.' And that, to me, is humanism. And when you see him at the very end, walking off into the snow, I think anybody who is halfway intelligent has got to know that in a day and a half he's going to be dead.

I don't think anybody would ever believe how *Quintet* evolved. It started out as a kind of surrealistic thriller with reference to the Irish underground, not specifically, but that's the only country I know of today that has this anarchy on two almost distinct social levels. It took place in the underbelly of a city, where these dogs roamed but didn't terrify the people living there, and yet you wonder why aren't they afraid of those maneating dogs? And then this killing, this man trying to uncover the mystery. We were going to shoot it in the underbelly of Chicago, looking kind of like *Odd Man Out* and *The Third Man*. Then we found this location in Montreal, and I decided we would freeze it, advance the period. After that the game developed, though both it and the dogs were always there.

Even before that, the germ of the film actually started in Rome. I had had about an hour of walking round a hotel room, looking out of windows and into courtyards. I was waiting for someone to pick me up, and I was having a drink standing beside a door to another suite that was locked. Standing near this door, looking across those open courtyards, I was watching two men carrying on a conversation out there. Suddenly I started hearing a man and a woman talking in the next suite, not totally distinctly but enough. So I was watching one thing and hearing something else; and the idea came that if these people I heard were plotting an assassination, and those I was watching were the victims...where did that put me? I think it's impossible for me to transmit to you the connection, but it did as a matter of fact kind of follow through to *Quintet*—although it never really occurred to me until this moment—when Essex *hears* and *sees* something similar. These elements do come in to stay, and consequently *can* become confusing to an audience. Maybe it's my own arrogance that says you don't have to understand them. We accept everything in our own lives, yet we want order in our fantasies.

Your idea that the game in *Quintet* might represent mainstream Hollywood, with the judges and arbiters as producers and critics, and Essex as myself, the lone independent...well, if that is a fact, it is so subconscious that I would never allow it to surface. But that's what a film should be. If it works for you, if you can see those analogies, then terrific. I mean, it's like looking at a painting. Or...take a tiger, wandering through the jungle in India at the end of the day, and suddenly there's this absolutely magnificent sunset. Does the tiger stop and look at that and say, God, how beautiful, or does he not? I think probably not. Which makes the difference between our brain and the tiger's. On the other hand, I don't know that he doesn't *feel* something. I know that temperature controls what animals feel and whether they're hungry or not. So how do we know that they don't eat certain leaves at certain times, which is the equivalent of you getting drunk or changing your perceptions? I think that if I had thought specifically of *Quintet* as a metaphor for filmmaking, I would have been afraid of it.

The danger of these kinds of conversations and interviews to me is that if I start explaining or thinking about...I don't really want to know *why*. The minute I articulate it, I say, oh yeah...and then I begin to believe what I say. I narrow everybody's view of what that film can be. Because if I say it means *this* to me, you are arbitrarily and almost necessarily bound to look within the range that I have set for it. Take, for instance, my own image of the way that *3 Women* ended. One sees seals, or sea lions, basking on rocks, just kind of lying around. And I see *3 Women* as if those three female seals had kicked the last male off that rock and are much more comfortable...but at the same time you know it means the end of the species.

Health began when a fellow who'd edited a health food magazine for some years came to me with the idea of doing a film about health foods. I liked the idea, but as we worked on it for a long time, on and off, I felt that just to deal with the health food thing directly was not going to do much. There's nothing wrong with people being concerned about nutrition and health. And I didn't want merely to parody the commercial aspects that are so terrible. So we brought in the political situations and it sort of grew.

The character played by Glenda Jackson isn't exactly Adlai Stevenson, but most of her speeches were paraphrases, and some of them were exact Stevenson speeches. That speech from the tower, for instance, was one of his; and she sounded very much like him, he had a very high voice... not that anybody is going to remember these things. He was the first political figure that really impressed me. But when we were cutting, we got very nervous about that tower scene. Originally there was much more continuity to what she said. But we felt that the film suddenly stopped to say okay, here's the liberal message. So we started slicing into it until you only heard sections of the speech and there was no sense of continuity to what was being said. So that could very well explain why, as you commented, the Stevenson who so impressed me sounds at times just as much like Ronald Reagan.

You see, when I make films... it's like color running in a garment. You might have a nice blue figure on a shirt, and you put it in hot water, and suddenly it just runs through the whole shirt. That kind of thing happens. But beyond the political element, the idea of shooting *Health* in Florida was very important. I don't think I would have made that film in Chicago or anyplace else. Everybody around there was in their eighties, or they certainly looked it. And all those people in St Petersburg, those old people down there—again, what the film was *about*—they behaved so well, they're really good Americans, they do what they're told. They're told to work hard, to save their money, to go to church, and then they can retire when they're 65.

Retirement means that they can go to Florida, they don't have to worry about the cold weather any more, they walk up and down the beach. But there's no sand on those beaches, it looks like sand but actually it's just rather hard, ground-up crust. And I see these people walking up and down the beach, just going right into it. I can almost see them disappear until they're a part of it. I think it's a terrible way to die. Because when people die in old age, in retirement, actually their life has ended a long time ago, it's like an elephants' graveyard, just walking up and down until they disappear.... Randy Newman did a great love-story song... 'Who'll buy a house? And then we'll go to Florida till we die....'

When I started the Lion's Gate company five years ago, it seemed an ideal set-up. I never sat back and said, Now I want to have a company. But as I acquired hardwear and softwear and people, it was a matter of self-defense against the Establishment, which is no good. But I felt even then the danger that we'd grow and grow until we became the thing that we set out to oppose. I mean, it's true of every liberal politician who ever lived, by the time he's 70, he's conservative. You become what it is you set out to fight against. I think that if I had an observation in mind while filming *Health*, being among all those old people down there—and I think it carried over into *Popeye*—it was that in order to attain power, every nation, group, large culture, or what-have-you has to have a slave class. And the slave class of America is the middle class.

I don't suppose it was planned, but it was very clever. People escaped from Europe because they were tired of being poor, and they go to this new land of opportunity, and then they realize.... We have really created a slave class. That is, the absolute power of the United States is the middle class. They do everything exactly right. They put their money in savings banks at low interest rates. The churches have been exempted from paying taxes, so they gather more money. The churches and the insurance companies are the richest forces. They're the ones that then are able to exercise the power, and people behave. They buy a new car every two years, because they're told that's what they're supposed to do, and that keeps the basic economy going. I think it's going to be very interesting to see what happens now that the automobile is really over, a finished thing.

The people in *Popeye* are like that, being exploited by a dictator whom they've never seen. But I don't think it makes a hell of a lot of difference what I say in these films. I didn't promise you a rose garden. I have no alternative, I can only show you what I think the ills are, and the fact that they overcome me too. And maybe that's the most positive thing that can be done: to focus attention so that if enough people see they will solve their problem. I have this great optimism that always translates into pessimism. But I'm not sure that that's wrong. In *Quintet*, we take this man who absolutely has the spirit of the human being in him, saying, By God,

I'm not going to lie down and die just because everybody tells me I have to. I'm going on. You say, That's noble, boy. Then the music starts and this triumphant thing, and the guy goes off and dies.

Talking about my work this way...I think most people would say my films are very different from each other. There was a time when I believed that was true, but I don't believe it's true now. Just intelligently, I have to realize that it can't be true, it must be the same, coming from one source. If you talk long enough, press hard enough, then all the films of any film-maker, good, bad, or indifferent, finally become to some extent at least variations on a theme. The complexity of our brain cells is such that no two brains are alike. There *is* a great similarity in our feelings and basic responses to things, but no two are exactly alike. And everything that's happened, everything you see, that you're exposed to, every feeling, every disappointment, every success, all those various emotions cram up in this computer, and that information is there. I think if I were to do...I guess it's science fiction...I would say that if you could go every five years or so and have your brain wiped absolutely clean of all the information that's in it, you could probably live forever. I think that what we die of is too much information, when we finally get so much information and counterinfor-mation that it all comes out and you say, 'Oh well, what the hell....'

On *Quintet,* I actually drew the plans for that network of cities, how they worked and how the trains communicated from one to the other, and how each sector contained a million people, and how there were five sec-tors and each one was five levels deep, and then there were five of those that made a cluster. And suddenly they became almost molecular structures. In that sense, all these films of mine are science fiction....

A Foolish Optimist

HARRY KLOMAN AND LLOYD
MICHAELS WITH VIRGINIA
WRIGHT WEXMAN/1983

DURING THE PAST 15 years, Robert Altman has produced an extraordinarily large and varied body of work, all of which bears the mark of his idiosyncratic vision. From genre films like *McCabe and Mrs. Miller* and *The Long Goodbye* to highly subjective projects like *3 Women* and *Quintet,* he has shown himself to be one of the few contemporary directors who has been able to work within the Hollywood system of distribution while creating an oeuvre which is manifestly the expression of his own sensibility.

To achieve his relative independence from the pressures of Hollywood commercial orthodoxy, Altman has produced most of the films he has directed, even creating a studio, Lion's Gate, where he could develop his characteristic techniques, including multitrack sound systems and multi-narrative editing systems. At Lion's Gate, he also established a home for the group of actors and technicians he had gathered around him: cinematographer Vilmos Zsigmond, associate producer Robert Eggenweiller, actors Keith Carradine, Shelley Duvall, Elliott Gould, Henry Gibson, Nina Van Pallandt, and others. The studio also allowed him to produce films for other directors such as Robert Benton, Alan Rudolph, and Robert Young.

Recently, Altman sold Lion's Gate, moving on to still more unconventional projects. During the past few years, he has directed two off-Broadway productions, including *Come Back to the 5 and Dime, Jimmy Dean, Jimmy Dean,* which was subsequently released as a feature film. More

From *Film Criticism* vol. VII, no. 3 (Spring 1983): 20–28. Reprinted by permission of *Film Criticism.*

recently, he travelled to Michigan to direct a university production of Stravinsky's opera *The Rake's Progress*.

Though some commentators have found Altman's method confused and his vision unduly mordant, for others his work expresses an emotionally complex and encompassing reading of the modern scene. Though the fragmentation that characterizes his films may express the sense of breakdown found in a great deal of contemporary art, his sensibility, like that of Jean Renoir and Walt Whitman, is ultimately optimistic, finding virtues in empirically based sensation and emotion which more rational approaches to experience lack. His relaxed style, which involves tracking camera movements, zoom lenses, overlapping dialogue, and improvised performances, allows him to create moments of beauty marked by evanescence. These emotional peaks are set against the sterile, intellectualized games which form a motif in all of the films and are dissected at length in *Quintet, California Split,* and *M*A*S*H.*

Committed to a vision of life which is organic and cyclical, Altman has faith in parental affection and childlike spontaneity. Hence, many of his films deal with families: from conventional ones in films like *A Wedding, A Perfect Couple,* and *Popeye,* to more contemporary versions of "improvised" families in films like *M*A*S*H, McCabe and Mrs. Miller, 3 Women,* and *California Split.* His concern with familial structures emerges in the camaraderie which, for him, is an integral part of the filmmaking process itself. "It's like a family," he has said of the group that surrounds him on the set. "Nobody's perfect; but there's all that affection."

The following interview with Lucy Fischer, Virginia Wright Wexman, Harry Kloman, and Lloyd Michaels, took place in the director's Pittsburgh hotel room during the Society for Cinema Studies conference in early May, shortly before an evening screening of *Come Back to the 5 and Dime, Jimmy Dean, Jimmy Dean.* Relaxed and genial, Altman nonetheless balked at points when he felt pushed to "intellectualize" about his work. The interview overall, however, was a lively and productive one, with Altman trying his best to speak to the interests of four different questioners.

V.W.W.

FC: *How do you respond to having been called the true "problem director," that is, difficult to assess?*

RA: I'm not difficult. My work may be difficult, but if in fact it is difficult, it just further enforces what I have to say: that all I make films about is what I see and the way things appear to me. And when people want categorization, when they want pigeonholing, I refuse it.

FC: *A lot of your endings have given people problems, like the ending of* Nashville. *Did you see that as in any way a hopeful ending?*
RA: I saw that as both sides of a coin. When they say, "It Don't Worry Me," after that assassination, I think it indicates how quickly you can get over something and become apathetic about it. But I think it also talks about, in equal intensity, the fact that people carry on. I'm always accused of being a pessimist, and I really think of myself as an absolute and foolish optimist. Maybe that's a pessimistic statement when I put that adjective there.

FC: *Can you think of a particular scene in a particular film that critics reacted to as being very cynical but which you thought was much more optimistic?*
RA: Well, the ending of *Nashville*, I think. The ending of *Quintet*. The ending of *Brewster McCloud*. Things don't end for me. The only end I know about is death. So unless a death is involved, why do we suddenly lose interest in those people just because they get divorced or married or ended that little segment of their lives? Those people are continuing to live. I think the image at the end of *Quintet* is hopeful. When the young girl sees the goose flying north, she says, "What is it?" She's frightened by it. It's something she's never experienced. And the man says, "My God, it's a goose. I didn't know there were any left." At the end he says he's going north, and he's told he'll freeze to death. And he says, "Well, you may know that, but I don't." So I think it had to do with spirit, the spirit of a hopeful ending. I also believe the man is going to freeze to death.

FC: *The optimistic side always seems to have so much to do with nurturing and generations, and images of parents and children. Something like* Popeye: *the family looking for a father and a grandfather image. You even used your own grandson in the role of Swee'pea.*
RA: I don't know. I never thought of that, although it's kind of interesting. The reason I used my grandson is because, logistically, he arrived at

the proper time and was the proper age. He happened to have been born with Bell's Palsy and the one side of his mouth was paralyzed for a few days after birth, which is a very common thing. And when these kids come out that way, every time they laugh or cry, why then you have that real funny look, like Popeye. And also I didn't want some stage mother that I didn't know to suddenly freak out and say, "Oh, my God, you've got my kid in a boat with an octopus!" I wanted as much control as possible, and by that I mean trust. My daughter knew that I wasn't going to put the kid in any jeopardy.

FC: *Could you say a little more about the nature of your optimism? What do your hopes rest on?*

RA: Well, I don't have any goals. I consider myself an artist, and I don't have anything to say. I just show what I see. This is the way it looks to me. Bring your experience to it, and it's going to be different. I'm as sentimental as anybody, and I'm as unsentimental as anybody. I get into an arena and I start dealing with very eclectic things that are in that arena. Consequently, rarely am I following one person, which to get a real mass audience for a film you've got to do.

FC: *Tennessee Williams once commented that in America success and failure are equally catastrophic. You have become a celebrity, but there have been times in your career when your reputation has fluctuated. How does that affect you, the rise and fall of your commercial success?*

RA: Obviously it has to have an effect, but I don't think I pay attention to it. If I had been able to put somebody else's name on many of the films I've made, the critical reviews would have been absolutely 180 degrees changed. But it works both ways. The celebrity gets my films attention and people write about them, but they're also analyzing or criticizing the whole body of work, and you can't escape that. It's tough.

FC: *Your films are more financially successful in Europe than in America. Why do you think that is so?*

RA: I don't think they're more financially successful. I think they're more critically successful. In Europe, there's more of a polarization among film writers and critics and filmophiles. They're denser, so they tend to embrace these kind of films more than American critics do. American critics are spread out. They cover a spectrum from intellectuals to people who review films. And now you've gotten into a whole new breed of critic, the television critic, who tries to develop a personality. In Europe, you get the same discouraging reviews, but they get more passionate about it, so it gets more attention. But the biggest European audiences, in the provinces in France, don't know who the hell I am.

FC: *You often deal with conventional genres in your work, transforming them to fit your own purposes. What about your attitudes toward those original films, the genre films that were so different?*

RA: In my formation, I saw a lot of films, but I've never consciously gone after a genre and said, well, let's tear this one up. But it always occurred to me that maybe things didn't happen exactly that way. I mean, let's talk about the private eye. It doesn't exist. In *The Long Goodbye* my intention was that the greatest crime that could be committed against Philip Marlowe, who was a romantic, is that his friend broke faith with him. So he killed him. I remember one of the first screenings, a lady said, "Oh, I loved your film but isn't he going to get into trouble for that?"

FC: *You've said that you want your films to reflect your "view." What is your "view"?*

RA: I don't know what it is. I have to look at something and—I'll quote Sherwood Anderson: "a truth is a truth as long as it's allowed to float freely. The minute you gather it into your bosom, it becomes an untruth."

FC: *You began this interview by calling yourself an artist. Now you seem to think of art as a reflection of popular culture.*

RA: I am an artist, possibly of popular culture, but I use the word with a small "a," as opposed to being a propagandist. I am not telling you the way I think things should be. I am not going to try to sell you on my philosophy. I try to show you the way things appear to me, so consequently you have to pick up my philosophy and politics, but I'm not necessarily showing the propagandistic side of it.

FC: *But you do have a way of happening on images that have a certain reverence, regardless of whether you're trying to convince or persuade.*

RA: But most of those things are unconscious. You can justify anything if you sit there and work your logic around a word. But I try not to do that.

In most cases, something is suggested, or I see something and say, "Hey, that's right." I don't consciously think about it. Because if I start thinking about it, I can justify it; and if I can justify it, it becomes intellectual; and if I transmit it through the film intellectually, it's going to be received intellectually. And if I transmit it emotionally, it'll be received emotionally. That's why I think it's very dangerous to give interviews. I think it's very dangerous to have this kind of conversation, to talk about your work, because once you start to understand it, a certain section of it is gone.

FC: *Can we ask you a couple of questions about technique, then, particularly your technique in directing actors?*

RA: I don't know what my technique is, other than to recognize that the artist that's creating at that particular moment is the actor, and not me. So I'm trying to do anything I can to encourage that artist to feel safe to dig and go as far with what they're doing as possible.

FC: *Do you employ different techniques for directing on stage as opposed to making films?*

RA: I don't think my work is any different. In both mediums, you are basically transferring content to an audience through the medium of actors. The process is logistically different because the rehearsal period for the stage is the same as the editing period of a film—their functions are just chronologically reversed.

FC: *When you make a film, do you have an audience in mind? For example, you said you thought 3* Women *was going to be as big as* Annie Hall. *But how would you think a deep, brooding, psychological film would be popular with audiences?*

RA: Because I'm an optimist. I think every film, as I finish it, is going to go through the roof, the cat's pajamas. I thought *Images* was going to be one of the biggest things of all times. I was absolutely positive that children would totally understand *Popeye* and love it, and I found that to be absolutely true.

FC: *Do you truly hold faith in American audiences to respond to intelligent films?*

RA: Well, I don't think about it. I don't get exposed to real life, and when I do I get terribly depressed. I was in a shopping mall in Dallas once, and I looked around and counted in my brain that there were 500 people, and not one of these people would have the slightest idea what was going on in any of my films. But, of course, I'm wrong about that.

FC: *Your films each have quite a distinctive visual look. Do you plan that out ahead of time?*

RA: I think that's the first thing. I'm doing a film this summer in Phoenix, and what I'm struggling with and thinking about all the time—I do this when I'm asleep, or at night or in the morning—is formulating how it's going to look. Then, once that's decided, you forget about it. But each project itself sort of dictates its own look—either by things you can or cannot do, or the nature of the thing itself. In *McCabe and Mrs. Miller*, we built and controlled everything. In *Nashville* and *Brewster McCloud*, we were out in the streets. I cannot tell everybody in the city of Nashville not to wear red on Thursday because I don't want red.

FC: *Yet there's a certain look to* Nashville. *It's photographed a lot in telephoto.*

RA: And that's for a reason. Sometimes you don't want the camera seeing so much. *Buffalo Bill* was photographed entirely in telephoto, even those big wide shots, in order to compress images. Sometimes I had the camera a quarter of a mile away doing a scene to get all those guys sitting on a front porch. Long lenses change the image and evoke antiquity. I use the zoom lens constantly. To me it's just a matter of magic: You're able to focus attention.

FC: *Despite some criticism of your use of it, you seem quite fond of the zoom lens.*

RA: Oh, yeah. I use it constantly. To me, it's just a matter of being able to focus attention. In *California Split* we had a rule—and there's always exceptions to these rules—that the zoom was always moved in. Because you get into a crap game in Las Vegas and you get to betting the money and watching the dice and suddenly they could take Abraham Lincoln and George Washington and Winston Churchill and Adolf Hitler and put all these people around the table and you'd never notice them.

FC: *There's a wonderful zoom at the end of* McCabe and Mrs. Miller. *How did that come about?*

RA: I went back and forth with the zoom into her eye and into that vase and the idea was to diminish—just to take all that experience and put it inside her head so that it looked like you were looking at a planet from a spaceship.

FC: *What were you striving for in your use of multiple sound tracks?*
RA: I think you have to train an audience that they don't have to hear everything. We go through life doing that. You look at somebody's face, you know what they're going to say. It's just a courtesy to let them finish. I learned about sound myself, but too many people don't have the time to do that. We don't take the time, or we become too obsessed with it. I think the problem is, like with all things, whoever has the veto power in a film doesn't know enough about it. I found out early in my career that I didn't know enough about cameras, and that the cameraman was telling me things I couldn't do. But we did do them. So I learned about that myself.

FC: *An actor you once worked with said, "Altman has a thing about negotiating."*
RA: Who was that, Duvall?

FC: *Ned Beatty.*
RA: That was over a thing that I offered him, but I wouldn't discuss the amount of money involved. We do those things for a very strong reason: that is, to free the actors from a lot of outside influences that will inhibit their art. And I insist on a sense of equality. I'm trying to destroy the pecking order which always exists in one way or another. In *Health*, Betty Bacall, Glenda Jackson, Carol Burnett, Dick Cavett, and James Garner shared the same dressing room and the same makeup room. The women could change their clothes behind a curtain—or the men could, since they were the ones most concerned about that sort of thing.

FC: *Let's discuss your contributions as a screenwriter. Joan Tewkesbury said that in* Nashville *you contributed all the political elements. There's a moment when the Geraldine Chaplin character gives a theory of assassination. Is that an idea of yours?*
RA: She was a connection. I wrote all of Geraldine's stuff. She was supposed to be a kind of tour guide. Her remarks were supposed to be a dippy,

panacea answer to a problem that's insoluble, and yet it's so innocent there's probably a lot of truth in it.

FC: *And in* A Wedding, *Geraldine has a similar kind of moment where she makes statements about weddings.*
RA: But those statements all came out of an etiquette wedding book. I mean, they came directly out. We just put the words in her mouth. In *Brewster McCloud* everything the Birdman says came right out of a textbook on birds. The statement about the time of mating being very important because the bird cannot support the weight of greatly enlarged gonads: That's in the book. Almost every announcement in *M*A*S*H* over the loudspeaker came right out of the almanac that year. Every one of those movie ads, other than the last one, *M*A*S*H*, was read off the poster of the film.

FC: *Some directors would say that unless a director is writing a script, he doesn't have the right to tinker with a writer's words.*
RA: That's bullshit. That may be right for them, but if a writer says to me he doesn't want something changed, "Go out and point your camera and direct my film," I can't do that. I've taken more liberties and made more changes and violations on my own screenplays than I have on anybody else's. You can see the screenplays on *3 Women* and *Images*, I tampered with that as much as anything.

FC: *In* Brewster McCloud, *a film that you did not write—*
RA: That's a film I totally did write, but I bought a screenplay and the writer insisted there would be an additional $25,000 payment if he didn't get sole screen credit on it. But that's the only case like that.

FC: *Why did you choose to direct those films in which you are not credited among the screenwriters?*
RA: Because I liked them. When I read *Thieves Like Us* I did not know that it had been made into a film before. I wanted to bring that book to the screen exactly the way it was. So I hired someone to write the screenplay and I said just give me that book, and the only change we made was in the ending. I guess I had less to do with the writing of *Thieves Like Us* than any of my films, but that's not true because when you say writing you're talking only about words.

FC: *Let's turn to American filmmaking today. Spielberg gets financed, Lucas gets financed; they both make millions. Some people call these empty-headed movies. Yet you call yourself a serious artist making serious films. It must be discouraging.*

RA: Why? I'm not discouraged. I make money. I live very comfortably. Steven Spielberg had a hell of a time getting *E.T.* made. I don't feel any remorse. It's what I do. It's not for anybody else. I'm disappointed, but I think there's room for those movies. Harold Robbins can write all those books he wants, and you can put them on the racks at airports, but I don't find that a terrible thing. Those publishing companies still print books of poetry.

FC: *The success of the "slasher films" doesn't push out serious artists?*

RA: No, because there are too many ancillary avenues right now, and also I don't spend that much money on a film. I think this is really the best opportunity for new artists that we've had. I think it's much easier than it was in the seventies.

FC: *Do you go to a lot of movies?*

RA: I see very few. I haven't seen *ET*, I haven't seen *Star Wars*, I haven't seen *Raiders of the Lost Ark*, I haven't seen *Gandhi*, I haven't seen *Sophie's Choice*.

FC: *Because you're too busy?*

RA: No, because I'm always disappointed.

FC: *Really! What disappoints you?*

RA: I don't know. I just always expect more. I just don't want to be disappointed.

Secret Honor

PATRICIA AUFDERHEIDE/1985

DIRECTOR ROBRT ALTMAN, WHO earlier produced
[Donald] Freed and [Arnold M.] Stone's play [*Secret Honor*] and
who produced the film as a teaching exercise at the University of
Michigan, shares Freed's concern for the quality of public life
today and his conviction that art can signal an alarm. In the following interview he discusses his motivation for making this
film, and the process of transforming a play into a movie.

CINEASTE: *What attracted you to this material?*
ROBERT ALTMAN: I thought that through the vehicle of Richard
Nixon, we could reveal what has to be done to arrive at public office today.
Democracy is being cheated by today's technology and the celebrityism
that goes along with it. We do not have the best people for the job. It has
become like getting a lead in a soap opera. And there is a defeated psychol-
ogy that goes along with it, because who has the power? Not the president.
It's those guys who put up millions of dollars to get someone elected, who
would like to sell a candy bar to every Chinese citizen.

CINEASTE: *It seems that most people have forgotten what Watergate was all
about.*
ALTMAN: We forget our history quicker all the time. Now we forget what
Ronald Reagan says within 24 hours. It's a serious situation, and I'm afraid

From *Cineaste* vol. 14, no. 2 (1985): 13–14. Reprinted by permission of *Cineaste*.

the proof of it is that the majority of people who should see this film aren't going to.

CINEASTE: *Do you think that's because it has a political subject?*
ALTMAN: No, not exactly. I don't deal in propaganda, I never have; I think this is art. But if someone paid attention to this film, they would have to reassess in themselves a lot more than most people will do.

CINEASTE: *So it's not a problem of reluctant distributors or exhibitors?*
ALTMAN: That's a problem, but they're in business and they have to make a profit. The real problem is that there isn't a big want-to-see factor in *Secret Honor*. Even with a strong positive review, some people will read it and choose not to go on that basis. If the review is written clearly, people will understand that the film will force them to reassess their thinking process.

CINEASTE: *So this film is about unpleasant truths?*
ALTMAN: In the sense that art always deals with truth, it does that. Not The Truth. A truth. Somebody's truth. It is in contrast to nostalgia-type productions about some historic figure, productions that put you in a comfortable relation with the character. They're balm. This one takes a situation and says—in a tradition that goes back to Jonathan Swift—look at this.

CINEASTE: *Does the prospect of a limited audience make it harder for you to keep working?*
ALTMAN: No, all I need to sustain me in my vision is one person. One person who says, I got it, I was really moved. We'll never get our money back on this film, but we didn't do it for that reason. And the response is good. In fact I never made a film that got such a critical response. Harold Pinter—I'm working with him on a production for next year—thinks it's the best film that's ever been made.

CINEASTE: *Why have you chosen recently to make films from stage productions?*
ALTMAN: Because it's material that ordinarily doesn't get enough exposure except to theater buffs. It's a challenge to take what the playwright

has to say and to adapt it in such a way as to reach a vaster audience. But it's not just a question of numbers. If I can say something in the form of theater and in a song and in a film and in a painting, I can reach through different senses to communicate. If you could get people to see something they can hear on radio, if you could figure out how to make it smell . . . !

I'm not talking about changing people's minds. You can't ever teach anybody. You can allow them to learn. But they have to make the effort, and that's the problem with making truth commercially. Now people want the constant assurance that they will be entertained.

As communications becomes faster, instead of taking advantage of it we start to close our ears to it. We choose to listen not to somebody's truth but to something that verifies a familiar position. Look at the criticism I get from liberals about *Secret Honor.* They tell me, "I couldn't stand it, because you made me feel sorry for the guy." They don't want to deal with the truth of the matter, which is that he is a human being. As soon as you reduce things to two dimensions it doesn't mean anything. The comic-book hero and the heavy diminishes both types. The project I'm working on with Harold Pinter is about torture, and we've talked about this. You have to give someone their humanity in order to hold them accountable.

CINEASTE: *How was it to work with University of Michigan students in producing this?*
ALTMAN: It worked very well, because they were able to see the play, and then to see how the film differed from it. By the time it was over they were disillusioned. They learned filmmaking is work, that standing on a ladder, and working 14 hours straight, is not glamorous.

CINEASTE: *How did the film differ from the play?*
ALTMAN: In a theater, people mostly have to depend on what they hear, and no two people see the same thing. The actors deal with all those people at once. On film everything resolves down to a single sightline, and everyone sees exactly the same thing. It means that the performance has to be different, and you can and must direct what they look at.

CINEASTE: *Was the use of TV monitors an invention for the film?*
ALTMAN: Yes. I got the idea about three days before shooting. It solved the practical problem of cutaways. And then I realized that it allowed me

to go deeper. In fact, where the idea started doesn't make a lot of difference now. The key is that there is a core truth in him peering into that monitor.

CINEASTE: *Are there themes in this film that reverberate with other of your films? A similarity in critique of American culture?*

ALTMAN: You can find parallels from here back to *Nashville*, and to *Brewster McCloud*, and *McCabe and Mrs. Miller*. But I think the strongest parallel is that they all address a particular kind of truth. Whenever I start a project I say to myself, now this is new. I've never done this before. And before I finish, I realize that there's only one thought, and I'm singing the same song.

CINEASTE: *What is that one thought, that one song?*

ALTMAN: I don't think I want to know what that is. Whether it's because it would make me too aware, or pretentious ... I just don't want to know. Anyway, if I told you, I'd be wrong. I say it in my work.

Altman '91

BEVERLY WALKER/1990

IN MID-SEPTEMBER I drove up a steep Malibu hillside to the working home of Robert Altman. Reportedly, he was back in Hollywood to make a new film called *L.A. Shortcuts*. I was eager to hear about it.

I spotted him immediately, slimmer than photos suggest, moving among his staff in a big, glass-enclosed room overlooking the Pacific. Though we'd never met, conversation began easily. One can imagine what a calm, secure presence he is for actors.

Replicas of van Gogh paintings done for his latest film, *Vincent & Theo,* lined the wall along with the British poster. The film largely received excellent reviews overseas, and the director admitted that the upcoming American release would be important to him, predicting, "It will do me some good." He could've only meant that *Vincent & Theo* proves he can make commercially viable pictures again, spelling easier access to financing and distribution.

No American filmmaker of the last 25 years has suffered the wrath of Establishment Hollywood like Robert Altman, a visionary maverick who simply couldn't play by the rules. From the release of *McCabe and Mrs. Miller* in 1971 through *Popeye* in 1980, he was our most controversial director, the center of a schism between critics and serious filmgoers on the one hand, and the purse-holders of the industry on the other.

From *Film Comment* vol. 27 (Jan.–Feb. 1991): 5–10. Reprinted by permission of Beverly Walker.

A native of Kansas City, Missouri, Altman struggled for 15 years on the margins of moviemaking, finally hitting it big in 1970 with *M*A*S*H*, starring Donald Sutherland and Elliott Gould. Though it contained certain innovations which later became trademarks, at bottom the film was a raucous, male-centered comedy set in wartime—a Hollywood staple.

Altman confounded industry bosses with his followup piece, an offbeat comedy called *Brewster McCloud*. The bosses, who thought that in Altman they'd found a deep vein of gold to be mined for years to come, were dismayed. That dismay would grow more profound: *McCabe and Mrs. Miller* was just too much of a revisionist Western (and audiovisually radical besides), and didn't "go through the roof" (which would've brought forgiveness). *Images* (1972), about a psychologically disturbed woman (Susannah York), was dismissed, but hopes perked up with his next few films, particularly *The Long Goodbye* (1973) and *California Split* (1974). Though they defied generic conventions, still they were about guys and did business. *Nashville*, released in 1975 to critical hosannahs, calmed the waters enough to lead to a big budget for *Buffalo Bill and the Indians, or Sitting Bull's History Lesson* (1976), starring Paul Newman. But *Nashville*'s box office, while respectable, came nowhere near matching its critical success, and *Buffalo Bill* achieved neither. By the time of *3 Women* in 1977, the unease about Altman had reached hurricane proportions.

Box-office performance was not the only issue—maybe not the major one, either. In addition to the director's stylistic experimentation, there was his propensity to portray women sympathetically, even make them the center of some of his movies. And most of his female characters were real contenders, neither passive victims of some type of male violence nor supportive sidekicks to a man who engineered the action. "I'd rather face a thousand crazy savages than one woman who knows how to shoot," says the guy in *3 Women* (Robert Fortier) who is ultimately done in by the troika.

The way Altman lived and worked, mostly with a coterie of the same people, was also a bone of contention. The press gleefully reported on his freewheeling lifestyle; his oft-stated disdain for unions and studios, not to mention writers ("A script is an embarkation point"); his dreams that inspired the movies. This made him great copy but also a giant-sized target. Worst of all, while other directors swallowed their pride and visions, and buckled under to the rising power of development executives, Altman

continued making patently uncommercial films with total autonomy —
four in less than three years: *A Wedding* (1978), *A Perfect Couple* (1979), *Quintet*
(1979), and *Health* (1979).

Then *Popeye* happened.

Rights to the original E.C. Segar comic strip were owned by Paramount,
which assigned Robert Evans as producer. Even before Altman came aboard,
the project had generated considerable trade babble, which steadily esca-
lated during the film's production on Malta. As usual, the director was
doing things his own way. These included hiring iconoclastic songwriter
Harry Nilsson for the music, and Canadian designer Wolf Kroeger to create
an ingenious town set. Squabbles with screenwriter Jules Feiffer came and
went, though the relationship was ultimately harmonious, but inclement
weather and special-effects snafus prolonged shooting. The budget boiled
over and with it, gossip. Paramount had been cool to Altman in the first
place; now they froze.

When finally unveiled, *Popeye* proved so original that neither the film
media nor marketing mavens quite knew what to do with it. Though it
looks like a cartoon, it is, of course, live action; and though the characters
don't *look* realistic, they feel that way. The movie has a soufflé-like delicacy
and lightness that comes from a perfect synthesis of all the elements,
including a gurgling baby — Swee'pea — that ought to melt the heart of
any mogul. Above all, it is an enchanting love story of Popeye and Olive
Oyl, heartbreakingly incarnated by Robin Williams and Shelley Duvall,
respectively.

Popeye did good business, but not enough to offset a brushfire of hostil-
ity toward Altman that caught wind throughout the industry. Too, this was
1980, when box-office figures began replacing any other consideration of a
film's worth. Very, very bad timing. Altman was, in essence, blackballed as
only the movie business can do it: No one returned his phone calls. In 1982
he sold his production company, Lion's Gate, and left the West Coast.

During the remainder of the eighties, while Hollywood atrophied, Robert
Altman challenged himself anew. He directed theater and opera in such
diverse spots as Lille (France) and Michigan; he adapted plays for the screen,
sometimes with great distinction (notably, *Come Back to the 5 and Dime,
Jimmy Dean Jimmy Dean*); when funds were lacking, he went to super-
16mm and television. Not only did he direct a superb production of *The
Caine Mutiny Court-Martial* (1988), starring Brad Davis, but, proving that the

boob tube is a noble medium in the right hands, he created *Tanner '88* (on videotape) with Garry Trudeau of *Doonesbury* fame.

At about the same time *Vincent & Theo* was being released in Europe, two of his finest seventies movies were reissued to great success: *McCabe and Mrs. Miller* in London and *The Long Goodbye* in Paris. Commentary from almost every sector of the critical/political spectrum called him "beyond a doubt one of the great creators of American cinema"; one of our "most talented . . . consistently original . . . intelligent" directors; "one of the U.S. cinema's few genuine individualists." Both EZ-TV in Los Angeles and the Anthology Film Archives in New York screened the *Tanner* miniseries; an Altman retrospective was mounted by the American Cinematheque (L.A.) and another is planned at the Sundance/United States Film Festival in January. All this for a man who has not made a mainstream, studio-based film in a decade, but who is very much alive and kicking.

Such a rising stir suggests not just belated acknowledgment of a great director, but actual *starvation* for something of worth in a new decade that dispiritingly suggests a perpetuation of the old: the hi/lo concepts, sequel fever, and ersatz emotion of the eighties continue unabated. In short, what Robert Altman's about is in short supply these days. We need him.

So the onetime lion of Lion's Gate is back, perhaps a little wiser: He's named his new company Sandcastle Productions, "to signify the impermanence of what we do." The self-protective posture is well taken because he told me immediately after entering his office that *L.A. Shortcuts* had been cancelled by Paramount.

Based on some Raymond Carver short stories, the new-film-to-be was meant to start in a couple of weeks; that's what the people in the room outside were still working on. A large cast had been assembled, whose names Altman ringingly read off from a piece of paper. "I'm afraid I'll lose them if we don't get going soon," he said in a voice so flat you knew he was sitting on a volcano of emotion.

Truly, I felt like weeping. From *McCabe and Mrs. Miller* in 1971, Altman has been my favorite American director. There are others I admire and respect, but his films pierce the soul, their moments indelible: Warren Beatty's McCabe comforting a young prostitute who has just stabbed a man; Lily Tomlin's yearning glance at Keith Carradine in *Nashville*; Shelley Duvall and Robin Williams making goo-goo eyes at each other while she sings, "He's mine."

In reseeing many of his films (more than half of the 29 features are not on videocassette), the only one I upgraded was *Jimmy Dean,* which is far better than I remembered. *McCabe, 3 Women,* and *Popeye* seem just about perfect, each mesmerizing in its own way, and *Thieves Like Us* is very fine. I still found *M*A*S*H* unpleasantly macho and remain at odds with *Nashville.*

My biases didn't perturb the director, who said he understands the absence of consensus about his work, even among diehard admirers: "When I make a film, my intention is for each person to see it differently. Really, the film doesn't *tell* you anything, it just stimulates something that opens up a channel of perception or feeling; it's a catalyst. The viewer furnishes the 'art.'"

Or the anger. Altman's painterly films with their fractured narratives and wacko characters simply drive some viewers crazy. Plot and heroics are not his bag, and for those who need them, he's infuriating. For marketing executives who're looking for a catchy one-line description, he's maddening. For others like me, his films are extremely satisfying on aesthetic, emotional, and intellectual levels—which is rare.

Preparing to interview and write about him turned out to be unexpectedly vexing, however. Like other charismatic directors who came to prominence in the early 1970s—Coppola, for example—Altman has been thoroughly mythologized. The personal myth is so pervasively intermingled with the work that it is almost impossible to track and separate them. Moreover, unlike directors such as Ingmar Bergman or François Truffaut, there is little empirically based autobiographical evidence (as opposed to conjecture), though his work is unquestionably personal, his signature unmistakable.

To step into Altman's universe is to confront a complex tapestry wherein aesthetics, philosophical musings, form and content are interwoven intricately with lifestyle and working methodology. It's hard to know where to begin even if one feels understanding and kinship. Unsurprising that the one major book published about him to date, *Robert Altman: Jumping Off the Cliff* by Patrick McGilligan, is largely a compendium of complaints and allegations by people who worked with him for years before suffering terminal disappointment. Altman felt such a book was virtually an obituary to his career, and declined to cooperate. He heard the voices calling him to take on the mantle of Orson Welles, but he didn't heed them. Above all else, he is a man of action, a doer, and he had some plans.

It's pretty tricky to interview someone with this history and under these circumstances, but he really does convey strength and determination. "Somebody will give us the money" for *L.A. Shortcuts,* he said; "it's only 12 million dollars." Then he sat down, folded his hands, set his jaw firmly, and looked at me — ready for questions.

Right after *M*A*S*H* in 1970 Altman made a very different picture with a powerful metaphor about, yes, existence. In *Brewster McCloud,* Earth is a prison whose constraints man endlessly dreams of escaping. Flight will do the trick temporarily, though performing, too, provides perspective and detachment from the hurly-burly.

In the movie's finale, a young man (Bud Cort) puts on homemade wings to fly around the Houston Astrodome during a show, but after a couple of orbits his energy flags and he drops to the ground, dead.

Foolish boy, we might murmur; but that was hardly the sum of Altman's statement. The spectators think Brewster's fall is just part of the act and they applaud enthusiastically, while other performers, equally ignorant, come out for bows around the boy's inert body. It is a chilling and unexpected ending to an otherwise shaggy-dog comedy.

The precarious nature of the artist/performer has been dealt with in other Altman films. His second feature, *The James Dean Story,* in 1957, was about the most legendary dead actor of our time; Ronee Blakley's country singing star in *Nashville* is assassinated; and in *Vincent & Theo* the artist dies without ever having sold a single painting — a point Altman underlines by opening with the multimillion-dollar Sotheby's auction of *Sunflowers.*

In these and other films like *Buffalo Bill and the Indians* or, arguably, *McCabe and Mrs. Miller* — where McCabe is clearly "putting on an act" — fans, managers, spouses are scathingly depicted. An exception of sorts is the sympathetic portrayal of Theo in the van Gogh film. This character serves as a bridge between the artist on the one hand and parasitic dealers and gallery owners, as well as the buying public, on the other. Conversely, Vincent is an example of the artist-as-devourer because he certainly helped ruin his brother's life — also underscored by Altman.

I saw *Brewster McCloud* for the first time while preparing this piece, and it immediately illuminated Altman's work as well as his life: his near-mirac-

ulous ability to stay afloat, not merely to survive but to express himself sig-
nificantly. His long struggle to become a filmmaker, begun in the
mid-fifties, had left him with an acute sense of what he was up against.
M*A*S*H's incredible success must've struck him as a fluke, gambler's luck.

It seems to me that from *Brewster McCloud* on, most of Robert Altman's
films are cautionary tales about people with illusions—though he himself
has few, and probably tries to resist the siren call of those.

Since Altman has often been called the most Icarus-like of directors, it's
de rigueur to bring it up. He smiles at the mention of *Brewster*; it's one of
his personal favorites. But he's uncomfortable with the analogy, and
dances around the subject for a bit before emitting a deep sigh. "Yes," he
nods, "the Brewster story is prophetic. You fly too high, get your wings
singed, run out of energy. Brewster was doing just fine and then he simply
ran out of steam.

"He overreached, I guess. But overreaching is exciting. 'Course, it's also
what kills you, but what the hell. . . . I've been criticized for not knowing
how to do an ending—and I don't: the only ending I know is death. But I
don't think death is stopping; it just eliminates that particular computer."

Then he lightens up, chuckling as he recalls another of *Brewster*'s scien-
tific theorems which compare men with birds. The scientist, played by
René Auberjonois, intones, "If we build enclosures to protect both men
and birds, will men allow birds in or put them out?" Altman remembers
the words *exactly*. And: "The importance of song to a bird can be partially
determined by how long the bird devotes to it."

Altman rewrote the screenplay (by Doran William Cannon) upon which
Brewster is based, and it is unquestionably as meaningful to him today as
in 1970. He points out that, as he was making *Brewster*, its studio, Metro-
Goldwyn-Mayer, was being dismantled.

Man is like a bird and needs freedom; a movie's a song; a studio can be a
cage. Then there is the extremely pessimistic ending of *Brewster*, with its
juxtaposition of the dead performer and the laughing/clapping audience.
Altman raises an eyebrow slightly, as if his meaning were self-evident, and
says, "People who watch don't die."

People who watch don't die. There is a trace of real bitterness in that comment. Perhaps it is the quintessential vise of all artists: how to reconcile
the ability to make the art with the need for appreciation—from onlook-

ers—which allows the artist to continue. And almost nowhere is this more crucial than in cinema, because of cost. Movies must have paying "watchers."

I ask Altman how he got the nerve to make films like *3 Women, Quintet,* and *Health,* which have no conventional storyline. He gives all the credit to Alan Ladd Jr., head of Twentieth Century Fox when the films were made. "He had great faith in me; he put his own job on the line."

A long pause ensues, during which I don't feel the need to point out that Ladd's backing of these films did not stand him in good stead within the industry. Then Altman continues: "But I don't feel guilty because I didn't have anything else to offer at the time. I'm a collaborative artist; I want to see things I've never seen before. Anything that triggers me, if it fits, I wear it."

So this acrid view of the watcher is also an asset, because it blinds him to certain realities of the marketplace and strengthens his resolve to say things his own way.

Which brings us to *Vincent & Theo,* a film whose exquisite, voluptuous images intensify a harrowing story of two brothers—one an artist, the other a seller of art. It is Altman's most searing, overtly despairing film ever, and it has been widely interpreted as his own personal statement.

But on this mild September day, Robert Altman rejects such facile presumptions. "Well, the story happened. Those people existed and the conditions of their lives [were] probably worse than I depicted, since they were not aware of the totality of their lives. We all adjust the past to suit ourselves. . . .

"But I am not Vincent van Gogh—I'm the luckiest person I know. I have had many successes, and I'm able to look in the faces of people after they've seen my films, faces which glow. One time in Paris a guy came right up to me . . . I thought he might hit me . . . and he started babbling about 'that movie called *3 Women,* when the yellow skirt got caught in the door.' That is my reward.

"I've had my ups and downs, but I'm on the top of a rollercoaster and van Gogh never got off the ground. He overcame so much. He was not a gifted draftsman; he had no imagination, no ideas. But his incredible passion did come through, not to the dealers but to people, eventually, somehow. It's an astonishing phenomenon and it tells you something about art. Art is not a skill, though that's part of it. It's a passion."

Yes, and that point is made all the way through *Vincent & Theo.* Art is about emotions, not ideas, and art does not merely replicate reality. Van Gogh is overwhelmed by the field of sunflowers—the frame of the movie itself cannot contain it—and he is able to paint them only when he plucks a handful from the earth and sticks them in a vase.

It's interesting to note that whereas Kurosawa, in his *Dreams,* depicts van Gogh as a joyfully mad painter in love with, and at one with, nature, Altman shows us the pain, frustration, and bewilderment.

Altman also rejects the notion of *Vincent & Theo* being more linear or conventional than his other pictures. "When I saw it in Toronto, I thought it was bizarre, the way the blocks are put together. When I was planning the film I knew the audience would have a lot of information about van Gogh, and for that reason I wouldn't have to deal with too many linear things, I could pick and choose, show glimpses. I took the position that the movie itself was a show about Vincent and Theo and the paintings, done by me. That's how I organized it in my mind."

Altman has long referred to his films as "paintings" and the actors as "living pigment," so *Vincent & Theo* provided a unique opportunity for synthesis. The film's performances—Tim Roth as the painter, Paul Rhys as his brother, and Wladimir Yordanoff as Gauguin—are vivid and unclichéd and, as in most Altman movies, do not secretly beg for our sympathy and understanding. They exist "existentially," as it were, and command us to take them straight, like a shot of strong whiskey.

The way Altman depicts human beings is his most critical attribute as an artist. Every aspect of filmmaking art is put at the service of his perception of people: the famous use of overlapping sound, his probing closeups, canny cutting. Who else would have given us Shelley Duvall? Many stars, in particular Warren Beatty, Cher, Elliott Gould, show us something of themselves in his films which we never see again.

"When an actor comes in to see me, of course I have an idea of what the character should be. But I want always to see what the actor brings to it. If the vision were just mine, just a single vision, it wouldn't be any good. It's the combination of what I have in mind, with who the actor is and then how he adjusts to the character, along with how I adjust, that makes the movie."

Then the actors really are extremely, urgently important to you, I commented, and he replied, "They are *everything.*"

Though his printed words don't show it, Altman's body language and tone during the interview often revealed discomfort with the questions and resistance to analysis. I apologized for "trying to pin you down when you don't want to be."

"I'm telling you all I know!" he laughed. "I open myself up to my work as much as I possibly can, and if I feel an obligation to disguise a thought, I do. But I don't intellectualize it, not as I'm doing it."

Utterly uninterested in heroes and heroism, Altman gives us the walking wounded—characters who are scarred, foolish, vain—somehow never quite smart enough. His closeups lay out their foibles with the delicacy and precision of a brain surgeon. Yet he does not mock, judge, or romanticize them.

How, I asked, does he finesse all this? A look of pleased astonishment suffused his face and he said, "But that's my trick, that's what I strive for. That's *me*." Enough said.

Robert Altman and *The Long Goodbye*

MICHAEL WILMINGTON / 1991

The Filmmaker

ROBERT ALTMAN IS ONE of the American cinema's most innovative mavericks and one of the most high-profile filmmaking talents to emerge in the 1970s. He was nominated for Academy Awards for directing *M*A*S*H* (1970), *Nashville* (1975), and *The Player* (1992).

A prolific television director through the 1960s on such series as *Combat* and *Bonanza*, Altman progressed to feature films with *Countdown* (1968) and made an auspicious international showing with the antiwar satire *M*A*S*H*, which was named best film of the year by the National Society of Film Critics and received the Golden Palm at the 1970 Cannes Film Festival. For the next six years, he was one of the most critically admired filmmakers in the world, delivering such extraordinary films as *McCabe and Mrs. Miller* (1971), *Images* (1972), *The Long Goodbye* (1973), and *Thieves Like Us* (1974).

His reputation peaked with *Nashville,* a multileveled look at the country-music industry. *Nashville* was named best picture of the year and Altman was selected as best director by both the National Society of Film Critics and the New York Film Critics Circle.

Afterwards Altman's career took a few dives and spins. While he could still reap critical appreciation for *3 Women* (1977) and *A Wedding* (1978),

From *Movie Talk from the Front Lines: Filmmakers Discuss Their Works with the Los Angeles Film Critics Association,* ed. Jerry Roberts and Steven Gaydos (Jefferson: McFarland & Company, 1995), 253–73. Reprinted by permission of Steven Gaydos and Jerry Roberts.

most of his films in the late seventies and early eighties failed to find a wide audience. In fact, his two films with Paul Newman, *Buffalo Bill and the Indians, or, Sitting Bull's History Lesson* (1976) and *Quintet* (1979), were box-office flops.

Through the eighties, Altman turned to the stage for material and filmed several critically appreciated but narrowly distributed films, including *Come Back to the 5 and Dime, Jimmy Dean Jimmy Dean* (1982), *Streamers* (1983), and *Secret Honor* (1984). He also returned to television, where his political satire, *Tanner '88* (1988), was widely regarded as one of the best programs of the year. Altman's late-career television work also includes *The Laundromat* (1984), *The Caine Mutiny Court-Martial* (1987), *The Dumb Waiter* (1987), and *The Room* (1987).

The success of *The Player,* an outstanding satire of the manipulations behind the operations of a major Hollywood studio, returned Altman to frontrank prominence. It was named best picture of the year, and Altman was selected as best director, by the New York Film Critics Circle.

Altman's use of mobile cameras and his ability to elicit extemporaneous performances from a wide variety of actors and to imbue his best films with a quirky sense of irony have made him one of the most distinguished postwar American directors. His best films expose the sham of American institutions and subvert hypocrisy on a general basis.

Reasons for Selection

Robert Altman is one of the most important and creative figures of the 1970s and, indeed, of right now. Like many of the best directors who emerged in the seventies, Altman had a problem making it through the eighties. How does a creative or innovative or audacious or offbeat or off-center American director make it through a period when his kinds of films are not appreciated, not sponsored, not encouraged, and when, in fact, the basic emphasis was on the mass audience's simple emotion, on simple stories, and on glowing technical expertise?

Altman always stood for something different. He stood for going out there, for exploring—more specifically, for going out there in terms of how the actors were handled, of the spontaneity of his ensemble performances, and of how the camera was handled. One of the aspects discussed with *The Long Goodbye* is a kind of major visual innovation that Altman started with this specific film: a floating kind of camera work.

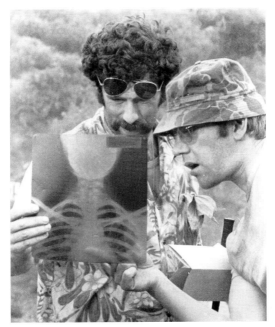

Elliott Gould and Donald Sutherland,
*M*A*S*H*, 1970

Carl Gottlieb, David Arkin, Tom Skerritt, John Schuck, Donald Sutherland,
and Elliott Gould, *M*A*S*H*, 1970

Julie Christie and Warren Beatty, *McCabe & Mrs. Miller*, 1971

Warren Beatty, Julie Christie, and Robert Altman, *McCabe & Mrs. Miller*, 1971

Robert Altman, Elliott Gould, Nina Van Pallandt, and Henry Gibson, *The Long Goodbye*, 1973

Barbara Harris, *Nashville*, 1975

Lily Tomlin, *Nashville*, 1975

Ronee Blakley and Henry Gibson, *Nashville*, 1975

Shelley Duvall and Robin Williams, *Popeye*, 1980

Whoopi Goldberg and Tim Robbins, *The Player*, 1992

Tim Robbins, *The Player*, 1992

Robert Altman on the set of *The Player*, 1992

Tim Robbins and Greta Scacchi, *The Player*, 1992

Tim Robbins and Frances McDormand, *Short Cuts*, 1993

Lily Tomlin and Tom Waits, *Short Cuts*, 1993

The Long Goodbye is, of course, based on the Raymond Chandler novel. The film was regarded in its time as scandalous simply because the whole Chandler milieu was updated to southern California in the 1970s and because Elliott Gould was seen as an eccentric Philip Marlowe, which indeed he is. The screenwriter, however, is Leigh Brackett, who, along with William Faulkner, adapted what has turned out to be the most highly regarded of all the previous Marlowe adaptations, Howard Hawks's *Big Sleep* (1946, with Humphrey Bogart).

In both using Brackett and then casting somebody like Elliott Gould and the rest of a typically eccentric cast, Altman was both making a statement on the genre and on how that genre collides with the reality of the time. There are lots of levels to *The Long Goodbye*; there are lots of ways to appreciate it. And it is a film that, to a certain degree, you have to work to get into. Maybe that is why it was not as appreciated in its time as it should have been, but why its reputation has held up.

MICHAEL WILMINGTON: *I just wanted to mention some of the people in that ensemble because it is kind of a very strange cast. Jim Bouton, who plays Terry Lennox, some of you might not remember, was basically known at the time as a pitcher for the New York Yankees and author of a book called* Ball Four, *a tell-all book. And Nina Van Pallandt was—what association did she have with Clifford Irving?*

ROBERT ALTMAN: Clifford Irving was the guy who wrote the fake Howard Hughes biography and went to jail for it. And she was his girlfriend, and she got in the news quite a bit. She had been a folksinger before that in Europe. I saw her on *The Tonight Show* when she was being interviewed by Johnny Carson because of that Clifford Irving scandal, and she was considered sort of a femme fatale. And Bouton was considered sort of a rat because of this book he wrote. He made some money and ratted on all his friends. Anyway, this was the first film for both of them.

MW: *Now, Mark Rydell, who does a great job as Marty Augustine, is better known as a film director. He directed* On Golden Pond, The Rose, *and* For the Boys. *Henry Gibson, who plays Dr. Verringer, was a comedian out of* Laugh-In, *and he also does a great bit in* Nashville.

RA: Dan Blocker was going to play the Roger Wade part, and he died from what was known as one of those botched operations. Dan was also a very,

very close friend of mine. And I abandoned the picture at that point. I was in Europe, and I said I wasn't going to go through with it. Then Sterling Hayden came up as an idea. Sterling was sort of a character living in Europe then, and he couldn't come back in this country because he owed so many taxes. Or he could get into the country, but he couldn't work. So we had to kind of pay him surreptitiously, and we had a lot of intrigue. And you might have recognized Arnold Schwarzenegger in that. I think that was the first film he ever made. I don't think he talks about this film very much. He didn't talk in this film very much, but he had almost as much to say as he does in most of his films.

MW: *Actually, I think he may have done one other film before this. I think he did a film called* Hercules Goes Bananas *[a.k.a.* Hercules in New York, *1970], in which he was billed as Arnold Strong.*

RA: Yeah, he was Arnold Strong. He was introduced to me as Arnold Strong in this.

MW: *I'd also like to say a few words about the technical people behind this film because with Altman there's always an ensemble—whether it's the actors or the crew people. And recently I was a few days on the set of his current film,* The Player, *which is a terrific film. It's probably one of the best backstage Hollywood movies I've ever seen. It'll be out sometime next year. And I watched it through a lot of the preparations. But in this particular film there's kind of an ensemble going that was associated with Bob [Altman] from his early days—people like Tommy Thompson, Vilmos Zsigmond, who was also the cinematographer on* McCabe and Mrs. Miller, *which is often described as one of the great color films of the seventies. [Vilmos Zsigmond was named best cinematographer of the year by the National Society of Film Critics for his work on* The Long Goodbye.*] Lou Lombardo, who is the editor, was associated with Bob for a long time, and he's really one of the great editors. He did* The Wild Bunch.

RA: Alan Rudolph was the second AD [assistant director] on [*The Long Goodbye*].

MW: *This is a film which really conveys the atmosphere of its time and its period better than very few [sic] that I've seen. It's kind of a double-period piece because Marlowe comes out of this Southern California of the forties that*

Chandler was talking about, but the milieu that he's in is the Southern California of the seventies. And there's sort of a collision between the two, and that's one of the basic, primary things in the film. And I wondered if you can talk about that and how you developed the whole idea?

R A :   The approach we decided to use was to make the book. I don't know if any of you read *The Long Goodbye*, but it's almost impossible to comprehend. I honestly never finished it. But I became fascinated with the way in which Chandler used these plots in stories not for the story's sake but to hang a bunch of thumbnail essays about this city, the time. And that's really what my feeling is about the basis of what his writing was. There was a book that was at the time called *Raymond Chandler Speaking* [edited by Dorothy Gardiner and Kathrine Sorley Walker], which was a small volume of his essays and letters and just writings of his. And I gave that book to everybody who worked on the film. I said, "Don't worry about reading *The Long Goodbye*, but read this about Raymond Chandler." And Leigh Brackett, who had written the screenplay, made certain changes—liberal changes from the book—and I tried to reflect more on Raymond Chandler than on his story. The character of Roger Wade to me represented Raymond Chandler. In the book I think he got murdered. I don't think he committed suicide. I had him commit suicide because Chandler tried to commit suicide, but he didn't have the guts to shoot himself. He couldn't stand the thought of it, so he went into the shower and shot the gun off five times, hoping the ricochet would get him. But all it did was alert the neighbors, and they called the police. And he never succeeded in that. So he just waited and died, you know, another suicide like the rest of us. I said, "Let's take this guy out of the forties because there's no such thing as these private eyes. They don't exist as such." And we put him in 1973. We called him Rip Van Marlowe. He was still in the forties, but suddenly he was in this period. And we made that the main kind of texture we were trying to deal with. And also we wanted everybody to know it was a movie.

M W :   *Well, there's also a kind of a critique of macho in the film, too, or machismo, in a variety of the characters, going straight through from Marlowe to Wade—who's kind of Hemingwayesque, too—as well as Chandler. And then Marty Augustine, of course, who's completely off the wall. And how's that character in the book?*

RA: There wasn't much. He had not much character to him in the book, as I remember. He was more of a plot device. He was a name. He was, you know, the gangster.

MW: *Well, how did you develop that character with Mark Rydell?*

RA: Mark and Johnny Williams, who did the music for this, they had finished a film with John Wayne, *The Cowboys* [1972] or something, and here we were all in Europe at this time. And so I asked Mark to play this. Then, I remember, we were at my house, and we decided to go down to the beach and have dinner, and we went to some place. And this girl who played Jo Ann—the girl who got the Coke bottle—was waiting on us. And I noticed this profile in the light, and I said, "Look at this girl." I think we were drinking a little bit—probably. And I said, "Look at that nose." And I said, "Here's what we ought to do." And we kind of came up with this Coke bottle thing at the time.

So I asked her, and I said, "Listen, this is going to sound funny to you, but we're making a film, and we'd like to put you in this movie." She says, "OK, bud, move on." And we said, "No, no." We finally convinced her, and then it turned out that none of us had any money or any credit cards, so she didn't believe us, but anyway we did put her in the film, and this was her first film.

MW: *So you kind of worked out that character with Mark?*

RA: With Mark, and everybody collaborated. I mean, Elliott particularly was real helpful.

MW: *Now, where did you get the idea of casting Elliott as Philip Marlowe? Because that actually was the one thing at the time that critics jumped on. Elliott Gould had a very familiar persona. He was sort of lovable, dopey, and a nebbish at the time. And when he was cast as Philip Marlowe, a lot of people really couldn't look past that.*

RA: Well, I think, however, that most of the people who objected, they weren't talking about Chandler's Philip Marlowe. I think they were talking about Humphrey Bogart or Hawks's Philip Marlowe.

MW: *Who's very, very different from the book—Hawks's Philip Marlowe.*

RA: Yeah, he is as well. So, but Gould—I didn't want to make this picture. I had just finished a film called *Images*. I made *M*A*S*H* and *Brewster*

McCloud and this little film, *Images*, in Ireland. And these guys who had the rights to this—Jerry Bick and Elliott Kastner—who kept pushing me, would I do this? And would I do that? And I said no. Then I read Leigh Brackett's script, and there was this thing that she had put in this script where Marlowe kills his friend, which, again, also wasn't in the book. That was interesting to me. And they said, "Well, we're going to change that, of course." And I said, "OK, I'll do this on one condition: that you don't change that ending and that we don't cast Robert Mitchum"—who was, at that time, I guess, the ideal Marlowe. And I love Mitchum, I think he's wonderful. Gould had worked for me in *M*A*S*H*, and he just seemed right. They went for it to get the picture made, I guess.

MW: *Looking at him this time, he seemed a lot more like a forties character than I remember thinking of him at the time.*
RA: Well, we put him the forties, you know. He smoked all those cigarettes. By all means he should be dead now, but he's not.

MW: *What about the stream-of-consciousness cracks that he's using?*
RA: A lot of that was improvised, and he came up with that phrase, "It's OK with me." And we sort of used that as the key thing with all of these things that were happening. If you remember, in the early seventies there were quite a lot of social changes going on.

MW: *Do you want to talk about that for a second? Because this is a film that's very, very saturated in its time.*
RA: I had a really nice trip down memory lane. I haven't seen this film for over ten years. I don't think things are any different, but they seem to be, I guess.

MW: *One of the reasons why I was excited about showing the film is that you were telling me about certain various camera techniques that you developed in this film that you hadn't used before.*
RA: Well, in the first place, this print is fading. This film's not 20 years old yet. It's 18 years old or something like that. It's gone. And I'm just thinking about how many others have the color gone from the negative. At this time, it would have cost them $9,000 to make a color separation, and they just wouldn't do it. And so this film is gone. I don't know what held it up,

but it finally came out on cassette just recently. I think it's available now some places, but most people don't know about it.

But I had done a thing in a few scenes in *Images,* this film I had just finished before *The Long Goodbye,* in which I had used the camera going counter to what the action was. And the idea struck me. I had liked it so much in *Images* I thought, God, we could do a whole film this way because it puts the audience in a little different position. And the idea was that the camera was always moving laterally, in and out, just in different directions, but never where it should have been necessarily. The cuts aren't clean. We weren't getting good framing. And we weren't trying for it. If the close-up is on the line, it should be—if it came on his back or somebody's blocking him, that was OK, we did it. And the idea is that it puts the audience in a position of, well—we're telling you that we're not going to serve this up to you. You better pay attention and watch it and follow it because you may miss the most important things. And we dealt with the dialogue that way. We dealt with the plot that way. And it frustrated a lot of people. A lot of people don't like this film at all. If this were a regular paid audience, half of them would have been gone, I think. Half of you would have been gone. But that was the idea of putting a little tension back into the audience. It's just that simple thing: You gotta pay attention or you're going to miss it.

MW: *Well, everything you're talking about implies that this movie, in addition to being a Hollywood genre project, which is the way it starts out, is a very experimental film. And obviously that experimentation comes out of the period. There was a period in American studio moviemaking from the late sixties through the mid-seventies—maybe Jaws and Steven Spielberg helped to kill it off—when there was a lot more experimentation in subject matter and acting techniques and in camera techniques. Could you talk a little bit about that period?*
RA: Well, no. What we were trying to do is say, "C'mon, how many of these can you see? How many private eyes, the blonde?" And, I mean, in every one of these films, the plots are the same, the suspense is the same. Everything is just pressing buttons that we know that work, get you to cry, or frighten you. And it's not hard to frighten you. You can jump at somebody, and they respond. So I was trying to always approach these kinds of stories differently. I saw no point in making this story. This story was meaningless, I felt. I felt that Chandler was not meaningless. And I felt that the

film was almost an essay, an education, to the audience, to say, "Stop looking at everything exactly the same way." And the fun of films for me is the discovery in seeing things. It's not in necessarily getting caught up in how believable this is, but to make fun of ourselves. So we constantly made references. And told the audience, "Gosh, this is a movie. This is just a movie. Another lousy movie."

MW: *Was that a reference to* The Third Man *there at the end, when he goes through the trees?*

RA: I don't recall what a lot of the references were, but anything that would occur to me that reminded me of films, I would just use it. I mean, we just did it. It wasn't really thought out in great detail. It wasn't the preparation. There was not an art director on this film. We would just pick these locations and arrive and move the stuff around. And so it was not finely crafted, as all of the films that we see today are. One of the best things that you can say about many films is, "Boy, they're sure made well." But so what?

MW: *You talked about the fact that the film is about Chandler and you had his ruminations given to everybody in the cast. Could you describe your take on the core of Raymond Chandler, since he's become almost a bigger cultural figure now than he was in the forties?*

RA: I feel what Chandler did was use the detective story or the private-eye pulp stories to hold the audience there. And while he had them there, he gave them all these little thumbnail essays that he kept hanging up on the line. Probably in one of the best passages I feel in *The Long Goodbye* was Chandler's first description of the Eileen Wade character, of Chandler's blonde. And I was more interested in the casting. I was more interested in getting Chandler's blonde than I was in getting some actress that could cry and work her way through those things. I mean, I wasn't looking for a skilled actress, although Nina turned out to be just wonderful. And I think Chandler did this. And I think I was doing the same thing. And that's where I felt my affinity to Raymond Chandler. So the whole thing kind of fit together.

By this time, I had made not very many movies, but I had made a few, and I had made a lot of television shows. And when I used to make television shows, I would look at these scripts and I would think, "Jesus, I've got to stop this. I can't do this." And I would try to think of some old movie, and I'd say, "OK, this will be the secret agent, or this will be this kind of movie." And with all those television shows I would do, I would try to put references in to tell the audience, "This is just another lousy movie." And [*The Long Goodbye*] just afforded the opportunity for me. And it just fit.

AUDIENCE QUESTION: *I've noticed that if you have any singular trade-mark, it's the ability to have a lot of characters talking all at the same time. And yet you still get certain things that they're saying that the audience should be hearing. I wondered how you came out with that concept, and whether it evolved or was just something you came up with for* M*A*S*H *and then just did with other films?*

RA: No. In many of the Howard Hawks films, overlapping dialogue was used. Jack Warner fired me one time. I made a picture called *Countdown*. He was out of the country, and he came back, and he saw it, and he threw me off the lot. I mean he literally locked me off the lot and would not allow me back in. And he said, "That fool has actors talking at the same time." And—my feeling is—of course, movies come from theater and theater is based on words because those people are always quite a distance away from you. So the structure of the words is very important. And in our lives we don't hear everything. We hear what we want to. We don't have to. We make our own minds up. We hear a smattering of a conversation, and we kind of get it, and that's really all we need. And I feel that once an audience has to work to help make the story by the way they perceive it, and they're picking things out—their own clues out on the way—that it becomes more enjoyable for them. They become a participant. You come and meet the screen halfway. And so, it's just trying to further that. I mean, I think it's dreadful what they do on television now, or have been for twenty or thirty years, which is, they say they got to repeat the line, and they got to be sure the audience gets everything. Well, the audience gets everything. But when you're told, and everything is underlined, you stop working. You sit back, and you don't really care. How many television shows, or even films that you now put on the VCR, can you get up in the middle of, walk out and come back in, and you never miss anything. I mean, you can pick it up—you weren't there when he said, "Oh, so-and-so killed her." You come back in and say, "What happened?" And he says, "I don't know, what do you think?" "Well, she probably killed him." You go right along with it because you're doing this. Well, I just tried to do the same thing and put that same thing to work in the films.

MW: *But there are specific devices that you also used to get overlapping conversations, like multitrack [sound recording].*

RA: I made *Thieves Like Us* after this with it. Anyway, this was shot with just a regular single microphone and boom and that sort of thing. But in *California Split* I actually had built for us eight-track machines because that's the way they were doing music then, and so I could separate on microphones. And we don't even put looping clauses in the contracts with actors anymore. On most films today, the actors will come back in, and they sit there and every line, 80 percent of the lines are redone because the producers—they want clarity, they want to be sure that everybody understands. I think there are various ways to get it.

AQ: *How did you approach the filming of Los Angeles in this film? How do you think about the role of the city in it?*

RA: I didn't pay much attention to it. I wasn't trying to do very much. The beach. You know, we did the Malibu thing, and up in the Hollywood Hills. I didn't pay a great deal of attention to it, I'm sorry to say.

AQ: *Mr. Altman, I remembered when this film first came out that you had a heck of a time getting it into theaters. I think it was released and then it was withdrawn, and then there was a new ad campaign or something about that. Could you comment on that?*

RA: United Artists—they didn't like the film very much. They opened it in Los Angeles and in Chicago and a few other cities. They did not open it in New York, and their ad campaign showed Elliott Gould with a 45 looking like Mitchum, and people went in to see a real honest-to-God thriller, and they didn't like this. They thought this was silly and they left. So I had big arguments with the distributors. And I said, "You know, you've got to let people know that this is a comedy, or this is a satire, or something. You got to tell them the kind of film it is. Not the kind of film that it isn't." I'm probably going to have this same argument next month on the film I just finished [*The Player*]. I mean, nothing's ever changed. But then we went ahead and *Mad* magazine did a kind of an ad for us.

MW: *Jack Davis.*

RA: Jack Davis did some [artwork]. We opened in New York, and this picture became a big, big hit in New York. And had that been the original opening, the film, we feel, would have gone through the country and would have been a big moneymaker. But it was too late because these other markets had already been dissipated.

AQ: *You did a movie [inaudible].*

MW: *OK, I'll repeat the question. A question about* O.C. and Stiggs, *a long-shelved teenage movie. What happened to it? And a question about Tina Louise.*

RA: Tina Louise? Oh, I thought she was wonderful. We did a film six years ago called *O.C. and Stiggs* [in which Tina Louise played the sexy school nurse]. And it was during the time when a lot of these teenage exploitation films became a big marketing thing. And this film came up, and I thought, well, good, I'll make this film. And it was a spinoff from *Mad* magazine, but I made it. And it was really a satire on teenage exploitation films, and what it really was, was an adult exploitation film. And, so, immediately, test marketing had just then become the cat's pajamas. And, so, they took this film to 400 kids from Canoga Park and asked them about it. And, of course, it didn't test well, and so they never released the film. That picture was simply never released.

AQ: *The magnificent movie* 3 Women—*has that been restored? And will it ever be on video?*

RA: You know, what they put on video goes in direct relationship to what the marketing did. The picture that made the most money and the most people saw is what they make the most prints of and what they push. It should be the other way. But nobody does that.

MW: *Talking about* 3 Women—*Bob has a lot of great stories. My personal favorite is about how he conceived the story of* 3 Women.

RA: Well, *3 Women* was a dream, literally. I didn't dream the movie, but I dreamed I was making it. It was during the time I was going to make the film *Easy and Hard Ways Out*, with Peter Falk. And it was a comedy. It was a book about guys working in a computer-manufacturing business, and it was a big comedy. I think it was the David Geffen Company that was going to pay for it, and they wanted me to direct. There were some airplanes in it. And this movie was made later, I think, with Eddie Murphy.

MW: Best Defense *[1984]*.

RA: I said, "OK, these airplanes that crash." I said, "I wanted that done in the Six Day War," which had just happened about that time in Egypt and Israel. And they said, "Oh, no, you can't do that." So, I just said, "I'm not going to do this. You guys are trying to manufacture this thing away from what it is." And so I quit. I was kind of in trouble because I didn't have a job, and my wife was very sick at the time. Very sick. But she's become fine. And I was living at Malibu. And I didn't know what I was going to do. I'd lost this picture. I had a lot of people working for me at the time, and I was, literally, out of money. And I was quite worried. I went to bed. My wife was in the hospital—an emergency hospital. My son, Matthew, came and got in bed with me, and I had this dream. I dreamed the title for *3 Women*. I dreamed of the people: Shelley Duvall and Sissy Spacek. I dreamed that it was a film about personality theft, and I would wake up in the middle of the night, and I'd take a pad from the side of my bed, and I'd write down this thing. Then Bob Eggenweiler and Tommy Thompson would come into my bedroom, and I'd say, "We want to shoot this thing in the desert, so why don't you guys go down and look for a location like this?" Then I would go back to sleep, and I would come back up and write more notes, and then finally in the morning I woke up. Of course, I didn't write anything in the middle of the night. There's no note pad at my bed. But my bed was full of sand from Matthew sleeping in the bed because it came out of his ears. And I dreamed that I was just making this film, and I got up and I became very depressed. So I called Scotty Bushnell, who worked with me, still. I said, "Listen, I read a short story last night, and I think it's pretty good. How does this sound to you?" And I kind of vamped this thing. They said, "Can you get the rights to it?" And I said, "You bet." And I really developed it. Nine days later we had a deal, and we were on our way to Palm Springs. That's how *3 Women* was born.

AQ: *Can you talk about postflashing in* The Long Goodbye, *and the lighting perhaps?*

RA: Postflashing, which we did in *The Long Goodbye*, is when you take the negative of the film and you expose it to light before it's shot. And you expose it to certain percentages. We had done a little bit of that before. And what it does is it cuts the contrast down and it fogs the film, actually. We did it in order to get this kind of glare that I wanted from Los Angeles in this. It was ignorant, I later decided. And we fogged this film 100 percent, and we shot all of it that way. And I'm sure that it also helps the deterioration of the negative. I think we advanced it about ten years ourselves.

AQ: *Isn't that a scary thing to do?*

RA: Yeah, but it's pretty much controlled. And, again, so what? What can go wrong? I mean, you saw the scratches on this film. You know, when we're making the thing, and if you saw scratches like this, we'd shoot ourselves. You'd say, "We can't release the film." But the prints are out in theaters for only five days and they're looking like this. You take a chance and so what? So what goes wrong? As I say, it's just another lousy movie.

AQ: *Were you influenced by any particular European filmmakers during the making of your films in the early seventies?*

RA: Yes, I was influenced to make *Images*, for instance. I never would have made it had Bergman not made *Persona* [1966]. Fellini was an influence. I could name lots of filmmakers that I like. But I think probably, in retrospect, that the most influence of other filmmakers that I've had are bad ones. And you learn and you say, "I'm never going to do that." So you eliminate a lot of stuff that traps. My feeling about this kind of art—or all art—is that you pick up all this information. You pick up information that you don't even know you have. And if you trust it, it'll come there for your use when you want to use it. So I don't really know when I can consciously say I'm going to make this just like something I saw—then I try to avoid that. My feeling is to really go by the instincts and dreams in sleep. I mean, many times we've had a problem about, "What are we really going to do tomorrow?" And I'll just say, "Tomorrow? When it comes time that we'll have to do it, we'll think of something." And I've never been really stuck. When something does happen, and I think a lot of times you just giggle and give in and let what information you have in your head, in your computer, fight its own way out instead of being so methodical and so careful. They make these films now—and I'm not criticizing—I mean, I don't think I can make the films like *Batman* with this kind of technical expertise. I think I'd fall asleep. It takes so long to make everything so perfect. And when it's all so perfect, what is it? I mean, I found that in all of this art, what I'm looking for the most are errors and mistakes. If I shoot 200,000 feet of film and I cut it down to a two-hour film, what stays in the film are the mistakes—all the little things where the actor stumbles or somebody does something interesting. Shelley Duvall in *3 Women* closed the door and her skirt stuck out the door, and we said, "Do that every time." You know, things go wrong because that's human, and the audience identifies with that. I just feel if you get too clever and too smart and everything is calculated, it comes out that way. It comes out very rigid and you know, it's a yawn.

AQ: *Given your feelings about underlining things for the audience and also given the rather loose improvisational style of your movies, how would you respond to people who find that your own style in its own way is rather manipulative, especially in the use of your zoom lens?*

RA: Well, it *is* manipulative and, you know, may not even be very attractive to some people. I promise you that everybody is not going to like this picture or any film—I mean, any film I've made or anybody else has made, because if you don't tune into it, if you don't go with it, why should you like it? I think that. And, of course, it's manipulative. Sometimes, I wished it was not. I see things that I think, "God, I hit that too hard." But I feel that in making all these pictures you've got a big frozen pond of thin ice, and I've got to walk from one side to another, and it takes a hundred steps. As long as I don't step too hard in any of the hundred steps, I'm OK. But if in one place you go too hard, the whole thing's gone. So, the zoom lens, the attention to it, the moving in—many times I'm doing that to show you that I'm doing that, so that I know that you know that that's what I'm doing. And, again, I come back to the thing of *so what?* I mean, I'm not trying to create those other kinds of films. That's not to say that if everybody made films this way it would be dreadful. Filmmakers are like painters. You can like this painter and not like that painter. You can admire this painter and not be moved by them. You can say, "God, the craft in this is wonderful." All of these things are open to you. There's no right or wrong.

Sometimes—usually, generally—I try to take the position of, where do I want to put the audience? I say, "OK, this is where the camera is." And I'll sit there and shoot the scene. I'll shoot it maybe six, seven times, and always I shoot the entire scene. I don't stop and do one close-up for three lines—and any time I say always, that's a lie. There are always exceptions to that. And I sit there and I try to say: "This is where the audience is. This is where I'm going to look at it from." And I try to almost create an event and then shoot it the best I can from that position. I'm hoping that the audience falls in tune with me and goes with it. Most of them don't.

MW: *Given that you're talking about the camera style, there is something really unique about your working relationship with your cinematographer and your camera operator on the film. I'm wondering if you can describe that a little because there's kind of a documentary aspect to it as well.*

RA: Yeah, there is a documentary aspect to it because I'm not trying to deny the fact that the camera is there. I'm not trying to carry you. I just don't make those kinds of films. For the last ten years, I've been working with two Canadian cameramen, Pierre Mignot and Jean Lapine. I shot a film called *Fool for Love*, on which Robby Müller was the cameraman because these guys weren't available at the time and I had to start. And he's a great cameraman. I mean, really a great cameraman. And we got down to New Mexico and started shooting, and suddenly I'm seeing these beautiful pictures, but I don't know how to make this kind of movie. And I stopped after nine days, and I said, "You know, we have to get divorced." I said, "You're making a beautiful movie. I don't want a beautiful movie." And by that time, Pierre was finished, and he came down and shot it. And it's a terrible thing to happen. But there was no communication about what we both wanted. We were just making two kinds of movies.

So I tell Pierre or Jean or whoever the cameraman would happen to be, and I let him go. And I say, "If you find something interesting, shoot it." I know what I need to cut to make the movie, what I need to have. But when he's shooting, if he sees an actor doing something or something's happened, he can go for that. He does not have to go where we said it's going to go. That's why my lighting isn't as good. Real good artistic cameramen don't like to work with me too much because they've got to have the room lit for 270 degrees—at least one eighty. And mostly when they light for a position where the camera doesn't move—I mean, you can do just beautiful stuff. But the minute you move this far, the lighting is atrocious. So the lighting has to be general so it can cover my moving from one side to another. And all these things come to bear on it. It's just a matter, again, of choice. It's not a matter that one way is better than another. It's just different.

AQ: *If you were starting out now, how would you go about making the films that you wanted to make?*

ALTMAN: I don't know how to answer that question. I just show up and go to work and follow my instincts. That's what I did on the last film I did, and that's what I did on the first film.

AQ: *I'm wondering, how do you now—and in the period of* The Long Goodbye—*keep track of what the cameraman is shooting? Do you or have you ever used a video?*

RA: I use now a video assist. I give one to the sound. Black and white. Very small video assist. I have one that is very mobile, one close to me. I don't record on it because I don't want people to look at it and run back and see what it was. And all that does is tell me what framing he has, so I don't have to go up and say, "Did you get it when she smiled?" or "Where was your lens when this happened?"

I'm looking through the camera all the time. I watch the actors live, usually. But I always have the reference of what the shot is. When we do the next take, I'll say, "Do it the same way, except when you come to the close-up, don't go for the close-up. Go over to this other person." Or something like that.

AQ: *How would you start a film like that, that's not a mainstream Hollywood film, as far as money and so forth?*

RA: It's just a matter of persistence. In other words, there are certain films I don't make because I feel I don't want to and I couldn't. I think I would fail. So I have a very hard time making films. I came back from Europe a year and a half ago with a script from Raymond Carver. I bought a bunch of Raymond Carver short stories, and I put together a script, and I wanted to make a film called *L.A. Short Cuts* [which was released in 1993 as, simply, *Short Cuts*] based on those—it has about 27 characters in it. I've got a terrific cast for it. I'm very happy with the script. But I can't get anybody to put any money in it because they read it and they say, "Oh, well, this is kind of depressing." And I said, "Well, it's not going to be depressing. I mean, it's a comedy." And they said, "Yeah, but there's too many people in it." And it's very difficult. So I have to just hold out. And I made another film, *The Player*, while I'm waiting to get this one done. And I'm starting back again on *L.A. Short Cuts,* and I'm going to keep trying to do it. I may never get it done. But it's just a matter of persistence. You know, you gotta go with your hat in your hand, and you've gotta get down on your knees, and you gotta be nice to a lot of people that you don't want to be nice to. It's difficult.

AQ: *You gotta compromise, in other words?*

RA: Well, either that or you gotta lie a lot. You don't have to compromise. You compromise it a little bit. Compromise is all right. It doesn't make any difference. A lot of these things don't make any difference whether this happens or that happens. It's the idea that you just have to stay with what it is that you feel is right because if you do something that you don't feel is right, you won't do it well anyway. I think the worst thing that could happen today—wasn't so 20 years ago—but the worst thing that is happening today is that a lot of first directors are getting shots. I mean, there's a lot of pictures being made. I'd say an extraordinary percentage of people making films are making their first films. And they are $35 million films. And that's a great break for those people. But, boy, if that film fails—not if they fail—if the film fails, they may just as well go back to being a box boy because they're not going to get another shot. And at least in my time, with the television and all of the kind of work with the number of films that I've done, there's at least a backlog that people—no matter whether they like my films or not—they know I can get one finished. So you gotta be kind of careful not to just accept a film just in order to have a film because if that film fails, you've really nailed your own coffin. I just think it's a matter of being persistent to do what you want to do, what you feel. And that's what you'll do. Then you'll do something that's correct that you're able to do.

MW: *One of the things you told me when you were taking* L.A. Short Cuts *around [to studios] was that certain executives would tell you that there wasn't enough hope in the film.*

RA: Well, they said, "There's no hope in this film." I said, "Listen, none of these women know each other, so why don't we call all the women

Hope?" And the minute I said it, I knew I'd made a grave error. But that source is not interested in my film.

AQ: *Is there something that can be done so at least the negative in its present state can be kept from further deteriorating? Or is there some way that someone can sort of rescue the negative a bit? And question number two: How did you work the cat [in* The Long Goodbye]? *Because that was amazing.*

RA: I didn't; the cat trainer did. But that was five or six cats, different cats that they'd trained to do different things and they'd respond to certain things. The cat was good, though, wasn't he?

But you know if that were written into a script — that scene — it's ten minutes. He's dealing with that cat for ten minutes. If that were written into a script and you took it to any studio executive and said, "This is the first scene," they'd throw you out because you can't do that sort of thing.

Marty Scorsese is doing the most active work about saving these films. Every time he makes a deal with a major company, part of the deal that goes along with it is that he grabs a couple of films and gets a real pristine print out of it. They get them on nondeteriorating stock. They're saving a lot of them.

With *McCabe and Mrs. Miller,* Scorsese did that. I saw him a year or so ago on a plane, and he said he's just gotten this print of *McCabe* which is just great and it is beautiful. And now they're going to laserdisc. And *McCabe* is now on laserdisc, widescreen format, letterbox, and it looks quite beautiful. So they can all be saved. Then again, you have to watch out because it's like Congress when they make a law about what films that they'll have: A committee will tell you what films can't be colorized. Well, the committee is a bunch of box-office people that would look at the selection, and *Top Gun* will be designated a classic because it made more money than *To Sleep With Anger.* It all goes back to money. It all goes back to commerce. And these people who own these companies and run these companies, they do not care. And this isn't to say they're bad people. They're in the business. But they don't understand. And I don't think they're capable of understanding that people take the work they do seriously. And the audience also takes the work to heart. A lot of the audience takes this work very, very seriously. You know, there's this wonderful stuff out there. And 40 years from now this film won't exist.

M W : *What about the negative of this film, though? Do you know that the color is deteriorating?*

R A : I have no idea. I don't know where it is. United Artists has broken up. God knows who owns the negative of this film, even. I just know that most of the films, the prints that I've seen, had the colors gone from them. And I assume that the negative is in better shape. But it's very expensive for them to take that film out—find it in the first place—take it out of the vault, get some people to work on it. Suddenly, there's somebody who has to sign that check and they say, "What are we doing this for? This film is worthless. It didn't make any money the first time out. What do we want with this?"

A Q : *All the actors are really great in the film, and Sterling Hayden was the best. Was he hard or easy to work with?*

R A : Oh, he was great. Sterling was wonderful. And his wardrobe, as he came walking up to my house—because he had to come into California illegally or something—it was some weird stuff. And those were his own clothes. And I said, "OK, well, that's your wardrobe. Try to wear it every day." He was terrific.

A Q : *My question is, do you just want to make films? Or do you want some-thing to last? And I say that not necessarily about film preservation, but when you say things like, you know, "It's just another lousy movie."*

R A : Well, when I say, "just another lousy movie," I don't mean that. I'm saying I don't put a great deal of weight in these things. They mean a great deal to me. I mean, I love all the films I make. When people ask what's your favorite film, I really can't answer that because each one of them is a success. I've not made a film yet that I do not consider a success. By that I'm talking about the collaboration of the people who made it. These films are what we set out to make. People may say, "I hate that *Quintet*. I don't get that." *Quintet*? I love *Quintet*. And I can find five people who agree with me. I say this because I don't think there's a lot I can do about it. But the real personal treasure that comes from this, the real personal pleasure, is the process of doing this. The finished product is great. And an evening like this is very moving to me. I mean, I'm very thrilled. I could, you know, be in tears if somebody says a catchword because this just brings back all kinds of—it's my life. So I treasure these things very, very much. But if they were all gone and disappeared, I don't think, it's a big deal. But I think if the memory of that process were eliminated from my brain, it would be a great loss. There are more important things.

GEOFF GILMORE: *I did want to thank you very much for coming tonight. I did want to mention that the preservation officer of the [Academy of Motion Picture Arts and Sciences] is here, and the preservation officer of the UCLA Film and Television Archive. I think they're both interested in talking to you about preservation of this film. So, again, thank you very, very much for coming. Thank you very much, Michael.*

MW: *Thank you.*

The Player

JANICE RICHOLSON/1992

IN MAY 1992, ROBERT Altman brought *The Player* to the 45th Cannes International Film Festival, where he won the Best Director award and Tim Robbins won the Best Actor award for his performance in the film. The following interview incorporates Altman's comments at a general press conference and a panel discussion of American independent filmmakers.

CINEASTE: *What sort of statement is* The Player *making about Hollywood?*
ROBERT ALTMAN: Hollywood is about greed and making as much money as you can and trying to get rid of all the artists. Of course, they can't really get rid of us—we just keep picking up and going on. In *The Player* the studio executives would like to get rid of the writers because they cost so much money. But they're needed—somebody has to create the basic blueprint. When Hollywood runs out of films to copy or make remakes of, they'll have to turn to writers, who are the people coming up with all the real films.

CINEASTE: *What's special about* The Player *that makes it a success at the box office, and will Hollywood become more receptive to financing and distributing your films in the future?*
ALTMAN: *The Player* is an experimental film. It's also a freak—we just got lucky. As far as I'm concerned it's just another movie. It's now hot and well

From *Cineaste* vol. 19, no. 2–3 (1992): 61. Reprinted by permission of *Cineaste*.

received, and I'm thrilled by that and happy that the film will make a lot of money. It gives me the power and resources to make the films I want to make. That's something I rarely get.

CINEASTE: *You had a number of name performers appearing in* The Player. *Did their presence have anything to do with the film's success, and how did you get them to appear?*

ALTMAN: Their presence is just another element. We don't really know if their appearance made the film a hit. But you'd be surprised the number of actors who will work in your films if they believe in you. I had 65 stars work for virtually nothing. Everybody was paid the minimum union scale, and then all the money was donated to the Motion Picture Home.

I just told them, "I'm making a film about a studio executive who murders a writer and gets away with it. It has a happy ending." They laughed and said yes. They just wanted to raise their hands and be counted. It was like signing a petition. I think we were making a political statement about Western civilization and greed and people who take, take, and take and give nothing back.

CINEASTE: The Player *had several layers of action to the story. Is this an expansion of your* Nashville *technique?*

ALTMAN: In every film I make, including this one, I think my object is to put density and layers in the film so that, instead of trying to make a broad audience picture by appealing only to the lowest common denominator, by having so many layers there's something for everybody to respond to.

CINEASTE: *Is the 'happy ending' of* The Player *your parody of Hollywood formula films?*

ALTMAN: It's impossible to do a parody of a parody. It's true that there's a happy ending. Griffin Mill walks into his rose-covered cottage with his wife, whose boyfriend he has murdered, and she seems to be very pregnant. I assume that the child in there is Damien and that, when this baby grows up, he will be the ultimate head of all the studios.

CINEASTE: *Do you think Hollywood films have to follow a formula to be successful?*

ALTMAN: As long as audiences support formula films that are all the same and have these happy scripts with happy endings, I think there will be people to make them. Only the audience can really stop Hollywood from making them. I complain a lot about the Hollywood system because it's a system of copying art. The majority of films that are made are set up, as though they say, "We'll make this kind of film, we'll copy it." The director is hired, then fired if he doesn't copy it the way they want him to. The majority of American films are manufactured products. We're talking about the difference between art and product. That's what I think this is really about. It's hard to get money to make a film because most of the money goes to marketing — selling boxes that are empty rather than being concerned about what is going to be in the box.

CINEASTE: *How can audiences be influenced to demand more quality and innovation in films?*

ALTMAN: Maybe we should stop publicizing the 'Number One Box Office Film' on the front page of every newspaper and on every television station. I wish they'd cut all that out entirely. Don't put those figures out. Why does the public have to know how much money is made? It's unfortunate that we've set up this sort of system. Every time you pick up the newspaper or turn on the TV, they say, "The number one box office moneymaker of the week is . . . ," say, *Basic Instinct*. That gives a message that the best picture playing at the moment is *Basic Instinct*. It may or may not be the best, so the mass media are serving commerce, not the audience or the art. That's the biggest problem.

CINEASTE: *What's the answer, then? How can cinema overcome the limits of commercialism?*

ALTMAN: I think the cinema should be more like the publishing business. Publishers produce books by Harold Robbins and Danielle Steele, but the same company might also put out a book of poetry. The film industry doesn't do that.

CINEASTE: *During the last ten years or so, you've worked largely as an independent filmmaker. Why?*

ALTMAN: If you're an artist, you have to be an independent. Independents make films that start with their own artistic integrity. You have to do what you want. Nobody's going to agree with you. Hollywood will say, "Why should I make this picture? You have no evidence that this picture can produce money for our company. It doesn't fit into our computer. We have no template that fits over it." That's why it takes so long. If you're not breaking new ground, you're not an independent.

CINEASTE: *Your work has always had an experimental, risky quality. Are you consciously choosing projects that allow you to explore new ideas, genres, or techniques?*

ALTMAN: I always try to find something to do that I've never done before or that's about something I've never seen before. Any time you do something that doesn't have a pattern already made for it, it's very difficult. It's been very exciting to do that. It's fun. If I didn't have fun doing it, I don't know why I'd do it. Any idea that is experimental, that doesn't have an absolute paved road to follow, is of great interest to me.

For me, the joy is doing something I've never done before. I may stretch too far, and I may make a film next time that doesn't make any money. But that's never the reason I make a film. It's just this learning process. I've got to be on the edge, and I've got to do something that I don't know how to do. That's the fun.

Death and Hollywood

PETER KEOGH/1992

ROBERT ALTMAN: I hadn't heard of this project [*The Player*] until 1 March a year ago. I hadn't read or heard of the book; it was just presented to me by my agent, who said there's a script out there you might like and they're looking for a director. I read it and said, I would do this if the circumstances were right.

PETER KEOGH: *Didn't you think it was perfect for you?*
It was good casting to put me in it. We thought we'd get a certain amount of tension from the film, that it wouldn't just be ignored, mainly because of my presence. But we've had a great response to it; I've never seen anything quite like it.

Were the stars a help?
That was one of my primary ideas. I said, if we do this, let's see if we can't do what I did in *Tanner '88,* the television series about the man who ran for president, where we mixed real people with our fictional characters. It seems to me that it would be very difficult to do a film in Hollywood about the movie business and not see any movie people walking around or sitting in restaurants. And we always had the mandate to use actors for the *Habeas Corpus* film and the dailies.

It was easy to get people to do it: I just called them up and asked them. I gave them a capsule of the script and said, it has a happy ending: It's

From *Sight and Sound* vol. 2, no. 2 (June 1992): 12–13. Reprinted by permission of *Sight and Sound* and The British Film Institute.

about a studio executive who murders a writer and gets away with it. And they all laughed and said count me in.

But I think the reason those people did that so graciously was that they wanted to stand up and be counted. They wanted to join the protest. And the protest is against the greed factor. I'm getting mail from people who work in museums, who say, my God, this is the museum system, or this is the magazine business, this is the way my goddamn editors are. So if I'm correct in that, we should do big business outside. For the Hollywood people, it's just a home movie: Oh look, there's so-and-so. It's good for gossip: Who is Griffin Mill really supposed to be? For me, he isn't supposed to be anybody.

I don't know these players any more, they're all too young, they were on tricycles when I was in Hollywood last. I can't remember their names or connect them to the faces. And by the time I do remember their names, they'll be gone.

Has Hollywood really changed so much? Surely since the 20s it's always been a place of greed?
Yes, but they used the artists. They knew they had to have the artists to make the product they were selling. No matter how much they bullied them or how greedy they got, they were still making movies. As bad as those guys were, they'd go on hunches. Hunches are probably using all your senses, conscious and unconscious, and making a decision. Now the hunch is gone, because the room up top is empty. You've got all these players who keep sending projects upstairs, to get a 'no.' When it gets up there what comes back is what was sent up—the data on how well it's going to do.

What we make now are pictures that worked before; they're in the business of making copies. The artists are the ones who have to feed the marketing machine—we have a joke about it in the film when he says, it's pretty interesting to eliminate the writer from the creative process; if we can just get rid of the director and the actors we've got this thing beat.

Do you read your reviews?
It's interesting to find out how people perceive these things—there are always other points of view. And there's timing. I can do a picture that I think is terrific and somebody doesn't like it. I think, why don't they like it? And I try to figure out for myself what it is. A lot of times it's simply the timing.

You're not confused about why people like this film?
I don't know exactly why they like it. There are a lot of reasons. I think
maybe it's because the timing is right. I fully believe that Hollywood is a
metaphor for our culture and our society. I think that the film is a reflection of what's happening in the election: People are tired of and object to
people who just take, take, take and don't give back. In other words, when
their object is just to make money. That's why this film is being received
so well.

You think it's the Jerry Brown of movies?
Absolutely.

*In a way, though, the film seems your least political and most removed from
political reality. It's a self-enclosed, reflexive artifice from the opening tracking
shot to the implied circularity of the ending.*
To me, it's like a painting; I do a certain subject. But I do think the film is
politically oriented; it's a metaphor for politics. I think the audience has
so much information now from all the media, so much is talked about
Hollywood and how much people make, it's like the basketball and baseball players. Then these guys who run the corporations, the Steve Rosses
and the people making $64 million in salary. It's shocking to people. And I
don't see these people putting it back in.

*Much of the pleasure, though, is in the film's play with form, artifice, and
illusion.*
It's exactly the same thing. This picture is very much like *M*A*S*H* in its
content too—in terms of what the general buzz is in our society.

In style and form?
It's the same ending as *M*A*S*H*—that's where we got the ending from.

*You've always resisted happy endings in your films, or at least an ending that
ties things up neatly. Isn't* The Player *an exception to this in its closure?*
It's structure is like a snail; it turns back into itself just like a fantail shrimp;
it reflects itself. Now I can really see what the structure is, I can almost
parse it. I'm sure that for the next film I do, I'll keep some of these things
in mind. What I learned is now filtered in with my own lore and consequently the next film will be changed.

Is there any character in this film that you identify with?
No, not really, though I see pieces of myself in all the characters. I can understand what their motivation is and what they think about themselves.

One scene in The Player *expresses the film's implicit voyeurism—when Tim Robbins is talking to Greta Scacchi while peering through her window.*
That's why the scene was done that way. The June Gudmunsdotter character is the one I had the most difficulty with in the script. I decided we shouldn't introduce her until very late; we're trying to set up a point of passion with her. So their first conversation is over the telephone. In the conversation, I indicate that Griffin is starting to flirt with her and they kind of connect. But how to do that? Then I realized that if I show him watching her and she doesn't know she's being observed, he can create a fantasy about her. That's the way we get interested in people. And I was always playing with the primal idea that when a guy goes in and kills another man, he takes the woman; the guy goes in and rapes the town and kills the soldier and takes the woman. So I was trying to use that. And to justify what Griffin does. So I felt that to make this woman so interesting to him, I'd let him create her. I took the position that June Gudmunsdotter too doesn't exist; she could be anybody, but he sees her in a certain way that fascinates him because of what she offers him, because she's not part of his world.

I think for the guy she's living with, she's the perfect woman. You go your own way, you don't see her much, you don't have to take her to the movies with you. I assume she cooks for him, she sits there, she sleeps with him, but she doesn't bother him.

It seems that Kahane was offering her to Griffin. Michael Tolkin said that the Greta Scacchi character was one of your areas of disagreement.
It was. You see, he wrote the book, and the character he had in the book made sense, but to me, she was too ordinary. I felt that we should make her a movie character. I tried to explain it to Greta: You're not a real person, you're acting in a movie, you don't have to find out the truth in this woman because there isn't any truth, she doesn't really exist. So you have to find what it is that becomes intriguing to this guy. Is it her philosophy, what she says, her vulnerability and openness? He hasn't seen anything like this, everything in his world has reason.

To this day, I don't know what it is I feel about her, but I was very insistent when I set it up this way.

Is she like a blank movie screen on which you can project your desires?
Absolutely. That's the way I felt about it. I know Tolkin had it differently, but . . . (shrugs).

It seems that with her, Griffin might even be redeemed.
He's about to be redeemable. He has a compulsion to confess to her; he feels guilt about this thing. He's not a murderer, he's a manslaughterer. If he hadn't seen her when he talked to her, I wonder if he would have gone so far as to kill the guy? Maybe her presence brought out a primal thing in him?

Which ending do you prefer to Habeas Corpus? *I would think the Julia Roberts/ Bruce Willis version, because it disrupts the verisimilitude and reminds us that it's a movie.*
If I was going to make that picture, which I wouldn't, she would have died in the gas chamber and he would have got there too late. Which was the way the author pitched it. That would have been my kind of movie. But that picture doesn't sell any tickets and this picture probably would. It's a sort of *Fatal Attraction.*

There seems to be a motif of ritual murder or sacrificial death in your movies, as well as in Tolkin's.
What other films is that in?

Let's see . . . McCabe and Mrs. Miller. Vincent & Theo.
Well, yeah. See, death is the only ending I know. A movie doesn't end; it has a stopping place. That story, those people don't die then: They live on and have terrible lives if it's a happy ending, or if it's a sad ending, they may survive it and recover and have happy lives. So death is the only ending and I deal with death as an ending. The people I have die are usually the wrong people, the ones you don't expect to die. That's the way it seems when people die—when friends of mine die, it's not the person I expect, it's always somebody I didn't expect. So that's another little truth thing I feel, and I feel compelled to use those kinds of things.

In your films, the gifted individual is invariably crushed by the system. Do you feel that's inevitable?

I don't know. I don't feel there's any justice in death, in who dies and who doesn't. And I'm not sure who's better off—the person who dies, or the person who doesn't. If you say happy ending, let's talk about *The Player*. If you're following Bonnie Sherow in *The Player,* it's not really a happy ending; if you follow Griffin Mill, it is. But if you think about it, it's not really a happy ending because this guy has lost his soul; he's become nothing. And with her, this could be a happy ending: Even though she's sad right now, she's out of this fucking mess and maybe she'll find some expression in life that will give her more happiness.

There seems a pattern in your films of women being humiliated, as with Bonnie in this movie.

Well, she got that way because she was trying to support something she thought was right. And she was defeated by it.

Other examples are Nashville *and* M*A*S*H. . . . *Feminists have given you a hard time about this before.*

I think I've supported the feminists. I'm not showing you the way I think things should be, but the way things are. That is the way women are treated. I got a lot of flack after *M*A*S*H* in 1970; they said, oh, it's terrible the way you treat. . . . I say, it isn't the way that I treat women, that's the way I see them treated. So I'm making your point for you.

In the past decade you've been doing a lot of theater and opera.

Well, not a lot. We've been working on *McTeague* for four years now. It'll be on in October.

One more question; it's an essay question. In 1970 M*A*S*H *initiated a renaissance in American film, which ended in 1980 with such debacles as* Popeye *and* Heaven's Gate. *Do you think this film might accomplish the same thing as* M*A*S*H *did two decades ago?*

I think you'll see it switch back; I think the times are going to demand it. These people doing copies are going to go broke and be fired and somebody else will come in. And maybe somebody else will say, hey, wait a minute, what they're doing is wrong. Maybe we've got to go back to the artists again.

So do you have a bunch of films ready for this renaissance?
Yes. I hope I'm around. I hope it happens real quick.

Do you have a new project in the works?
I don't have a film financed, though I've been trying to do a Raymond Carver project.

Which story?
Nine of them. I put them together with a couple of stories of my own connecting them, a tissue, like *Nashville*. It's nine stories that crisscross back and forth. It's viewed as having too many people in it—I've got a terrific cast. They also say that the story is too depressing and I say, well, this is a comedy. They say, you mean, the kid dies and that's funny? No, it's not funny, but it's a comedy. It's like the blues: The blues don't inflict pain, they relieve it, yet they do discuss it. Any one of those Carver stories done as a full-length movie could make you go off and shoot yourself, but when they overlap.... They don't have anything to compare it to; they have no way to market research it. So they won't do it. But I will get it done. I just have to find the right guy.

The Movie You Saw Is the Movie
We're Going to Make

GAVIN SMITH AND
RICHARD T. JAMESON/1992

What ideas did you have about visual style when you read Michael Tolkin's screenplay [The Player] *of his novel?*

Early in preproduction I decided to do that first shot as a long take satirizing long takes. Setting up the time jump of the [different writers'] pitches and still doing it in one take, so it became very cinematic, in that there weren't any cuts in it. Some of the characters tell you what I'm doing — they talk about long takes, *Touch of Evil, Rope,* those things, which tell the audience what it is they're about to see: This is a movie about movies, of movies. This is a way of telling them, There's a lot of mirrors here.

You start the movie with slates.

Well, I left the slate on the shot. I kept the face of the clapper out of [frame] because I knew there was a chance I might do that, but I wasn't sure. Then I went with the Charles Bragg lithograph, "The Screen Goddess," so that became my initial title background, the mural behind the desk.

In what way did you incorporate genre film style into the film?

All the scenes were constructed as scenes reminiscent of other films — but without being specific about the films. Film style in general; in terms of lighting and look, to remind the audience that this is a movie, that this is about movies and ultimately this becomes a movie about itself. That's what the total package is.

From *Film Comment* vol. 28, no. 2 (May–June 1992): 22–30. Copyright © 1992 by the Film Society of Lincoln Center. Reprinted by permission of *Film Comment*.

What were you thinking of particularly in the scene where Robbins talks to Scacchi on his mobile phone while he watches her from outside her house?
I did that simply because their first contact was a telephone call; it didn't seem very interesting to cut back and forth [between them, or go to] split screen. And I thought, because we were using all these space-age devices.... By seeing her through the window, it sets up a voyeuristic situation—which is what films are anyway—and also feeds the eroticism of the plot that was to develop between the two of them.

In that initial phone scene, we were also trying to set up the fact that this was a guy in the movies and she was somebody who didn't care about the movies, probably never saw a movie. We were trying to create an alien character so that he could see through her a crack in his world that maybe he could get out.

You interweave scenes of dreamlike unreality and others with an almost documentary feel; the film slips in and out.
I just think that's what I do. My initial intention was in the movies within the movie, the *Lonely Room* dailies with Lily [Tomlin] and Scott [Glenn] and the *Habeas Corpus* sequence, that they should look like a James Cameron film or a Spielberg film, anybody's film except mine. But when I got there to do [the *Habeas Corpus* finale], I didn't shoot it that way. My son, who is the production designer, I probably should have let him direct it—he had designed the set, he had laid out a storyboard about how that particular film was going to look. But when I got to do it, I just shot it my way.

If I had my way, there wouldn't be any cuts in any film. You would just start following the action and try to be where you want to be at the same time. But of course that's impossible, impractical. My camera style is very simple. I try to place the camera and allow the cameraman to shoot the scene that is happening in front of him, so that he goes to what is most interesting or what it is he wants to look at or what it is I want to look at, which is what I want the audience to look at. But I don't plan for any effect. We set the scene up, the arena, and we let the event happen and then we just film. I rarely put the camera where it can't be. I usually get in the corner of the room like a dying bull in the bullring and say, Okay, this is my spot, I'm gonna watch everything from here. So what I'm really doing is putting the audience in effect where I am. I'm not moving all around. Obviously, [sometimes] there are reverses. But I don't like to do those... and in most cases I don't.

There are scenes in the movie that are definitely cut and edited, *as noticeably as certain scenes are done in one take. Did you have equally deliberate reasons for certain scenes emphasizing editing, even to the point of parody at times?*
Oh sure, the editing for instance in the first Whoopi Goldberg scene in the interrogation, or in the scene where Jan the secretary [Angela Hall] comes in with the Schecter brothers [Michael and Stephen Tolkin] and Fred Ward is there, we cut each person as they spoke, stacatto, almost like it was one of those old movies, the way they cut information. But I had the material to edit it that way. Many of the scenes I had no coverage on—I couldn't have even shortened a scene. The intention was to give the audience something in each of these scenes that they are somewhat familiar with the style of. When I had to take [Robbins and Scacchi] from the airport to [the desert spa], I used three shots in there that are like commercials: the pans to the windmills and then the snake and then into that big oasis. I needed the sense that they were going someplace, but that was set up because you've seen that in those kind of pictures—look at the shots in *Tequila Sunrise.*

And you're continuing to play the movie game, because the pan from their car to the snake, as though the snake were a sinister symbol—
But it's also just a snake in the desert. Yeah.

Why the visual puns—panning to pictures of Hitchcock and framed movie posters?
That's all punctuation. Commas, pauses, and dashes that also comment on what you're seeing at the time; to evoke in your memory banks those kinds of things. When I go to Hitchcock, the next cut is the longshot of the guy walking out by the deck and the music comes in and what it's saying is, We're doing one of those kinds of films now.
    It's not an endorsement. I'm not referring to movies that I like. I'm not talking about the directors I admire, necessarily. I'm saying this is not from my standpoint at all, but from everybody's standpoint. I do not happen to think the opening shot of *Touch of Evil* is anything but grossly pretentious. If I was going to talk about somebody who uses long camera moves, I'd probably talk about Ophüls. But I'm talking about what most people talk about. It's like I get my information from McPaper, *USA Today*—it's what C.W. says, not my own particular feelings. I picked the posters used in the offices. They weren't necessarily pictures I admire or don't admire—their texts somehow told you something about what this picture was about, about the cheapness of the thing.

What do you hope will result from the audience's awareness that they are watching a movie?

I don't have any idea. I think I do that in almost all my movies—constantly say, This is a movie. I wouldn't do this in, say, *Vincent & Theo,* but there the references I had were more to paintings.

There's also a lot of verbal punning, and since some of it bounces off your visuals, your color system, how much of that was introduced by you and how much of it was Tolkin, er, blue-skying in the dialogue? The progression from Robbins and Scacchi's phone conversation about different-color seas, through the death in a puddle that goes red with a shift of camera angle, to her comment at the funeral about "You were right, there was a red sea." . . .

We improvised that. All of the puns were from "icy" and "I see" and "ice queen"; he says "I see" and she says "No, blue sea" and he says "Red sea" and she says "No, no red sea." We happened to shoot those scenes in sequence. If we had shot the funeral scene first, the "red sea" reference would never have appeared.

The ending of the film is very different from the beginning in style—even more removed from reality.

It's like a lobster tail or shrimp tail that's turned back into itself. It's the ending of *M*A*S*H*—absolute flat-out same structure. We come to a point and then suddenly the loudspeaker says, "Tonight's movie has been *M*A*S*H*," and so on, and we give the cast. At the end of *The Player* what we are saying is that the movie you saw is the movie you are about to see; the movie you saw is the movie we're going to make.

And it's a "Hollywood ending."

Yes, and we're saying that happy endings are absolutely ludicrous, they're not true at all. We see the guy carry the girl across the threshold and everybody lives happily ever after—that's bullshit. Three weeks later he's beating her up and she's suing for divorce and he's got cancer. . . .

Why's there an American flag in the shot of Mill's idealized house?

The American flag happens to be there because it *was* there. I would never have put the American flag there. That was Dina Merrill and Ted Hartley's house; I'd been to dinner there a couple of weeks before and I said, This is perfect. The white fence was there, all we added were the flowers. We put about two thousand roses and flowers in that garden, flowers that don't even bloom at the same time!

Why is the last thing we see that big palm tree on the skyline?
Because I had to go someplace or I had to go to black—I need something to play out my end titles on and tell you that the movie is over. I went to the location and I looked around and said, Oh well, let's go to the palm tree. That seemed to be applicable. If the palm tree hadn't have been there, maybe I'd have gone into the gutter, you would have seen . . . I don't know what.

So it's just a release shot.
Yes. And palm trees—any collage of Hollywood has a palm tree in it.

Your associate producer Scott Bushnell used to have a lot to do with set decoration and costumes in Lions Gate days. Does she still?
She had a lot to do with everything. The sets—as I said, my son Steve was the production designer; the decor is entirely Steve's. The costumes—Scott to an extent, but Alexander Julian designed the suits. And now he's getting stiffed in the reviews: They all talk about "Armani-clad studio executives." Poor Alexander Julian.

Dick Mellen [Sydney Pollack]'s house: was that location dressed to a significant degree, or filmed as it was? There's so much that jibes with the watery, layers-on-layers design of the movie.
Steve moved those two streaming-bubble sculptures into the house, but other than that we didn't change it a bit—we just rented it and shot it.

Did you use the same place for the exterior?
No, the exterior was not even a house; it was actually the corner of Joffrey's, the restaurant that we did the breakfast meeting in. We shot that scene and then went up around the corner and got Sydney out there overlooking the ocean and shot that for the telephone call.

You made interesting use of the space in Mill's office—each time there's a scene there, it seems like a different place because you show a new angle or stage in a new area.

First we found the structure of the office, but it lacked certain things; then Steve designed it to encompass those, like the glass brick, that kind of art deco thing. We really had to go with the configuration of what was there. We took out the ceiling—luckily that building was being condemned, it was being torn down, so they let us do certain things. We had to give the idea that this guy was a big shot, had a nice rangy office. I wanted to be able to see as much out the windows as possible all the time because that's all that ever gave us the idea that we were on the studio lot.

Does the staging there just come out of the actors' organic choices?
Yes.

So for instance, in the scene in the office where the studio security chief Fred Ward is grilling Tim Robbins about his alibi: After Ward chose to be moving around behind Robbins, who remains in his seat, you broke that down into a fixed single on Robbins and a medium of Ward with the camera following his movements. Those choices are based on their blocking?
Yes. Any time you got somebody with a desk and somebody talking to them, you're really limited as to where to place your camera, so you have to break it up into shots and then try to induce any kind of movement to give the scope of the place.

You stage a similar grilling scene with Elliott Gould and Nina Van Pallandt in The Long Goodbye *the same way.*
Well, it's probably what I do, then.

It's more interesting than filming it in separation.
I think that's probably true. In terms of the look in this film, I think we all had *The Long Goodbye* a little bit in mind. Of my pictures, the two closest cousins this film has are *The Long Goodbye* and *M*A*S*H*.

Why is Mill's office lit with those dark brown/amber tones in the scene following the breakfast meeting?
It's [later in the day, almost] the end of the day. The next scene we went to, he got rid of the secretary, finds out who he thinks the writer is, and the next scene is night. So it's just my way of glissing into a transition.

Did you revise the script with Tolkin? The screenplay had been around for a while. What revisions did you want?
I don't remember, but we made changes that fit certain things I wanted to do. Then as the casting came in there were certain revisions made to take advantage of the presence of those actors.

The film is quite different from the book, although the book is in the film. The book is used in the film rather than it's a film of the insides of a book. There's more in the film than just that story. The novel is the nucleus.

One notable difference is the way the killing comes across. In the book it's pretty creepy and coldblooded, almost absurdist. In the film, even though it's violent and shocking in a way, you can understand the motivation, because Griffin's paranoia about the security of his job and reputation is emphatically invoked at that point. Plus the progression of the scene entails some accidental knockabout—Kahane [Vincent D'Onofrio] pushing Griffin to begin with....
A thing I kept asking myself was, If I were in his situation, what would I do? He's hollow, there's no soul there, it's not a question of identifying with him—but still you have to be aware of what he'd be going through.

Why do you have the light on the theater marquee go out as Griffin passes underneath?
Several reasons, basic things: to say it's now the end of the evening; nobody else is likely to be around; create a sense of mystery, melodrama—there's going to be one of those scenes now.

Were you perhaps suggesting that people like Griffin Mill are the death of cinema? Because what he does next is to kill a writer, a creative person.
Well, *you* can say that. And when I read it, I may agree to it. Because it may be true. But I wasn't thinking about that at the time.

Soon afterward, another writer [Brian Brophy] is delivering David Kahane's eulogy and he reads the last thing Kahane ever wrote. Did that passage indicate for you that he was a notable talent, that his death had been a real loss? Or was he a lousy writer?
Lousy. That stuff is typical of the kind of thing I read in almost every screenplay I get; it has nothing to do with.... Screenplays aren't literature. They're

just blueprints. And she [Scacchi] didn't even read what he wrote, so really how good could he have been?

Is June anyone to trust, though? She strikes me as the most ambivalent character in the film. Is she a moral reference point?
A-moral; amoral. She's a hedonist. She's somebody who only worries about what she wants to worry about. What she wants. And she gets it.

To me, she doesn't even exist. She's a hallucination. She's the character a guy like Griffin would dream up for the hero of his movie to get involved with. Someone who had nothing to do with the movies—except that she's the ultimate movie character. She's the movies.

Watching her, I found myself being reminded of Mrs. Miller in McCabe.
I know what you mean. Not that I had thought of it before, but yes.

And it's another English actress—well, Australian, but with that "English" accent.
She's Icelandic. Or is she? [*Chuckles.*] I would never have cast an American actress in that part; she had to be somebody foreign. I considered a Hungarian actress, I looked at a Pole. But you can't beat the way the English speak the English language; other accents are just too thick. But she had to be . . . alien.

The scene with her and Robbins at the house—both scenes, actually, though I'm thinking of the second, after Griffin has been shaken up by the encounter with the rattlesnake—were very intricate, visually. How did you arrive at your setups there?
I mostly like to shoot several angles of the scene from the same side of the room, and then later I can figure out how to put them together. I'm always hoping one of them will play for the whole scene.

But those scenes [at June's house] were the hardest to direct in the whole picture. The hardest to direct, to act, to write. Because it's very dangerous: You're breaking all the emotional rules. It's primitive stuff. You kill a guy and then you take his woman.

Was that his motive?
It could be *a* motive. Which is a gain from having the earlier phone scene the way we did: He had *seen* her, and he went to find the guy after that

and . . . you really can't say. He could now have another reason for the killing.

It certainly makes it all the more psychologically ambiguous.
And it's ambiguous from her point of view, too. Does she know what he has done?

It seems he tries to tell her during the lovemaking scene.
And she says, "I don't want to hear that."

Why did you shoot the love scene as you did?
It's the obligatory sex scene; the fucking scene. And I think it's a *great* fucking scene, by the way; the actors played it just terrific. But it's one of the elements, it. . . .

When I was interviewing actors and I talked to Cynthia Stevenson [who plays Bonnie Sherow, Griffin's girlfriend], I said, "Look, before we go any further with this, I want you to know ahead of time: You're going to have to take your shirt off." She said, "Why?!" And I. . . .

Let me tell you a story. After one of the screenings of this film, Paul Newman came up to me and said, "I know what this picture's about. It's about getting to see the tits of the girl whose tits you don't care about seeing, and not getting to see the tits of the girl whose tits you want to see." And I said, "You're absolutely right."

When Griffin is talking to June at the spa and telling her the elements that have to be in a film so they can sell it—suspense, laughter, love, hope, sex, nudity, violence, happy endings—well, *The Player* has all of those. But they're not necessarily where you figure they'll be. The nudity I figured to put in when the story-editor girlfriend [Stevenson] reads to him in the hot tub. And she's naked, because that's how you are in a hot tub. She's reading a sex scene to him, from a screenplay—and again, every screenplay has this ridiculous, impossible-to-film stuff in it, it's just ludicrous. She reads to him, and then she climbs over on him and says, "Can we go to bed now, I'm getting all wrinkled." *That's* the nudity. But in the real sex scene, I'm not going to show nudity, just a little bit of their faces.

If this film reflects on anybody, if anybody should be embarrassed by it, it's the audience. Because we're saying, Here's the stuff you wanted to see, we put it all in for you, here's what you want, but we won't show the things when you want them, the way you want.

But that's all any movie is. It's the scenes we want to show you. *The Player* is full of holes if you really start figuring out how long things take and what would be possible. And so is every movie. We don't show everything, we trick you into believing the time sequence, what's offscreen. . . .

In *The Long Goodbye*, we didn't show people what to look at. It was [*draws a Panavision frame across the air*], and you have to look among all these things, decide what's important; but you won't necessarily know it at the time.

Putting us in the position of a detective . . .
Or a voyeur.

Yet your scenes are very composed, somehow. I'm struck how often you begin from a detail, and pan or tilt up into the action, and then you somehow end on another detail, and there's a form implied.
I like scenes to be whole. I'll shoot a scene six ways, and every one of [these master shots] has a beginning and an end. I don't know which one I'll wind up using.

[In the scene when Bonnie confronts Griffin about his taking another woman to Mexico,] I had one take that I expected to use in the final cut. The camera was behind her, and when she says "Have a nice trip" and walks out of his office, you pan with her down the hall and end up looking at a movie poster: *The Hollywood Story*. But when we got to the spa scene, and Griffin's reservation card has just his initial on it — because this is a place where you *only* take somebody to fuck — "Mr. 'M'" . . . M inside quotation marks . . . just like on the *M* movie poster that you see on Griffin's wall when we pan Bonnie out of the scene from his point of view: "Have a nice trip," pan to "THE WORST CRIME OF ALL: 'M'." And I realized that that was a very nice connection, and so that was the angle I ended up using.

You must have been really thrilled, then, to have that dead fish turn up in the pond at the cemetery.
Oh, I wanted that fish. A dead carp. I mean, it's a funeral, somebody's dead, I can open on this. But I *didn't* anticipate that that wonderful cloud of bright tiny goldfish would come to feed on the carp. [*Chuckles.*]

Why did you decide on the transition out of the lovemaking scene by way of the mud bath? They're making love and then this knee comes up out of the mud....
I don't know—but it worked very well, didn't it? Oh, that scene, there was a *sea* of metaphors in there, you can just take your pick. But it's good, because here are these two people, they've made love, and now neither one is sure what's going to happen. How much does each really know about the other? And remember, the last time you see her [after Dick Mellen's phone call summons Griffin to the police station], she's sitting there, her face covered with dried mud, closeup. *No one* can know what's going on behind that face.

You also use sound very adroitly to achieve some transitions. The soundtrack foreshadows the rattle of the snake Griffin finds in his car.
Sure, but . . . that's part of the music. We also got something like that in the happy ending, leading into that *la-la-la* chorus when he feels her 8½-months-pregnant belly. Which is just fine, because in my opinion this is going to be an *Omen* baby—the ultimate studio head.

As long as we're talking snakes, I must say that it was only on a later viewing that I noticed: The S in the studio motto MOVIES NOW MORE THAN EVER *is made out of a strip of film that rears up like a cobra.*
I hadn't thought of that, but you saw it and that's okay. Every time I make a movie, I then get to read the reviews and find out what I've done—and it's all *true,* whether I thought about it or not. But sure, we had snakes all through. In her studio, all the images in her paintings, and him asking, "Do you have snakes in Iceland? Are you afraid of snakes?" and she says, "I never saw a snake"—and she's in the room with one right now. . . .

How much of the dialogue did you end up rerecording?
None. None of it. I never rerecord any of the dialogue in any of my films. Oh, I'll loop something later if a guy said "I'm going east" but really he's supposed to go west. Otherwise, no. Why do it?

It just seems that you have stuff in the film that's remarkably up-to-the-minute. When I first saw the film in November, and the mail-room boy tells "Martin Scorsese" [Alan Rudolph] he loved Cape Fear, Cape Fear *had come out only the week before. But it turned out to be Scorsese's biggest hit.*

Oh, I knew it would. But I did luck out on a lot of things. The Rebecca De Mornay joke—I had no idea Rebecca De Mornay would be in the first big hit of the year [*The Hand That Rocks the Cradle*]. Or the Rodney King joke in Whoopi's office—the trial's on now, so that's back in the headlines.

How did you get such a spontaneous reading out of Tim Robbins in that "Let's try not to talk about Hollywood for a few minutes"? It was so genuine.
Well, he's very *good*, isn't he?

I'm struck by how good, because I was just reading the New York *story on* The Player, *and in it you claim that the writers making pitches in that opening long take all improvised their pitches. Did you run through a few improvs and then semi-write the scene, or—*
No.

Well then, I have to say that the pitches are hilarious but Robbins's comebacks are even better: "I see, it's The Gods Must Be Crazy, *only the Coke bottle is a TV actress...."*
No rehearsal. Yes, he is terrific. And he's a *director*, too. I've seen his film [*Bob Roberts*] in four different cuts now and it's fantastic.

Speaking of directors, how did you come to cast one in the role of Dick Mellen? You initially cast Blake Edwards.
I got to thinking I needed someone with authority to kind of keep the actors in line on that location. I'm asking all these people to show up and essentially be dress extras. If it's Blake's house, if Blake's the lawyer—a lot of them agreed to do it because I'd said, "Blake Edwards is going to be playing the lawyer," and they'd worked for Blake in a lot of pictures, so it was "Oh, *Blake*—well sure!" Then Blake called me and said, "Gee, I've got a problem, I've got to be out of the country the day you're shooting." So I asked Sydney to be backup for Blake, and he said, "Of course, no problem." Either way, there'd be *two* directors on the set to keep everybody a little bit settled down.

And also, to have a director play a powerful lawyer amidst all those actors who were playing themselves as roles—it just seemed right for the equation. I can't really tell you why, but it did.

Casting Brion James as Levison the studio head was a bit of a surprise.
The replicant himself; the greatest villain in the movies. Who better to be running a studio?

How did you ever get Julia Roberts and Bruce Willis to agree to participate and cap one of the movie's running gags?
I asked them and they said yes.

And how do they feel about it now?
They love it.

Nobody asked for script approval. Burt Reynolds . . . he was getting ready for his scene and said, "This guy [Griffin] is a real asshole," and I said, "Yes, he is." Burt said, "Can I call him an asshole?" I said, "Sure." So he did. And for Malcolm McDowell's scene, he was complaining to me about how these guys [studio execs] say things behind your back; so he got to call them on it, onscreen.

Julia was very good. It was a really bad time for her; that wedding bust-up with Kiefer Sutherland had just happened six days before, and she'd run off to Ireland, and she was doing *Hook* at the time. She came in on a Sunday and did it and she was great.

So is The Player *your definitive take on Hollywood, as everyone is gleefully reporting?*
The Player is my take on a lot of things, but Hollywood. . . . What *is* Hollywood, anyway?

A guy like Paul Newman starts a company [selling salad dressing], makes $54 million in profits last year, and it all goes into a charity; you don't hear a lot about that. A guy like Steve Ross makes $63 million a year, a guy like Michael Eisner, Lee Iacocca, Barry Diller, those guys don't feed that money back. They gather as much as they can, and the profits don't have any real meaning. They can't spend that money. All they've got, they can say on their record they have the most chips in front of them when they die.

It's a terrible thing that's happened to our country, to our culture — and I'm talking about *all* of Western culture. And it's crushing the artists. People are avariciously out there . . . it's like what they did to the art market, selling paintings for $93 million and all that. It's just ridiculous. And that's what Hollywood's like. That's why I think this film presses a button. So many people have responded to it, not because of the Hollywood part of it, but because they see that that's the same as in the museum business or the magazine business or the journalism business, in the political business or in the lawyer business or in the Milken business or in the savings and loan business. It's all the same thing. There's no time or room for this wonderful stuff [art] that really entertains the population of this earth — not in terms of just entertaining them but it gives them pause to think, gives them reason to feel important, to be important, to put their own ideas together with existing ideas. It's a reason for being, the reason for it all.

Hollywood doesn't mean anything, it doesn't exist anymore. My film . . . nobody's even upset about it. One guy, Mark Canton, is the only one who got pissed off, because he's a fool. Most of these guys, they're sitting there doing a job, they're making money — they don't even have a sense of shame.

What is the atmosphere of Hollywood now?
The atmosphere is exactly as you see it in my film. It's a cutthroat atmosphere. These people are all after their own. It used to be every car in the parking lot at ICM had to be either a black BMW or a black Mercedes. Somebody bought a Lexus and now they're all Lexuses. They wear these things like you wear a necktie. It becomes the only important thing.

As for power . . . all these people, they've got nothing to do. Nobody can go by the hunch; nobody can go by the little man inside of them that says, "I've got a feeling about this." That's the only way you can really make judgments. That's the way, ultimately, when you go into the polls and vote for the President, you're gonna go on some gut reaction. It isn't anything that you could intellectualize. Because you're using all of your senses, all of your feelings.

You have the sense that in the old days the business was still run by showmen.
Yes. There was still greed, but it worked. The idea was that if you got a guy that was a good actor and the people liked him, and a good writer and a good director, let those people make the movie and then they'd figure out how to sell it. Now they try to figure out how to sell it first and then they try to make the picture they've sold.

I would not allow [*The Player*] to be test-marketed. There's not been one marketing thing on this film, and there never will on any film that I do. Which is why I'll never make a film for a major studio. When the majors came to bid for this film, we said, "Here are the rules: You cannot test-market this film." So two of them passed us up and the rest of them bid . . . not as high as they should have. Now they all wish, it looks like it's gonna. . . . [The Player *is being distributed by Fine Line Features, the division of New Line Cinema that handled* My Own Private Idaho, The Rapture, *et al.*—Ed.]

But still, this film hasn't been *released* yet. This film, less than 3,000 people have seen it—in the *world*. I've got more mail from those screenings than on all the other films I've made in my entire lifetime. Twenty, 30 films. More interest, more than I got on *M*A*S*H*, more than I got on *Nashville*. And everybody's writing about it; every goddam magazine that you could pick up has it as my "comeback." This is my *third* comeback, whaddaya gonna do on my next one?! "Oh, this is wonderful, you're getting the recognition, everybody loves it, it's gonna be great for ya. . . ." It's nice. But you know what's gonna happen next? I'm gonna pay for it.

But I *know* that. I know that these are the rules of the game, and that's okay with me. I'm not "angry with Hollywood." I'm not "a maverick." I'm not a person who "ran away in exile." I fiddle on the corner where they throw the coins. Where I can get my work done.

The business the major studios are in is not the business I'm in, and the business I'm in is not the business they're in, so how can I be mad at them? They don't want what I do and I don't want what they do. So I have to work—and many artists like myself—around the edges of this pie. And do it the way that we do it. If they called me in and said, "Do you want to do *Batman*?," what am I gonna say? I *might* say yes. But they're not gonna do that, because they want this thing structured in a way that hits their market research.

They didn't learn anything from Einstein: They know the train's moving, but they don't know that the station's moving, too. So where they're standing, they say, "Okay, we got that train, we know how to figure that angle"—they don't know they're moving along with it. And they're wrong, because when they say, "All right, we know what we have to do," they're wrong, because that time is already past.

Being in that situation, what is there in your background that has given you the ability to continue working through that?

It's just what I choose to do. What I can do and what I do do. But I'm no different from anybody else. I've had a better career than anybody you can name. You name somebody that's had a better shake than I have—I can't think of anybody. I have done almost 40 films. I have done theater, opera—I'm doing it *now*. I've had great commercial successes, great critical successes; there are schools that teach my films; almost all the films that I've made are still being shown somewhere in retrospectives. I've got a problem? I'm making a comeback? The best work I've done, the most creative work, has been between those peaks that the general public sees.

That work you have behind you now gives you strength. But when you were trying to break in, what kept you going through all the years of false starts?

I didn't know any better. There's birth pains and a struggle to get anything done, and when you're in that struggle you don't think about it being over or not happening, you just continue to struggle.

I'm trying to do the same picture . . . I've been in Hollywood 23 months. I came back February 20, 1989; I wrote and was planning to do a film, *L.A. Shortcuts,* based on some Raymond Carver stories. I never could get those made. I got this picture offered me—a year ago today I probably didn't know about [*The Player*]. I stopped, I made this film, it hasn't even been released and already it's a—

—big success—

—a hemorrhage. It's gotten everybody's attention. Chances are we struck a nerve with it. And it's great for me. But I still can't get *L.A. Shortcuts* made. Nobody has said, "Well, we'll make *L.A. Shortcuts* now because we see you're a success." So that old saw dies; that horse is a dead horse. I'm no different than I was two years ago. "It doesn't fit our marketing; it doesn't have a happy ending."

Hollywood is something that doesn't really exist. These corporations have nobody running them—that's the change. When Brandon Tartikoff takes over Paramount, and Joe Roth at Fox, and they both make announcements that they're only interested in making films that make money, only interested in the lowest common denominator—and they say that out loud; when Bridget Potter of HBO says, "We don't want to make *Tanner*

['92] because we don't have an instant audience for it"....And *Tanner ['88]*'s probably the most creative, the most breakthrough work I've ever done. But that doesn't mean anything to anybody. Everybody's thinking in terms of how much money it makes—and it isn't even the money. Suppose they're wrong? Suppose they make *L.A. Shortcuts* and lose their $12 million, $18 million on it—so what? They lose the money on *Hudson Hawk*, they lose it on *Bonfire of the Vanities* or *Shining Through* or *For the Boys*—what difference does it make? Their calculated judgments are no better than....Every breakthrough film that's ever been made has been a film that nobody wants to make.

The irony is that a lot of them realize that it's arbitrary. I remember some exec saying, "If I'd made the films I said no to and not made the films I said yes to, I'd probably have come out about the same."
Exactly the same.

So why not say yes to good ones?
Because they're afraid; it's easier to say no than say yes. The point is, there isn't anybody there. There isn't one person that if they were plucked out, they died—nothing's gonna change. Who's gonna be missed? Only the artist. When Marty Scorsese dies, WHAP, something's lost.

To go back to Tanner '88: *You said you thought it was your most creative work. Why?*
I think that we broke into new form. We used a mix of drama and comedy and reality and satire, fiction with nonfiction. It'll be emulated—I couldn't have made *The Player* if I hadn't made *Tanner*. We wouldn't be sitting here talking about this picture now if I'd made *The Player* as it was in the book. I took the tools and techniques and systems that I used—and learned, and were taught to me—in *Tanner '88*. And very few people have seen *Tanner*; probably more people have seen *The Player* already than have seen *Tanner*!

I hope that's an exaggeration. In addition to Tanner, *in the eighties you also filmed a number of plays. How did that affect your filmmaking approach?*
It's always interested me to do something that just came up, and to say, Geez, how do I do this? Also, it comes down to, these are the only things that were offered to me.

What sort of challenges did, say, a piece of material like The Caine Mutiny Court-Martial *present?*

I have to do *The Caine Mutiny Court-Martial* and I can't change the words. I had to use all the dialogue that was written; same way with *Streamers*. And I say, Can I do this and still make this a movie? *The Caine Mutiny Court-Martial* I would not have done, except that I looked at about 400 hours of Oliver North testifying and I thought, Shit, this is the same thing. Then, of course, I found that wonderful location, the gymnasium [at Fort Flagler in Port Townsend, Washington], with red marks on the floor, and I thought, This is a game. We put it into that dreamlike place and it happened.

I filmed *Black and Blue,* the Broadway musical revue at the Minskoff Theater last year. I put that on tape for Japanese pay television. Nobody knows about that; it isn't even going to get shown in this country, until maybe next fall on PBS. I'm *very* proud of that work. I'm doing an opera in October, a new opera in Chicago [*McTeague,* from the Frank Norris novel on which Erich Von Stroheim based *Greed*]. I'm one of the authors, and I look forward to that.

So I've got no complaints. But that doesn't mean that it's easy—nobody's going to come and just give me what I want. I got about five pictures I want to get made, and about one of them will probably get made. Maybe none of them will—but there will be some other picture. It's always been like that. Like I say, it's my third comeback. Or fourth. And I haven't been away.

What became of your plans to do TV versions of Nashville *and* Buffalo Bill and the Indians?

Nashville wasn't successful in big numbers commercially and the network decided they didn't want to run it in two nights. And *Buffalo Bill* was just generally considered a bad film, so nobody wanted *anything.*

So those versions weren't assembled?

The *Nashville* version was assembled in a workprint.

Was it preserved?

None of this stuff's preserved. It costs money to preserve—who's going to pay for it? Nobody knows where the negative for *Images* is; nobody knows who owns it, Hemdale, Columbia, blah blah blah—it's just gone. A year from now you won't be able to find the elements of *The Player*. Guys like Marty Scorsese who go back and save . . . he saved *McCabe* from disappearing, forced Warner Bros. into saving that—'cause the color's gone from most of those films. Scorsese, Jonathan Demme, really care about film, really care about preserving. I don't know how they do it. They do wonderful things. Now, with video, stuff does get saved and recycled. Fifteen years ago, your films couldn't be seen again.

Speaking of video, a couple of segments of Tanner *came out, but the rest. . . .*
That's HBO again, getting greedy. I finally got the rights back, and it's going to be put out, all six hours of it.

When'll that happen? We certainly want to mention that in our Life With Video section.
It's happening now. I'm sure they want to have it out for election time.

I taped it all off cable for myself back in '88, but loaned it to somebody and didn't get it back for two years. Of all the things I wouldn't want to lose. . . .
Well, keep it now that you got it.

The Player King

GEOFF ANDREW/1992

ROBERT ALTMAN IS IN unusually ebullient mood. Conspicuously delighted by the very enthusiastic reception for *The Player* at Cannes, he embarks upon a rant about one of his past producers (who, for legal reasons, must here unfortunately remain nameless). "He won't pay me a cent for the movie I made. He says, 'Fuck you! Sue me!' And now, after the success of *The Player,* he's going around saying, 'Oh, *I* produced an Altman film.' But this man stole from me, he lied to me, he's a despicable person. And the only way I can combat that is to tell the truth about him. And if he says I'm telling lies about him, then *he* should sue *me* for slander!"

If any filmmaker was the perfect choice to direct the movie adaptation of Michael Tolkin's novel—in which a high-ranking Hollywood studio executive is driven to murder after receiving anonymous death-threat postcards from a scriptwriter whose calls he has failed to answer—it was surely Robert Altman. (He did, however, come to the project only after several big-name directors, reputedly including Sidney Lumet and Walter Hill, had turned it down.) Few major American directors have had such a troubled, up-and-down relationship with the studio establishment in recent years; and few, presumably, of those who know the pernicious ins and outs of Tinseltown from first-hand experience feel they have nothing to lose by speaking their minds.

From *Time Out* no. 1137 (June 3, 1992): 18–20. Reprinted by permission of *Time Out Magazine.*

His openness is not, as one might expect, merely the embittered out-pourings of an artist belatedly welcomed back into the fold after years in the wilderness. For one thing, Altman—who during the '70s was widely acknowledged as the most adventurous and interesting filmmaker working in Hollywood—is long resigned to his fate ("I can't do what they want, and they don't want what I do") and seems far from bitter. For another, he has always made a habit of telling the truth as he sees it, irrespective of how much he might be damaging his career.

Even back in '63, for example, when the then 38-year-old director, who had served his apprenticeship in industrial documentary, was making a name for himself in television on series like *Alfred Hitchcock Presents, The Roaring Twenties, Bonanza,* and *Combat,* he told *Variety* that the *Kraft Suspense Theatre* he had been working on was "as bland as cheese" and little more than "show by committee"; that he'd had enough of "the agencies, the winking, the networks, the ratings. Anybody who thinks TV is an art medium is crazy—it's an advertising medium." Similarly, in the late '70s, he repeatedly criticised certain top-name actors (Streisand, McQueen, Brando, Redford, and Hackman included), making it extremely unlikely he would ever be able to secure their services, even if he wanted to. In the back-slapping world of Hollywood, such attacks—besides potentially alienating colleagues and friends—can be tantamount to professional suicide (after the Kraft affair, he was even dropped by his agency). Remarkably, however, Altman has managed to continue in work, mostly financed by television, cable, or European backers ever since the ludicrously lukewarm reception which greeted *Popeye* in 1980 (its hero's motto—'I yam what I yam'—might serve equally well for the director himself).

It's because he has kept himself so busy that he's understandably wary of *The Player* being seen as a "comeback" movie. Admittedly, during the '80s his output was far less conspicuous and included the clumsy *O.C. and Stiggs.* At the same time, however, most of his work—marvellous theatrical adaptations like *Come Back to the 5 and Dime, Jimmy Dean Jimmy Dean* and *The Caine Mutiny Court-Martial,* and the ground-breaking television series *Tanner '88*—was unfairly neglected, and one can't help feeling that his low profile was rather less to do with the quality of his work than with prob-lems of marketability. Happily, the new film—a dazzling comedy-cum-thriller and almost certainly the most honest, accurate, and complex movie ever made about Hollywood—looks set to change all that, even if only for a while. As Altman admits when I say he must be pleased with the way the film's been received: "Let's say I'm enjoying the absence of pain. Someday I'll have to pay for all this, but it's very nice while it's happening."

Where Michael Tolkin's original novel was a good if fairly straightforward psychological thriller about a man threatening to crack up under the stress of receiving anonymous, murderously vengeful postcards, the film uses Tolkin's basic plot as the starting motor for a far funnier, all-embracing satire on the greed, philistinism, and rampant egotism of contemporary Hollywood, a town where relationships, morality, and even the movies themselves are all subservient to the pursuit of power for power's sake. Menaced studio executive Griffin Mill (Tim Robbins) seems worried less for his physical safety than about how much his career (and the status that goes with it) might suffer should the postcard-writer publicly reveal a *faux pas* Mill can't even remember. Likewise, when Mill finds himself directly involved in the killing of a man, he makes no bones about moving in on the dead victim's girlfriend (Greta Scacchi), and cares only that a rival studio hotshot (Peter Gallagher) should not discover, and so take advantage of, Mill's suspected part in the crime. In this paranoid, power-crazed, Machiavellian world, the ability to pitch a good story and firm up a good deal is everything; reputation, rather than reality, rules.

"I made the film," says Altman, in far cheerier frame of mind than when I've met him in the past, "not to take revenge on or chastise Hollywood, nor to become the manipulator in a town that likes to manipulate. True, Hollywood is a place I know a lot about, so Michael's script was an opportunity to show a lot of the truth—which is what art is. My real motive in doing it was artistic; I just saw a chance to make something that was interesting, especially in terms of its *structure,* which is something most people don't discuss. If you could draw a graph of how the film works, you'd see it has a very unusual structure—though I didn't know if that would work until I'd finished the film."

What Altman appears to be referring to (he doesn't often elaborate on his more aesthetically oriented statements) is not only the way we are continually led to reconsider our feelings about Griffin Mill—sometimes we're gunning for him, sometimes our main response is contempt—but the fact that *The Player* is a film-within-a-film. (Moreover, we also see excerpts from two films being made within this film-within-a-film.) It opens on a painting of a movie lot, in front of which a clapperboard is snapped shut (to the sound of Altman's own off-screen voice ordering quiet on set) so that the action, itself set on a movie lot, can begin; and it ends with the story we've just seen being 'pitched' for a movie that Mill may one day produce ... to be entitled, of course, *The Player*. Within this circular framework are endless in-jokes, allusions, parodies, and star cameos that not only lend Altman's film an unprecedented authenticity but also help it to operate successfully on two levels — as a clear piece of fiction and as an attempt to document the state of the movie business today.

"The stuff about the clapperboard and the ending weren't there in Michael's original script," explains the director. "The script and the book are *in* the film, they're its nucleus, but they're not the same as the film. In a way, the film is about itself; it's a film about films about films, like a series of spinning mirrors. Similarly, the film is *of* Hollywood, but it's not really just *about* Hollywood. Hollywood is a metaphor for our society, which is based on greed — take, take, take, and don't give anything back to the system; lie and cheat. So though the film is about the stupidity of Hollywood, it's also about the moral problems of our society at large.

"The problem with Hollywood now is that the artists have lost a lot of their power. But that can only go on so long; eventually the public will just go away. Because when the artists are not there *directly*, what the studios make are just copies, and eventually the copies get so thin they can't be sold. So then the studios say, 'We'd better find another artist and we'll get something else to copy!' And the artists are always there; they get their heads cut off, and another one comes up. There's a lot of us."

Interestingly, back in '76, Altman pointed out that, for him, *Nashville* was not only about the country-and-western capital *and* America in the wider sense, but a metaphor for Hollywood during the '40s, a time when he himself was dreaming of making it into the movie business: "It's a place where people get off the bus," he said. "The money is generated, and there's a crudeness to the culture." But where *Nashville* dealt with both the successful stars, agents, and entrepreneurs, *and* the no-hopers — the fans, session musicians, and ordinary folk hoping that a little of the Grand Ole Opry glamour might rub off on them — *The Player* focuses most of its attention on the moneyed movers and shakers. But not, noticeably, the agents.

"Why leave out the agents? How can you do a parody of what's already a parody?" laughs Altman. "As for showing that executives can be human and that writers can be vain and vacuous, well, that's the way we are! To do a satire successfully, the satire basically has to be upon myself; I have to know that all of those things I laugh at in the characters also exist in me. While there is no single character I identify with, I do understand them.

"I don't have any perception of myself as being either in or out of Hollywood; I'm not, as people have said, 'a maverick' or someone who went off into exile. To me, Hollywood is a state of mind. I'm in Hollywood, I work in the business, in the system, but I'm also out of it. I'm not a major player, I don't sit at the table. You know, people don't like to talk to me because if you say something to me, I'll tell somebody else. I don't have a good memory and I found out that the best way to deal with that is just to say the truth the way I feel it at the time; and then I don't have to remember what I said!

"And similarly, I didn't base the characters on specific real Hollywood people. The truth is, I don't even know the names or the faces of that level of Hollywood executive; I haven't dealt with them. I know and admire Alan Ladd Jr. [who, as head of production at Fox, gave the green light to the risky *3 Women*], and he's certainly not represented in the film, but I really don't know anybody else like that."

What Altman does know, however, is actors. For every star who may have found some of his more outspoken pronouncements irksome there are countless others who have found his generously supportive, semi-improvisational approach rewardingly liberating. That, presumably, is why he was able to assemble such an unprecedentedly starry cast for *The Player*, with dozens of name talents—from Julia Roberts and Bruce Willis to Burt Reynolds, Nick Nolte, Jack Lemmon, and Susan Sarandon—contributing a day's work for next to nothing, to appear as often as not in wordless cameos or even, in about 25 instances, to end up on the cutting-room floor. Many—Karen Black, Cher, Louise Fletcher, Scott Glenn, Jeff Goldblum, Elliott Gould, Sally Kellerman, Lily Tomlin—had worked with the director before, some of them making their first noticeable impact under his tutelage, and so may have felt they owed him a favor; others, perhaps, simply didn't want to be left out. Whatever, Altman insists that casting the movie was no problem at all.

"I just called them up, and they said yes. I think for all those people it was like signing a petition, making a political statement against the greed. And there was nobody turned us down that I know of, though there were people who wanted to be in it and couldn't because their schedules didn't fit ours. When I started the film I had very few people committed—Tim, of course, and Julia and Bruce, who had parts we needed to settle at the very beginning—but it sort of built up. It wasn't very planned; whoever turned up, I'd tell to go eat at that table, and they'd ask, 'What should I do?' And I'd say, '*I* can't tell you! You're not one of my characters, you're playing yourself, so do anything you want to do.'

"Of course, one reason for casting them was part of the game: It's fun to identify all those faces. But mainly, it's because when I made *Tanner '88,* where we mixed fictional characters with real people, it was very successful. And I thought, I'm doing a film about Hollywood, so why wouldn't there be faces you recognize at the restaurants and so on?

"But the whole film is a game. Like the opening, nine-minute tracking shot [where characters pitch ridiculous scripts like *Graduate 2* and allude to lengthy tracking shots in Welles's *Touch of Evil* and Hitchcock's *Rope*], which is so *pretentious,* and tells you you're watching a movie about movies. Or like Griffin's recipe for the elements to sell in a film—suspense, laughter, love, hope, sex, nudity, violence, a happy ending; we do all that, so in a way ours is a bad movie, too! Or like we don't say who the postcard writer is, but you can work it out from when you hear him use a phrase on the phone at the end of the film which is a phrase you've heard before. You didn't get it?" Altman laughs. "You'll have to go see the film again!"

Though currently riding the crest of a wave, Altman is all too aware of the irony in the motto—"Movies, Now More Than Ever"—billboarded above Griffin Mill's company office. "That's a paraphrase an old Nixon campaign slogan! It *is* ironic in that in recent years I've got most of my financing from sources other than the studios. But there *is* a future for cinema, and I think it'll get very good in the '90s; we'll see big changes.

"I've *always* had trouble finding finance, and I still am. It should be a little easier now for a short while, because those guys are not very smart; they can only follow the crowd, so I have to take advantage of that. In fact, it looks at last like my plans to do a film of Raymond Carver stories, called *Shortcuts,* will come off. But you're only as good as the perception of your last film. Still, I've done very well really, right through the '80s, and all my life. I can't think of one person who's had a better career than I have. So when people ask if *The Player* is vengeful, I tell them I've had it great. I'm a very lucky man."

Altman on Altman

GRAHAM FULLER/1992

AT A SEMINAR ON independent filmmaking held in the American Pavilion during last year's Cannes festival, Robert Altman sat like Sitting Bull at a lodge meeting of fiery young bucks. Emphatically non-idealistic about the vagaries of getting personal films made in a system hungry for homogenized product, he dispensed the kind of cold wisdom that enables an old warrior to survive many war counsels and innumerable wars: in Altman's case 45 years in (and often out of) the American film industry. Each of Altman's fellow panelists—Stacy Cochran, Tim Robbins, Quentin Tarantino, and John Turturro—had come to Cannes with an impressive directorial debut, but Altman had come with *The Player,* his 28th theatrical feature, a layered, densely allusive, and beautifully crafted satire of the system in question, and the most entertaining and fêted American film of the year—you could call it Bob Altman's history lesson. Not bad for a 67-year-old director who, a few years ago, seemed destined to end his career in television, where he had spent his long apprenticeship in the fifties and sixties. That "comeback" has now been cemented by Altman's filming of *Short Cuts,* adapted from a series of Raymond Carver stories.

If Altman had proved mercurial in the previous 15 years, his place among the elders of American *auteurism* had already been assured by his work between 1970 and 1975, when he made *M*A*S*H, Brewster McCloud, McCabe and Mrs Miller, Images, The Long Goodbye, Thieves Like Us, California Split,*

From *Projections 2: A Forum for Filmmakers,* ed. John Boorman and Walter Donahue (London: Faber and Faber, 1993), 149–81. Reprinted by permission of Faber and Faber.

and *Nashville.* This was the period when Altman developed his style of mock documentary realism, characterized by overlapping dialogue, improvisation, offhand irony, and those floaty zooms into dead space and the quick of life. Although he has drawn "reality" into invented scenarios (think of the fake Haven Hamilton greeting the real Julie Christie in *Nashville* and then asking someone who she is), particularly in *Tanner '88* and *The Player,* it has been in filming the fictional as if it was the actual that Altman has consistently revealed the kinds of truths that have often eluded contemporaneous champions of *vérité* and hyperrealism.

The following interview is excerpted from two conversations I had with Robert Altman in 1992. The first took place in February at his Park Avenue office, the second in June at his Malibu beach house—a few miles up the coast from where Altman filmed Roger Wade (Sterling Hayden) walking dreamily to his death in the Pacific in *The Long Goodbye.*

GRAHAM FULLER: *Your first feature film,* The Delinquents *[1957], which is rarely seen, was shown on television last night. I watched it.*
ROBERT ALTMAN: You did? Oh Jesus, I don't think I'd have the courage to see it. It's pretty dreadful.

GF: *It's really a teen exploitation flick; certain scenes reminded me of* Rebel Without a Cause. *Was it simply an opportunity for you to direct a feature?*
RA: Oh, absolutely. That was all. I was living in Kansas City, doing the Calvin industrial films,* and I'm sure I would have done anything. A guy named Elmer Rhoden Jr., whose father owned a chain of theaters in the Midwest, hired me to do a film about juvenile delinquency. I wrote it in four to five days, staying up for two nights, drove the generator truck, and made the picture in 22 days or something like that. We had no money—I think the total budget was $63,000. I got paid $3,000. That whole coda at the end, warning parents about teenage delinquency, was added by somebody—I've no idea who. It was a weird experience.

Alfred Hitchcock loved the picture, and he wanted to put me under contract on the basis of it. I wasn't interested in that, but I did end up directing two Hitchcock half-hours.

---

*Altman worked on about 60 industrial films made by the Calvin Company of Kansas City in the early 1950s. Many of them included dramatic sequences.

GF: *Is it true that you refused to continue working on* Alfred Hitchcock Presents *because there was a script that you objected to?*

RA: Well, I did the first one—*The Young One* [1957]—which was Carol Lynley's first film. Then I did *Together* [1958], with Joseph Cotten. Then they gave me a third script, and I just thought it was bad. I went in to the producer and told her, "This is no good. I can't do this, and I strongly advise that you don't do it because it won't work." It turned out it was a script she had developed. That was the end. I was out of favor.

GF: *Were you confident that you would get a regular directing job in television?*

RA: I don't know if I *knew* I would, but at that time in your life you are pretty confident. I remember once I came out here and almost got a job directing the Groucho Marx TV show, *You Bet Your Life*. At one time I thought I was going to get a job directing *I Love Lucy*, but they found out very quickly that I didn't have enough experience. I would bring my industrial films with me, and I would show them to people. I carried projectors to parties and set up and generally imposed myself on people—I see myself in the young filmmakers who bring their work to show me now. I don't think it was ever the quality of my films that got anybody's attention, but the persistence of this nudging. I did know a lot of technical stuff. I knew about the camera, about sound, and about editing.

On the industrials, we had to do everything, and when I began working in TV, I was able to work fast, and so they liked me. If we'd finish an episode at two o'clock, which we did many times, the crew would be put to work on another show, because they were on a full day's pay. The trick was to stay out almost all day, so we started doing reflection shots and all kinds of complicated stuff just to fill the day out. I did hours and hours of syndicated television—*The Whirlybirds* [1957–8], *U.S. Marshal* [1957–8], *The Troubleshooters* [1959], *Sugarfoot* [1959–60]. *Bonanza* [1960–61] was the big time. I did Warner Bros. television, for which they paid only scale and was really the low-quality end, but I did it because they had a series over there called *The Roaring Twenties* [1960–61], and I really liked that. So I would go between *Bonanza* and *The Roaring Twenties*. Then I got *Combat* [1962–3] and started producing.

GF: *Were you frustrated during this period that you couldn't break into features?*

RA: Yes, but I was very content in my failure. I was not on the very top level of television directors, but I'd say I was on the second level. I was doing well and I was always totally enthused about everything I did. I would get into these projects and make mini-features out of them; I was copying features. I remember on one *Combat*, I said, 'OK, this is my *Foreign Intrigue* film.' On *Bonanza* I started them doing broad comedy in their second year.

Then I got a job at Universal as a producer-director and did an experimental film, *Nightmare in Chicago* [a.k.a. *Once Upon a Savage Night*, 1964], in Chicago. We shot the whole thing on the streets with natural light and high-speed film—that was new. Then I got fired—well, I resigned—and made a life-long enemy out of Lew Wasserman.

GF: *Do you think the improvisatory methods you later developed in features grew out of your long experience of rapid-fire, spontaneous TV work?*
RA: Everything you do today forms what you do tomorrow. In TV, I was working constantly with such dreadful scripts that I just found it was better to change them, or let the actors change them—at least make these ridiculous lines that they had to say more palatable.

GF: *You've favored single takes, where possible, throughout your career.*
RA: I don't do a lot of takes usually. My approach to shooting, even today, is that you set up an event, you determine the perimeter of your arena, and then just shoot it. I never got into nitpicking about performances—I always felt they were better when they were a little raggedy and a little spontaneous and realistic. When I was doing *Whirlybirds*, I wouldn't even read the scripts. I had a great AD, Tommy Thompson, who eventually came back and worked with me from *Brewster McCloud* [1970] to *Popeye* [1980]. He would pick me up in a car at 4:30 or 5 in the morning—I usually had a dreadful hangover—and drive me out to the location, which was usually an hour away out in the Valley someplace, and he'd tell me the story. The actors all knew their lines, so I never read a script. We'd just set up and do it.

GF: *Your feature career really got going with the astronaut film* Countdown *at Warner Bros. in 1968.*
RA: Yes. I got fired by Jack Warner. He was gone through the whole shoot, and he came back and viewed all the footage, and they locked me out of the lot. Bill Conrad, who was the executive producer of those low-budget

projects over there at that time, called me and said, "Don't come in tomorrow, because they're not going to let you in the gate." I said, "I'll go to the Directors Guild. I have the right to cut the film." He said, "If you exercise that, they'll just give you six days and you'll cut it, and then they'll take it all apart and nobody will look at it." Then I went to Spain on an independent project that I thought was going to get financed, and I sat in Seville for a month and the money fell out.

GF: *In 1969 you directed* That Cold Day in the Park. *It's already characterized by what became your very distinctive fly-on-the-wall, documentary approach to fiction. How did that style evolve?*

RA: I don't really know how I got to that. That picture was always kind of in my mind. I'm sure everything that everybody does is imitative.

GF: *That style is full-fledged by the time of* M*A*S*H *[1970], which had been shopped around a lot before you came on to it.*

RA: I think I was the 14th or 15th director it had been given to. Certainly that was the story, and I think it was probably true. I had been working for years on a project called *The Chicken and the Hawk*, which was a comedy about First World War flyers. (In fact, two or three years ago I paid a writer to develop it, but I couldn't get anybody interested in backing it—I doubt if it will ever get done.) I had certain ideas about how I wanted to shoot that picture, and when I read *M*A*S*H*, I saw a way to use the same kind of techniques and style I had in mind.

I did a lot of things in *M*A*S*H*. Originally, it had only eight characters who had speaking lines, and I just filled it with people who had never been on screen before. I got them from an improvisational theater group in San Francisco, and I had to write a line in for each one in order to get them hired. If there wasn't a line of dialogue in the script, Twentieth Century-Fox wouldn't hire them as actors. So I did a little rewrite and I was able to put all these people in as actors. I'm sure that had everything to do with the success of *M*A*S*H*. I had started doing that same kind of thing in television. I had a bunch of guys I called "panics," who were utility actors, and I would write one line into the script for them, and hire them as a reporter or whatever, to give some sense of reality to it.

By that time I was seeing Italian films, and I was striving toward that kind of neorealism. It seemed to me these things should be done that way.

I got away with it on *M*A*S*H*. I never would have at any other time, but there were two bigger war films going on at Fox, *Patton* and *Tora! Tora! Tora!*, and the whole studio machinery was very busy on those. *M*A*S*H* was this little $3.5 million film that was heading for the drive-ins. Nobody had any high hopes for it; there were no stars in it. I got away from the Fox lot out in the country and they didn't pay too much attention to us. I did that by staying under budget—I never let any red flags come up and so we really snuck that film through the studio system.

GF: *What elements in Ring Lardner Jr.'s screenplay of* M*A*S*H *had appealed to you?*
RA: I think that nobody was in that war situation because they wanted to be. Put into that arena, they did their best to survive. And mostly humor is what got people through.

GF: *But it's also a very cynical film. It's set during the Korean War, but in making it so bleak were you trying to deflate the official position on Vietnam?*
RA: Probably. I went through this whole thing without ever mentioning Korea, thinking I could slip it by. But the studio made me put that disclaimer on the front; they said, "You've got to say this is Korea."

GF: M*A*S*H *has been described as anti-Christian, anti-gay, and anti-women. Certainly, the humiliation of the Hotlips [Sally Kellerman] and Frank Burns [Robert Duvall] characters by Hawkeye [Donald Sutherland] and Trapper [Elliott Gould] does seem needlessly cruel. What's your take on this?*
RA: Certainly after *M*A*S*H* people said, "You're a misogynist." And I looked that word up and found out what it meant. But *au contraire*—my answer was and is that I'm not making this film to show you how I think things ought to be; I'm showing you the way I see them. And this is the way women were treated, this is the way gays were treated. This is what went on. The reality of that film was a reality of attitudes. It wasn't factual, but it was truthful. I was involved in all those decisions that made *M*A*S*H* seem cynical, but they had nothing to do with my own personal opinion.

GF: *Do you prefer to maintain a distance from these broader-scale pictures, like* M*A*S*H, Nashville *[1975],* A Wedding *[1978], and* The Player *[1992], as opposed to some of the more personal films you've made?*

RA: What I see becomes personal, so I am as involved in the fabric of those films as I am in the others. The difference between those films with many, many characters and small films like *Images* [1972] and *3 Women* [1977] is just the size of the canvas. Some are small paintings, whereas others are big, broad murals.

GF: *Images and 3* Women, *which do seem to be making personal statements, focus on strong female characters. On the whole you haven't delved so deeply into the male psyche.*
RA: That's true. At the time, of course, I was not aware of it. I don't sit and think, "Oh, I'll use a female character." That's simply what attracted me. I don't know if that relates particularly to my own life or experience. I don't know where that interest in strong female characters comes from.

GF: *Is it true that these two films came to you in dreams?*
RA: Not really, although I trust my dreams. About the time I was making *M*A*S*H*, I got to a stage where I would consciously go to sleep with a problem and say, "OK, the answer is somewhere in the information that's in my head; it's just a matter of getting it out—and it will occur to me." Rarely did I have a specific dream that would answer a question, but sometimes in the next day or week, that answer would disclose itself, because it was there—trapped in my head.

Images, I think, was an imitation of Bergman's *Persona*, which I was very impressed with. I *did* dream the exterior of *3 Women*, though not its content. I was living in another house down the beach in those days, and my wife got very sick—I was very worried she would not survive. Also, I was in desperate financial shape at that time, as I find I usually am. I'd just lost a project, a broad comedy I was working on called *Easy and Hard Ways Out,* with Peter Falk and Sterling Hayden—I wanted to set it at the time of the Six Day War, but the Geffen Company told me I couldn't do it, so I passed on it.

I came home from seeing my wife in the hospital the first or second day she was in, and I was really anxious. I knew I had to get a film. I went to bed and my youngest son, Matthew, came and slept there. I had this dream that I was making a film called *3 Women*. I said to myself, "This is really great." I'd get up and take the yellow pad next to my bed and I'd write down something, then go back to sleep. Then I dreamed the *3 Women* cast—

Sissy Spacek and Shelley Duvall, though Janice Rule wasn't in that dream — and would wake up again and make some more notes, and go back to sleep. At one point I called Tommy Thompson and Bob Eggenweiler, who was my location guy, into the bedroom, and said, "Now, we go look for locations for this film in the desert," and I described the set — sand and desert and heat. Of course, I woke up in the morning, and Matthew was already up and out of bed and in the ocean, where he spent all of his time — and the bed was full of sand. There was no yellow pad next to my bed. So I was having dreams within dreams. I got terribly depressed because I thought, "Oh God, that would be such a good movie and I don't know what it's about."

But I went down and fixed some breakfast, and called Scottie Bushnell, who has worked very closely with me for years. I said to her, "Listen, I read a short story last night that's pretty interesting," and I vamped on the telephone. I said, "It's called *3 Women,* and it's about this woman, living in Palm Springs or someplace like that, who advertises for a roommate, and a girl moves in. It's all about personality theft. These are perfect parts for Sissy Spacek and Shelley Duvall." Scottie said, "Gee, can you get the rights to this story?" And I said, "Oh, yeah." That's how *3 Women* started, though years before, around 1959, when I was painting a lot, I had painted a picture called *3 Women.* All this stuff that spewed itself out had been inside my head, of course, all the time.

So I didn't dream the story or the plot. I dreamed the *results* of it. We sense things through our skin, smells that we don't detect, visual things that we don't think we remember, things we hear that we don't know we've heard, and temperature — and all of these things add up to a hunch. I trust hunches, because I think they are the most accurate messages we get and because they are not something you can intellectually explain. Sometimes you fool yourself, and they don't work or they're invalid. But so what? Your percentages of hits and misses are about the same.

G F : *All right, let's get technical for a moment. One print of* McCabe and Mrs. Miller *[1970] I saw had a very blue tint; on another print it was kind of green.*
R A : Well, it should have been kind of yellow, blue or yellow. The prints are terrible now, although it's pretty good on laserdisc. I was trying to give a sense of antiquity, of vagueness, and to make this not a life that you're living in, but a life that you're looking through.

G F : *What particularly interested you about turn-of-the-century frontier life, or was it Edmund Naughton's novel* McCabe *that attracted you?*

R A : It was a very ordinary novel about this gambler, kind of a romantic character, and this whore with a heart of gold. And then the killers came along and they are a classic trio: the Giant, the Kid, and the Half-Breed. Everything that happened was in plots that we've seen and heard a hundred times before. However, there was something unusual in that book, and I think it was probably in the scene where McCabe was talking to himself about poetry. He tells himself that he's not a poet, that he can't put things down in words. It was very moving to me, because what it was saying was that this guy didn't know anything, and knew he didn't know anything, and was justifying his lack of knowledge by the fact that he wasn't smart enough. But he did know that those feelings existed. I remember that passage very well, and that's what made the whole story for me.

The story became an easy clothesline for me to hang my own essays on. The audience recognized those traditional things—the whore, the killers—so I did not have to dwell on them. Instead, I was able to say, "You think you know this story, but you don't know this story, because the most interesting part of it is all these little sidebars." The filmic approach to that occurred to me as part of telling that story.

G F : *Were you concerned to show that the West was rather different from the familiar myth?*

R A : I wanted to say that maybe it was *this* way. We do research for a western picture through photographs or drawings that people made at that time. You go through the photographic books, and you see a picture of a cowboy with a big hat. So the assumption is that everybody wore these big hats. Well, a glass plate for a camera cost about two dollars in those days, so you didn't go around and take snapshots everywhere. A photographer was very careful about what he took a picture of. My contention is that some guy comes into town, and he's got this big hat on, everybody in town runs down the street and they run to the photographer and say, "Hey, there's a guy out there with the goddamnedest looking hat you've ever seen. Go take a picture of it." So the photographer comes out and takes a picture of the man in the hat. I believe it was something that was very eccentric, or he wouldn't have taken a photograph of it.

G F : *But mostly they wore derbies, right? There's that famous photograph of Bat Masterson wearing a derby.*

R A : Well, most of the American West was populated by first-generation Europeans—Irish and some Italians, English, Dutch. All the clothes they had would have been European, and nobody spoke like they speak in Texas. It took a long time for the language to generate to that.

So in *McCabe* we took the vision that most of these characters were immigrants. I actually got a wardrobe of that period from Warner Bros., took it up to Vancouver and hung it up on racks, then assembled my cast and said: "Everybody gets to have one pair of pants, two shirts, one vest, sweater, light coat, one heavy or rain coat, one hat, and then there's objects that you can go and pick around." So everybody picked their own wardrobe. Of course, all this wardrobe had holes in it and was tattered to make it look aged and old. From this, I could tell the personality of each actor— the guy who wanted to be the most flamboyant picked the most flamboyant stuff, and so on.

There they were all lined up with these clothes with holes in them. I said, "Now, the needles and threads and patches are over here, and you've got two days to sew up your holes, because otherwise you'll die from cold up here. So they repaired all their clothes—because people didn't run around with clothes with holes in them—and suddenly that wardrobe became part of their characters, and they became part of the wardrobe's character. And everybody was eccentric, and yet everybody was the same.

G F : *Why was it necessary to have McCabe [Warren Beatty] ritually sacrificed at the end of the film?*

R A : Because I think he couldn't have survived. What I was really trying to say was that he won and he lost. My script and my film was originally called *The Presbyterian Church Wager*. In the book, Dog Butler [played by Hugh Millais in the film], the big guy with the goatskin coat, makes a wager with McCabe that he'll kill him. I took that out, because it became too theatrical, but we kept the essence of it—that, in gambling, you win a bet, but you also lose. I mean, everybody dies. So I just chose to end it that way. I have no idea how the book ended—I don't remember at all.

G F : *What were you trying to say about mythic western archetypes with* Buffalo Bill and the Indians, or, Sitting Bull's History Lesson *[1976]?*

R A :   It's going the opposite way from *McCabe*—it's saying that this idea of the West is all show business. When we were doing *Buffalo Bill*, Paul Newman said, "I'm not playing Buffalo Bill Cody—I'm playing Redford and McQueen and myself. I'm playing a movie star. These are guys who are given credit for doing these super-heroic things." But Buffalo Bill was a sham. He was originally a guy who moved cattle around, a scout for the Indians, which was just a job. Then Ned Buntline came along and started writing these heroic stories about him, and he had to play up to that role. Tom Mix, who was in the Pancho Villa wars, was probably more of a real doer of deeds than Buffalo Bill.

G F :   *You seem to have consistently addressed yourself to a debunking of American myths.*
R A :   It's just another look at them. They've become rigid. They don't move enough, those myths. They all become imitated to the point where they become like granite, and they're not interesting. I just want to say, "Suppose it could have happened this way." It's not debunking. What interests me when I start looking at a subject is that what we all accept about it probably isn't true. I'm just moving to a place where I can look at it from a different angle.

G F :   *You link* M*A*S*H *together with the loudspeaker announcements;* Brewster McCloud *with the ornithological lectures of the Birdman [René Auberjonois];* The Long Goodbye *with the theme tune;* Thieves Like Us *[1974] with the Romeo and Juliet radio commentary; and* Nashville *with the canvassing of the Hal Philip Walker third-party presidential campaign. . . .*
R A :   Right. The H. Ross Perot truck.

G F :   *What's the intention behind these devices—is it primarily to provide an ironic commentary?*
R A :   It's punctuation to me. For M*A*S*H, I had shot all this fragmented raw material and I knew I was going to have to have punctuation, cutaways. So I came up with the idea of those loudspeakers and sent my editor, Danny Green, out to shoot them. Of course, all the sound content was put in at the editing stage. I still look for punctuation or commentary, and I find it very helpful. I'm doing it in the Raymond Carver film, *Short Cuts*, that I'm about to start shooting.

G F : *What is your linking device there?*

R A : Television—one of those guys who are station managers and give these boring political editorials—and a thing about two women musicians. Layering a movie in this way gives me more options. If something doesn't work, I can cover an awful lot of sins by using these devices. A plot, to me, is a clothesline. For example, as I read *The Long Goodbye*, it occurred to me that Raymond Chandler's story was merely a clothesline on which to hang a bunch of thumbnail essays, little commentaries—because that's what he was most interested in. I thought, "This is exactly my interest in it."

G F : The Long Goodbye, *which was one of several Chandler adaptations to be made in the seventies, is still the only one to present a less-than-traditional view of the private detective Philip Marlowe. Were you unimpressed with the world Chandler created?*

R A : I liked Chandler's stuff OK, and Dashiell Hammett's. Marlowe is a character that didn't actually exist. He's mythical, not even based on truth. This was a script that was given to me when I was working on *Images* in London and initially I said, "I'm not good at this sort of thing." But Leigh Brackett, cowriter of the 1946 adaptation of Chandler's *The Big Sleep*, had written the screenplay and ended it with Marlowe killing his best friend. That I liked, and I also liked the idea of Elliott Gould playing Marlowe— although really the producers wanted somebody like Robert Mitchum. Finally, I agreed to do it with Elliott.

I never finished the book. I never understood it logically. If you really follow the plot, it isn't valid—it doesn't hold up—so I changed it. I got hold of a book called *Raymond Chandler Speaking,* which was a bunch of letters, essays, and other pieces he'd written, and I gave that to all my collaborators, telling them, "This is the book that we're making." I took out the murder of Roger Wade [Sterling Hayden] and replaced it with him committing suicide. It's a movie suicide—I was dealing with Hollywood, *A Star Is Born.* Chandler had tried to commit suicide by shooting himself in the bathtub and missed, hoping the ricochet would get him. So I tried to make the Roger Wade character Raymond Chandler in my mind.

Then I said, "How are we going to date this film? Am I going to go back and do a period film with a bunch of 1934 Chevys in the street and all that stuff?" I didn't want to do that. Instead, I called Marlowe "Rip Van Marlowe" and said he'd been asleep for 20 years. I tried to play up what was happening in 1973, coming off the sixties, and put him in the middle of it. It was a place in which he didn't belong. So suddenly we have Philip Marlowe in a world in which he's not even real, he's walking through it—and it's alien to him. That became the reason for doing the film and I became very excited about it. I love that picture. I think it's very close, in a physical way, to *The Player*.

GF: Nashville *has 24 characters. Was this an opportunity to present 24 little essays?*

RA: They're little soap operas that aren't particularly extraordinary on their own. They're common stories of ordinary people, but I show you such a mass of them that they comment on themselves. *Short Cuts* is the same structure as *Nashville*, basically, but the stories are much stronger and they also come from the same voice. I expect this film to be very interesting in some way, though intellectually I don't know how. I don't know what's going to come out of it; I haven't shot it yet. But I know that each individual story in it could make an hour or a half-hour television show, or even a full movie-of-the-week if you really wanted to flesh it out, though then they wouldn't be Carver's stories any more.

It's like the blues in a way. They're all depressing stories. But just by seeing pieces of them and lifting up rooftops to look at these people, and catching a part of their behavior, you get the essence of a full story. You get the feeling for those characters and their lives. But you never get bored with the story, because immediately I take you to another strand and you keep seeing pieces of these stories develop. Hopefully, they will all, in aggregate, present a spherical kind of structure that the audience will respond to.

GF: *Have you written the screenplay for* Short Cuts *yourself?*

RA: I wrote it with Frank Barhydt Jr., whose father had been my boss at the Calvin Company. That's how I knew Frank Jr. He came out here and edited a health magazine—it was his idea and his script that led me to do *Health* [1980].

GF: *The different plot elements coalesce very neatly in* Nashville, *even through omission. For example, when Barbara Jean [Ronee Blakley] is shot, Opal [Geraldine Chaplin]—the BBC reporter, the one person who needs to be there—is conspicu-*

ous by her absence. However, did you intend at one point to include material sug-
gesting Opal was a phony, not really a journalist at all?

RA: She had other scenes that didn't end up in the picture, but I don't
think any of them treated her differently. We didn't make any specific
indication that she was a phony. This was just something that Geraldine
and I knew, and I'm not sure we even discussed it.

GF: *Why did you ask your screenwriter, Joan Tewkesbury, to include the assas-*
sination attempt on Barbara Jean? I'm interested in this because you have Lady
Pearl [Barbara Baxley] talking about the Kennedy assassinations earlier in the
film.

RA: The development of the Lady Pearl reminiscences about the Kennedys
came after we decided to have the assassination. I don't remember the circumstances. Joan had written this blueprint for us, based on all these
characters, which really were the result of what happened to her when she
went and observed Nashville for 11 days.

Then one day I was in my office—I can even remember the quality of
the light—and I said, "Let's have this woman assassinated." Joan didn't like
it, and it infuriated Polly Platt, the art director, who quit the picture because
of that. But it seemed right to me; it was a hunch. I don't know where the
notion came from, but I was determined to do it. And without it, I don't
think there would have been a film.

Once we knew what that theme was, we were able to develop it through
the other characters. Again, it's the same thing of letting there be many
commentaries. Lady Pearl talking about the Kennedys was a harbinger of
what was going to happen.

In *Short Cuts,* I've got two characters who will furnish all the music for
me in the picture, Annie Ross and Lori Singer, who play a mother and a
daughter. This is not a Raymond Carver story; it's part of the connective
tissue of the film that I mentioned earlier. Originally, I had three stories of
my own that I put in *Short Cuts,* but I've cut them all out except the one
about these two musicians, one of whom, the daughter, commits suicide.
Everybody who has read the script says, "This doesn't make any sense. Why
did she commit suicide?" I say, "Well, I don't think we know why *anybody*
commits suicide, so I don't want to explain why in the film." I don't even
want to know why she does it, but I want the audience to furnish those

reasons in their own minds. Now, I am going to get a lot of heat over this. I can see reviews right now saying, "This is a stupid film because suddenly this woman kills herself and we never know why." But to me it's exactly the same situation as in *Nashville*: Why did Kenny [David Hayward] shoot Barbara Jean?

Right now, we have four or five assassins incarcerated in this country. With all of our technology and all of the wisdom and all of the things that we know, there's not one person who can tell you why any of those assassins assassinated or tried to assassinate the people they did.

GF: *It's been said that you are not interested in character. Looking at your films and examining the way you make them, it seems you are profoundly interested in character, but not prepared to analyze what this character is or is going to be until the actors have discovered it for themselves and let it unfold in front of the camera.*

RA: When I look at a film and I see somebody behaving in a certain way, that's what interests me. And I think the audience wants to see something that they haven't seen before, something that they can believe is true but they don't know why. That's what thrills me.

So in *Short Cuts*, I still don't know what behavior will lead to this suicide. I've talked to Annie Ross and Lori Singer about it and they don't either yet, but something will happen. They will come up with ideas or combinations of ideas or thoughts that will *expose* themselves in their behavior. And if this is done well enough, the audience won't feel like the suicide's come out of left field. Consequently, something will happen in the music that will start pointing arrows toward this event. Something will happen in other scenes with other actors that don't connect at all, that don't link with that, but will still form a link.

GF: *And if the actress Lori Singer explains to you afterwards the reason why her character killed herself, you are fully prepared to accept whatever it is?*

RA: She can have any opinion she wants about it, because whatever her opinion is, it's only going to be part of the answer. Because the reasons why someone commits suicide are so complex, and yet so simple—it's luck. If I have a message, it's not any profound truth, it's this: "I am going to expose an event to you in such a way that you yourself will get a hunch that will tell you about other things in your life experience."

GF: *It's that same sense of arbitrariness which permeates many of your films.*

RA: And this is not what you're supposed to do—this is not general drama fare. Everybody feels they have to have an explanation of why everybody does everything, and my contention is simply that that is not truthful. I don't know one person, and I don't know one person who knows one person, who is not eccentric. And if everybody is, in fact, an eccentric, then "eccentric" is the wrong word and it can't be used!

GF: *With* Come Back to the 5 and Dime, Jimmy Dean Jimmy Dean *[1982], which I regard as the best of the stage adaptations you filmed in the eighties, you returned—albeit not directly—to the myth you'd explored 25 years before in* The James Dean Story *[1957].*

RA: It was a reverse angle on that, different from what you would think. I didn't have a very good feeling about James Dean because of my distasteful experience working on *The Delinquents* with the actor Tom Laughlin, who had been trying to emulate the stories he'd heard about James Dean working with Elia Kazan on *East of Eden*. My interest in making *The James Dean Story* was not in idealizing Dean, but in going the other way. The film didn't turn out that way because I'd had a partner [George W. George], and it developed more into a sentimental, soppy thing.

So when the play by Ed Graczyk was presented to me and I heard the title, I said, "I don't want to read it, I don't want to do it, I'm not interested in James Dean." But I agreed to read it and have actors read it, and I got interested in it because it was not about James Dean, but about the phenomenon he caused and about which I'd made a documentary. What I'm trying to say is that everything touches everything else and influences it. *Come Back to the 5 and Dime, Jimmy Dean Jimmy Dean,* on the stage or on film, would have been an entirely different piece had I not had this other experience. So really it's all one piece of work.

GF: *This notion of serendipity seems very important to you.*

RA: Yes. When I got home yesterday afternoon, after looking at a location for *Short Cuts*, I lay down and turned the television on and *Popeye* was on. I was thinking not about what was happening on the screen, but everything that happened outside of the screen, the memories that it brought back to me, and I started watching a scene where Olive Oyl [Shelley Duvall] is packing her bag and sneaking out to escape marrying Bluto. As she closed the suitcase, a piece of one of the skirts she'd packed was left hanging out-side the suitcase. I grinned because I remembered the exact moment in time when we were shooting that. I'd said, "Let's do that," because there'd been a scene in *3 Women* when Shelley had caught her skirt in a door—we did that quite often in that film. Now, nobody in the world is ever going to make that connection between those two films, nobody can know the gen-esis of things like that—and yet it's thick.

The Presbyterian church that's at the top of the hill in *Popeye* is the same church from *McCabe*. Similarly, I took an actor, Bob Fortier, who was the town drunk in *McCabe,* the guy that did the dance on the ice, and made him the town drunk in *Popeye,* and he wore exactly the same wardrobe. These are the things that are interesting to me. I don't know whether it adds up to personal art—I guess all art is personal.

GF: *Did* Tanner '88 *[1988] grow out of the scenes with Michael Murphy as John Triplette in* Nashville?

RA: Sure it did. And *The Player* grew out of *Tanner. The Player* could not have existed had I not done *Tanner '88,* because it never would have occurred to me to mix real people playing themselves with fictional characters. While *The Player*'s not the same thing as *Tanner,* it *is* the same thing. You cannot pull one thing out and let it stand alone, because it does *not* stand alone. It is carrying all of the strings that are attached to all the other things in my life—and in the lives of Tim Robbins [Griffin Mill in *The Player* and star-director-author of the *Tanner*esque *Bob Roberts*], Julie Christie [the costar of *McCabe and Mrs. Miller* who played herself in *Nashville*], and Shelley Duvall. There's no way I can avoid the sticky stuff that connects one film to another.

GF: Vincent & Theo *strikes me as one of your harshest, yet least naturalistic films. It doesn't have that documentary feel about it.*

RA: My whole purpose there was to demythify art. If I have a Van Gogh painting and I want to move it down to Christie's, six guys in white gloves and one guy with a gun will come in here to move it. But there was a time when he just painted the damn thing, and it fell on the floor, and people stepped on it or left it out in the rain. I was trying to convey that the value of art is not in its existence, but in its doing.

GF: *Going on to* The Player, *did you in any sense feel it was an opportunity to settle a score with Hollywood? When it came out, there was all that talk of it being a* film-à-clef.

RA: I have no beef with Hollywood. I never have. They have not done things that I wanted them to do, and I have not done things that they wanted me to do. I've made enemies and I don't suffer fools gracefully. It's simply that I have an interest in doing certain kinds of work that I feel I do well and it doesn't fit with their marketing plans, generally. So it's only occasionally that I am able to get a picture through the machinery. Most of the hysteria about *The Player* suggests that I'm sitting there throwing knives at a bunch of old enemies, which isn't true. I hope that the film stands on its own as a piece of work. But, in general terms, it's fraught with allegory. It's an allegory on an allegory, set inside an allegory. And the arena is something that I know fairly well. But it's no different from the museum business or the newspaper business. Hollywood is the surrogate for what I am addressing, which is the cultural dilemma between art and commerce that's taking place in this country and in most Western civilized countries.

GF: *Did you feel that you were exiled from Hollywood in the eighties?*

RA: No more than I am today. I have the same projects I am trying to do today that I had last year, and the year before that, and the year before that—and nobody will fund them. A lot of people offer me *their* projects, but these aren't anything I want to do. They are not interested in what I have to say. They're interested in the fact that, oh, he's hot now, so let's get him to do something. But they want it done their way.

GF: *In the last ten years, Hollywood has seldom allowed directors, yourself included, to have any kind of artistic trajectory.*

RA: There's a scene in *The Player* where Griffin Mill says, "I'm kind of fascinated with the idea of eliminating the writer from the artistic process." He says, "Now, if we can just get rid of the directors and the actors, we've really got something here." And that's exactly what those studio guys are trying to do, though they don't even know they're trying to do it.

GF: *Are the studio types depicted in the film based on actual figures, are they amalgams of different people, or are they purely fictional?*

RA: They're nobody I know. They're very generic. I made no effort to make fools of the characters themselves. Taking cheap shots is too easy. I said to the actors, "If you're this character, think the way *you* feel the character that you've created is going to think." Those studio people don't think they're bad guys. I tried to show that they don't turn down projects because they don't *like* an artist, but because that's what their job is. Naturally, you don't like people when they turn you down, and you say, "Nah, they didn't get it. They're too dumb"—but that's not fair.

GF: *How did you arrive at the style for* The Player? *The beginning—when the delivery boy collapses—is reminiscent of* Nashville.
RA: I think that's just me imitating myself. The style of any film really derives from after the fact.

GF: *And then there's your homage—if homage is what it is—to* Touch of Evil *with the long opening shot.*
RA: I wanted to make that ridiculously long opening shot because so many people talk about these long opening shots as if they are some achievement in themselves. And in a way, they are, but they are all pretty pretentious—they are seldom done for narrative drive. In this case, I was trying to show the audience that this film was about movies and people who talk movies. The majority of people who see it are never gonna know that shot is eight minutes and six seconds, and it doesn't make any difference. I'm breaking linear time, but without breaking linear *film* time. It was the *effect*, cinematically, of cutting, but there was no cut in it, and it's seamless. Basically, it sets up that this is a film studio, and these are the characters, and this is the style of the film, because it's movies within movies—that's also why I had movie posters all over the place.

I have no idea how that opening shot first occurred. I never make models of sets and I never do storyboards—but I *did* have a model of that set built. I imagine I spent $5–6,000 on it, which was totally useless. I'd just sit and look at it and think, "Where can I put people?" Then I found out that the furthest extension I could have on a dolly was 25 feet. So I had a little model of that made, then I could make little camera pivots and I could say, "Well, from here I could go to there, but I'd have to come back here." And I just played with those puzzles. But I never resolved them. I never came up with a plan. I got into doing the picture and then suddenly, in the middle of production, it came time to go do it—and we went over and did it. All of that prethinking led to what the shot finally is. Things like that stylize the picture eventually.

GF: *You once said, "I'm trying to reach toward a picture that's totally emotional, not narrative or intellectual, where an audience walks out and they can't say anything about it except what they feel." Is that still a goal?*

RA: I don't think I'll ever attain that. What I'm really talking about is taking the linear references out of film and having something happen that works on the individuals in the audience so that the information they get from the film suddenly invades all the information they have accumulated in their lifetime, so they can only say, "Wow, that's so right." It's difficult in film, where you need a narrative. You can look at a painting for a split second or you can look at it for an accumulation of time, and it's still working on you. In film, one frame has to follow the other. I think the structure of *The Player* is rather remarkable. I use one part of the film as the clothesline to keep your attention. Hanging on that is the way the murder story is done, which is the way they are done in bad films. So I am emulating not good films but bad films, and—again—I'm hanging on that a lot of abstract thumbnail essays, so one supports the other.

GF: *I sensed that you were trying to emulate the bad film that gets made in the course of* The Player—*the* Habeas Corpus *film with Bruce Willis and Julia Roberts—and to use it as a vehicle to digress.*

RA: Yes, but the *Habeas Corpus* film was an exaggeration. It was a parody—it could never be made. The other, subtler scenes—the love scenes, the sex scenes, the interrogation scenes—were all picked off other bad movies, or even good movies. For the scene where Griffin and June [Greta Scacchi] are travelling to Palm Springs, I thought, "I'm going to have to transport the audience with them." So I said, "OK, I'm going to be Ridley Scott, but I only have a day or a day and a half to be him." So we shot it as three little commercial shots.

GF: *Both the hot-tub scene between Griffin and Bonnie [Cynthia Stevenson], his colleague and girlfriend, and the elliptical sex scene between Griffin and June give more and less than what we expect.*

RA: Paul Newman saw the film, and somebody asked him what it was like. He said, "It's a film about how you get to see the tits of a girl whose tits you don't want to see, but you don't get to see the tits of the girl whose tits you do want to see." I wanted to use that obligatory nudity, because otherwise the film isn't marketable. But I didn't want to put it where it should have been. So when I interviewed Cynthia Stevenson for the role of Bonnie, I said, "Now, before we even get into what this part is about, I've got to tell you that you've got to take your shirt off." She said, "Nobody has ever asked me to do that before. Why?" I said, "Because if I show you nude in a hot tub, in an unsexual situation, then I don't have to show Greta Scacchi, who the audience *does* think it's going to see nude." I wanted to make the point that these things are done for the wrong reasons.

During the lovemaking scene between Griffin and June I didn't want to have them just screwing. I wanted it to appear that they both were very much involved and that he felt obligated to tell her that he had killed her boyfriend, and she doesn't want to hear it. Some people are going to ask, "Did she know or didn't she?" I don't know. I don't know whether she did or not. And it doesn't really make a lot of difference. You figure out what works for you. It should always be ambiguous.

G F : *You've said that the ending of* The Player *is the same as the ending of* M*A*S*H.

R A : It is, yes. We had no ending for *The Player*, because all the endings were melodramatic, and we had to bring back the writer who threatens Griffin Mill, whom we had suddenly dismissed. Tim Robbins and I were talking about various endings, and we had many options, none of which was satisfactory. I said, "I know this is going to come to us, so it's not a problem." We were maybe three weeks away from shooting.

When I was editing *M*A*S*H*, I remember I had just put in those loud-speakers with the announcement of the war movies. I'd been driving through Malibu Canyon, and was just turning into my driveway when this idea came up that I would say, over a loudspeaker, "Tonight's movie has been *M*A*S*H*, that knock-'em, sock-'em, kill-'em . . ." — and so on. And I said to myself, "This is great. It's that idea of telling people, 'The movie you've just seen is the movie you've just seen' " — that this was all a film.

I told Tim that. And about ten minutes later, he said, "Maybe we should do the same thing in *The Player*." And I knew immediately what he was talking about. We celebrated. We didn't actually break out the champagne, but it was that feeling. I ran from office to office saying, "We've got the ending. Listen to this." It was the idea that Griffin gets on the telephone with the writer, who pitches him the film we've just been watching—and it's called *The Player.* It's saying that this is a movie about itself. I want the audience to see that many of the scenes, the way the actors acted it, the way the sets were, the way it was shot was *movies,* not life. The melodrama was movie melodrama, not real life melodrama.

I've always tried to show the audience that what it's seeing isn't real— and show them the device that shows that. I'm sure that this will appear in my opera, *McTeague.* Because if I don't tell them it's an opera, how am I possibly going to succeed in making them think people behave this way— walking around singing? They don't. So something has to mirror that. I think every film I do is like that. It's making something spherical rather than linear. The more and more of this I do, the more I want it to be like you're inside a universe, you're inside a sphere. There isn't any end and beginning to it.

G F :   *Tell me a little bit about* McTeague.* *Is it from Frank Norris's novel?*
R A :   Yes, and, of course, Erich Von Stroheim shot that entire book when he made *Greed* [1924]. It's a very operatic story. When Von Stroheim made it, he went to San Francisco and shot the cars and people in the street, so he wasn't accurate to the period of the novel. My wardrobe and the physical look of the stage set of *McTeague* is more authentic to California in 1908—still, most of the images and the tone of the opera are from that silent, black-and-white film, because when I look at *Greed,* I know more about those characters than I do when I read Frank Norris's book. So that has to have an influence on me—and I also *want* it to have an influence on me. I have no idea why, except that it seems to make a vague connection with what *my* history is.

G F :   *Perhaps it's because you and Von Stroheim each had a contentious relationship with the Hollywood studio system. Do you see yourself working within the studio set-up again?*
R A :   I doubt that will ever happen, because I have certain demands that I think they are not going to meet. I'm 67 years old. I wonder: Where am I

McTeague opened at the Lyric Opera of Chicago on 31 October 1992.

going to be ten years from now? I'm going to be 77. That's pretty old. So what have I got? Six, seven pictures left. I don't want to make a film just for the sake of landing a job. And unless I feel that I will have fun with the shooting of a film, and afterwards, when you kind of smile and say, "We really did a good job on that," then I don't want to do it.

Director Builds Metaphor for Jazz in *Kansas City*

DAVID STERRITT/1996

MOVIES AND JAZZ HAVE a long history together, from Hollywood oldies like *Paris Blues* and *Young Man With a Horn* to more recent pictures like *Round Midnight* and Clint Eastwood's beautiful *Bird.*

The newest jazz movie seeking a wide audience is *Kansas City,* with Jennifer Jason Leigh and Harry Belafonte in a story of love, crime, and intrigue set against the African American jazz scene of the 1930s.

What sets it apart from most jazz pictures is the fact that music accompanies much of the story, but never takes over and becomes the main subject of the film. This breaks the pattern for jazz-oriented movies—and that's perfectly all right with director Robert Altman, who has devoted his career to breaking patterns ever since innovative works like *M*A*S*H* and *McCabe and Mrs. Miller* gave him a permanent place in the filmmaking hall of fame.

Kansas City tells two meandering, sometimes violent stories that finally come together near the end of the picture. One centers on a disreputable white man named Johnny who tries to rob a black tourist, gets caught in the act, and winds up in the clutches of an elusive and dangerous nightclub impresario.

The other shows how Johnny's wife makes an inept effort to save him, by kidnapping the wife of a presidential adviser whose influence might

From *The Christian Science Monitor* August 13, 1996: 14. Reprinted by permission of The Christian Science Publishing Society.

somehow help Johnny out of his predicament. Much of the plot focuses on these women and the offbeat relationship they develop during the long, tense hours they spend together.

Jazz is central to the movie in two ways. The most obvious is its jumping, jiving presence in the background of all the nightclub scenes, lending vivid atmosphere to what could have been ordinary *film noir* crime and suspense episodes.

Just as important is the role jazz played as basic inspiration for the movie, which could be called a "melodrama" in the original sense of that word—a drama with music as an essential part of its fabric.

"It all began with an attempt to use jazz music as the score of a film," said Altman during a conversation at the Cannes International Film Festival, where *Kansas City* had its premiere. "People say if you use jazz, the movie has to be about a jazz subject. That doesn't work for me, because I don't want to make a film about [jazz] players. Then a few years ago it occurred to me that if I'm going to deal with jazz, that should be the structure of the whole movie."

Altman usually puts his films together in some unconventional way—and this has often involved music, as when *Nashville* worked country music into every aspect of its story, or when *Short Cuts* centered some of its most involving sequences on characters who deal with music in their everyday lives. But in *Kansas City* he wanted to try yet another new approach, making the movie itself into a kind of freewheeling jazz improvisation.

"A song is usually about three minutes long," he explains, "but when jazz guys work on it, the song takes 17 minutes. I decided to make a song out of the story of the two women. As it developed, the whole movie is jazz. Harry Belafonte is like a brass instrument—when it's his turn to solo, he does long monologues and riffs—and the discussions of the two women are like reed instruments, maybe saxophones, having duets. So it's really all about music."

This is an experiment nobody has tried before, and Altman admits it was risky to stake a Hollywood-sized budget on it. "I didn't know if it would work," he says, "and I don't know if it does work. But this is what I wanted to attempt. If people 'get it,' then they really tend to like it. If they don't—if they thought they were going to get something like *Nashville,* or if they think the story is too thin—well, that's too bad. The story is just a little song, and it's the way it's played that's important."

As a jazz movie with no major roles for musicians, *Kansas City* is certainly an odd piece of work. But in other ways it fits comfortably with Altman's prior career. In his most respected movies, from *M*A*S*H* and *Nashville* to *The Player* and *Short Cuts,* he has assembled many first-rate acting talents and allowed them an amazing amount of freedom in developing their own characters, actions, and even dialogue. In sum, he has often functioned less like an everyday movie director than a master conductor who orchestrates individual riffs and melodies into smoothly harmonious wholes.

Altman agrees with this analysis but stresses the intuitive and spontaneous nature of his work. "I don't start with that idea or sit down with a master plan," he says. "But after the fact I say, 'Oh, this is what I did!' And since all the material [for a film] passes through me, it's going to vaguely have my shape. . . . So, of course, there are connections between all my films. And yet I'm always trying to make a different film than I've made before."

When he speaks about new approaches, Altman is referring more to style than to plot. "I'm not so much interested in stories," he says. "With this movie, I saw clearly that it was like a song, and the lyrics are kind of thin, but I don't give you lots of details because I'm not interested in that. It's just a song!"

Also of interest to Altman is the history of jazz as an integral part of African-American culture. Running through *Kansas City* is an awareness of music as a key means of black expression, often coded with hidden meanings that insiders can thrill to while outsiders—including white ones—listen in blissful ignorance.

Reviews of *Kansas City* were lukewarm after its Cannes debut. Some praised its energetic music and glowing camera work, but others faulted its slender story and criticized some performances—especially Leigh's portrayal of the inept kidnapper, a plain and ordinary woman who's gotten the inexplicable idea that she's a look-alike for movie star Jean Harlow.

Altman takes the mixed reviews in stride. "Everything's an experiment," he says of his work. "If I knew how everything was going to be done, I'd always be late for work, because it would be dull. But this is exciting for me because every day I'm a little scared, since I'm not quite sure what's going to succeed and what isn't."

In any case, the response of real moviegoers is more important—and Altman would rather have spectators arguing over his work than quietly agreeing about it, since this means he's been as daring and "experimental" as he set out to be.

"If I can hook 51 percent," he says of his audience, "I've certainly won the day. If I get 'em all, I've probably made a really bad picture!"

INDEX